Cambridge English

ADVANCED
3

WITH ANSWERS

AUTHENTIC EXAMINATION PAPERS

Cambridge University Press
www.cambridge.org/elt

Cambridge Assessment English
www.cambridgeenglish.org

Information on this title: www.cambridge.org/9781108431217

© Cambridge University Press and UCLES 2018

It is normally necessary for written permission for copying to be obtained
in advance from a publisher. The sample answer sheets at the back of this
book are designed to be copied and distributed in class.
The normal requirements are waived here and it is not necessary to write to
Cambridge University Press for permission for an individual teacher to make copies
for use within his or her own classroom. Only those pages that carry the wording
'© UCLES 2018 Photocopiable' may be copied.

First published 2018

20 19 18 17 16 15 14 13 12 11 10 9 8 7 6 5 4 3 2 1

Printed in Malaysia by Vivar Printing

A catalogue record for this publication is available from the British Library

ISBN 978-1-108-43121-7 Student's Book with answers
ISBN 978-1-108-43122-4 Student's Book with answers with Audio
ISBN 978-1-108-43120-0 Student's Book without answers
ISBN 978-1-108-43123-1 Audio CDs (2)

The publishers have no responsibility for the persistence or accuracy of URLs
for external or third-party internet websites referred to in this publication, and
do not guarantee that any content on such websites is, or will remain, accurate
or appropriate. Information regarding prices, travel timetables, and other factual
information given in this work is correct at the time of first printing but the
publishers do not guarantee the accuracy of such information thereafter.

Contents

	Introduction	*5*
Test 1	Reading and Use of English	*8* } final test
	~~Writing~~	*22*
	Listening	*24*
	~~Speaking~~	*29*
Test 2	Reading and Use of English	*30* } not used
	~~Writing~~	*44*
	Listening	*46*
	~~Speaking~~	*51*
Test 3	Reading and Use of English	*52* – self-study week 11
	~~Writing~~	*66*
	Listening	*68* — self-study week 11
	~~Speaking~~	*73*
Test 4	Reading and Use of English	*74* – not used
	~~Writing~~	*88*
	Listening	*90* – in-class week 11
	~~Speaking~~	*95*
Test 1	Frames for the Speaking test	*96*
Test 2	Frames for the Speaking test	*99*
Test 3	Frames for the Speaking test	*102*
Test 4	Frames for the Speaking test	*105*
	Marks and results	*108*
Test 1	Key and transcript	*120*
Test 2	Key and transcript	*129*
Test 3	Key and transcript	*138*
Test 4	Key and transcript	*147*
	Sample answer sheets	*156*
	Thanks and acknowledgements	*167*
	Visual materials for the Speaking test	*colour section*

Introduction

This collection of four complete practice tests comprises papers from the *Cambridge English: Advanced (CAE)* examination; students can practise these tests on their own or with the help of a teacher.

The *Cambridge English: Advanced* examination is part of a suite of general English examinations produced by Cambridge English Language Assessment. This suite consists of five examinations that have similar characteristics but are designed for different levels of English language ability. Within the five levels, *Cambridge English: Advanced* is at Level C1 in the Council of Europe's *Common European Framework of Reference for Languages: Learning, teaching, assessment.*

It has been accredited by Ofqual, the statutory regulatory authority in England, at Level 2 in the National Qualifications Framework. The *Cambridge English: Advanced* examination is recognised by educational institutions, governmental departments and employers around the world as proof of the ability to follow an academic course of study in English at university level and communicate effectively at a managerial and professional level.

Examination	Council of Europe Framework Level	UK National Qualifications Framework Level
Cambridge English: Proficiency Certificate of Proficiency in English (CPE)	C2	3
Cambridge English: Advanced Certificate in Advanced English (CAE)	C1	2
Cambridge English: First First Certificate in English (FCE)	B2	1
Cambridge English: Preliminary Preliminary English Test (PET)	B1	Entry 3
Cambridge English: Key Key English Test (KET)	A2	Entry 2

The structure of *Cambridge English: Advanced* – an overview

The *Cambridge English: Advanced* examination consists of four papers.

Reading and Use of English   **1 hour 30 minutes**
This paper consists of **eight** parts, with 56 questions. For Parts 1 to 4, the test contains texts with accompanying grammar and vocabulary tasks, and separate items with a grammar and vocabulary focus. For Parts 5 to 8, the test contains a range of texts and accompanying reading comprehension tasks.

Writing   **1 hour 30 minutes**
This paper consists of **two** parts which carry equal marks. In Part 1, which is **compulsory**, candidates must write an essay with a discursive focus of between 220 and 260 words. The task requires candidates to write an essay based on two points given in the input text. They need to explain which of the two points is more important and give reasons for their choice.

In Part 2, there are **three** tasks from which candidates **choose one** to write about. The tasks include a letter/email, a proposal, a report and a review. Candidates write between 220 and 260 words in this part.

Listening   **40 minutes (approximately)**
This paper consists of **four** parts with 30 questions. Each part contains a recorded text or texts and corresponding comprehension tasks. Each part is heard twice.

Speaking   **15 minutes**
The Speaking test consists of **four** parts. The standard test format is two candidates and two examiners. One examiner acts as both interlocutor and assessor and manages the interaction either by asking questions or providing cues for the candidates. The other acts as assessor and does not join in the conversation. The test consists of short exchanges with the interlocutor and with the other candidate, an individual long turn, a collaborative task involving both candidates, and a discussion.

Grading

Candidates will receive a score on the Cambridge English Scale for each of the four skills and Use of English. The average of these five scores gives the candidate's overall Cambridge English Scale score for the exam. This determines what grade and CEFR level they achieve. All candidates receive a Statement of Results and candidates who pass the examination with Grade A, B or C also receive the *Certificate in Advanced English*. Candidates who achieve Grade A receive the *Certificate in Advanced English* stating that they demonstrated ability at Level C2. Candidates who achieve Grade B or C receive the *Certificate in Advanced English* stating that they demonstrated ability at Level C1. Candidates whose performance is below C1 level, but falls within Level B2, receive a *Cambridge English* certificate stating that they have demonstrated ability at Level B2. Candidates whose performance falls below Level B2 do not receive a certificate.

For further information on grading and results, go to the website (see page 7).

Further information

The information contained in this practice book is designed to be an overview of the exam. For a full description of all of the above exams, including information about task types, testing focus and preparation, please see the relevant handbooks which can be obtained from Cambridge English Language Assessment at the address below or from the website at: www.cambridgeenglish.org

Cambridge English Language Assessment
1 Hills Road
Cambridge CB1 2EU
United Kingdom

Telephone: +44 1223 553997
email: helpdesk@cambridgeenglish.org

Test 1

READING AND USE OF ENGLISH (1 hour 30 minutes)

Part 1

For questions **1–8**, read the text below and decide which answer (**A**, **B**, **C** or **D**) best fits each gap. There is an example at the beginning (**0**).
Mark your answers **on the separate answer sheet**.

Example:

0 A earns   **B** gains   **C** wins   **D** obtained

0	A	B	C	D
	▭	▬	▭	▭

Time and the rotation of the Earth

As all school children know, there are 60 seconds in a minute. But every so often, our planet **(0)** …….. a second. The addition of what's called a 'leap second' is **(1)** ……… to allow the Earth's rotation, which is gradually **(2)** …….. to catch up with atomic clocks – the world's most accurate time-keepers. This sounds simple, but according to scientists, because they only get six months' **(3)** …….. of the need to add a leap second, it's difficult to insert it into computers without mistakes being made, **(4)** …….. systems to fail temporarily. In 2012, a leap second was added on a weekend but it resulted in over 400 flights in one country being grounded as the check-in system **(5)** …….. down.

Some countries are in favour of abolishing leap seconds while others **(6)** …….. that the technical challenges are **(7)** …….. if everyone adds the second in the same way and at the same time. They say that we have always taken the Earth's rotation as the ultimate reference for timekeeping and we shouldn't break this **(8)** …….. without considering the consequences.

1 **A** designed   **B** targeted   **C** framed   **D** drafted

2 **A** delaying   **B** lessening   **C** slowing   **D** declining

3 **A** advice   **B** notice   **C** information   **D** instruction

4 **A** compelling   **B** making   **C** causing   **D** influencing

5 **A** came   **B** fell   **C** ran   **D** went

6 **A** argue   **B** disagree   **C** dispute   **D** question

7 **A** governable   **B** controllable   **C** manageable   **D** adaptable

8 **A** join   **B** link   **C** chain   **D** union

Part 2

For questions **9–16**, read the text below and think of the word which best fits each gap. Use only **one** word in each gap. There is an example at the beginning (**0**).
Write your answers **IN CAPITAL LETTERS on the separate answer sheet**.

Example:

0	*O*	U	T														

Solving problems while you sleep

How often do we struggle to figure **(0)** ……. a problem and then, after a night's sleep, we wake up knowing exactly what to do? We tend to view sleep simply **(9)** ……. a period of recuperation, but it actually has profound implications for a lot of human tasks, including a positive effect on problem-solving. Research now suggests that **(10)** ……. only are we able to come up with answers to life issues while asleep, but these answers are often better than the ones we might think of once the routines of our daily lives take **(11)** ……. . Sleep aids memory too, and it's believed that new information isn't processed and absorbed fully until we've had a good night's sleep.

So, if you're faced **(12)** ……. a difficult problem, set it aside, sleep **(13)** ……. it and return to it the next day. But **(14)** ……. made a complex decision, you **(15)** ……. like to revisit it after a second night's rest on the off-chance that **(16)** ……. could be a better solution waiting to be considered.

Part 3

For questions **17–24**, read the text below. Use the word given in capitals at the end of some of the lines to form a word that fits in the gap **in the same line**. There is an example at the beginning (**0**). Write your answers **IN CAPITAL LETTERS on the separate answer sheet**.

Example:

0	S	I	G	N	I	F	I	C	A	N	C	E						

A wise old owl

Many birds have special (**0**) …….. for humans but none is perhaps more respected than the owl. Owls, often seen as symbols of (**17**) …….. , have a powerful hold on human imagination.

SIGNIFY

WISE

There are many species of owl and most of them are solitary, nocturnal birds of prey that are (**18**) …….. by their upright stance. They tend to blend in with the colorations and even the texture patterns of their (**19**) …….. , which makes them hard to spot. They have a keen sense of (**20**) …….. and have special ears that can pick up sounds that are (**21**) …….. by the less sensitive human ear, such as tiny (**22**) …….. from small animals on the ground.

CHARACTER

SURROUND

SEE

DETECT

VIBRATE

Many owls have special feathers on their wings which allow them to fly silently. They are commonly believed to be able to turn their heads a full 360 degrees; in fact, although they have fourteen neck vertebrae in (**23**) …….. with seven in humans, they're only able to rotate 270 degrees.

COMPARE

All these features add to our view of the owl as being (**24**) …….. .

MYSTERY

Part 4

For questions **25–30**, complete the second sentence so that it has a similar meaning to the first sentence, using the word given. **Do not change the word given.** You must use between **three** and **six** words, including the word given. Here is an example (**0**).

Example:

0 James would only speak to the head of department alone.

ON

James ………………………………… to the head of department alone.

The gap can be filled with the words 'insisted on speaking', so you write:

Example:	0	INSISTED ON SPEAKING

Write **only** the missing words **IN CAPITAL LETTERS on the separate answer sheet**.

---

25 If there are fewer doctors on duty, patients may have to wait longer than usual.

DEPENDING

Patients may have to wait longer than usual, ………………………………….. of doctors on duty.

26 There's a danger those mountaineers won't be able to make it back to the hut before it gets dark.

RISK

Those mountaineers run …………………………………….. able to make it back to the hut before it gets dark.

27 Whatever time he leaves home, John always seems to get to work late.

MATTER

No …………………………………….. off from home, John always seems to get to work late.

28 It is Sam's responsibility to ensure everyone has left the museum before closing time.

CHARGE

Sam ………………………………….. sure everyone has left the museum before closing time.

29 Martin was going to host an event for the new students, but it appears he has decided against it.

MIND

Martin appears ……………………………….... hosting an event for the new students.

30 Up to now, I've never thought of working in any field other than finance.

OCCURRED

The thought of not working in the field of finance ………………………………….. now.

Part 5

You are going to read an article in which a young journalist talks about using social media to find a job. For questions **31–36**, choose the answer (**A**, **B**, **C** or **D**) which you think fits best according to the text.

Mark your answers **on the separate answer sheet**.

Keeping pace with scientific publishing

Science correspondent Joe Cushing considers old and new ways of publishing scientific research

Journal-based peer review – the process of subjecting a scientific research paper to the scrutiny of others who are experts in the same field – is generally held up as the quality assurance mechanism for research. It professes to be an essential filter which prevents publishing flawed or nonsensical papers, and indeed is often touted as such in reassuring tones when scientists talk to the media or the general public. Reviewing a paper can delay its publication by up to a year; is that a price worth paying to ensure the trustworthiness of the published literature? Well, yes and no. And picking apart such issues reveals a great deal about the state of scientific publishing, which is very much in flux.

I'm not yet ready to abandon journal-based peer review. I'd still like to see all papers pass some sort of checking stage before formal publication, but I feel the ground moving. The growing use of preprints (drafts of papers which are posted online without having been peer reviewed, found in digital archives) is a crucial part of that shift because they bring academics back to what research publication is all about: the rapid dissemination of new results so they can be read, critiqued and built upon. Publication in journals has become more about renown and career advancement, and this has perverted both the motivations of authors and the job of reviewers.

Competition for prized spots in highly-regarded journals drives scientists to do some of their best work and the best journals certainly publish plenty of outstanding research. But the excessive rewards for publishing in top journals are incentives to corner-cutting, as stories streamlined by the omission of inconvenient data are more likely to be taken up. And the job of the reviewer also becomes distorted: it is more often now to decide, not whether a manuscript is any good, but whether it is good enough for the journal considering publication. For top journals that can depend as much on topicality or newsworthiness as scientific quality.

These problems are well known, but the tragedy for science is that too few people are willing to break away from the present system. However, as the eminent biologist Ron Vale argued recently – fittingly, in a preprint – preprints may be a way out of the impasse because they don't entail a major shift away from the norm. That may seem an odd claim in view of the fact that preprint archives have been in existence for twenty years, yet preprints have not been adopted universally. This slow uptake is not only a reflection of the inherent conservatism of scientists, but also a result of the widespread misconception that journals won't accept manuscripts which have been posted online as preprints. There is also a fear that publication of papers without peer review risks opening the floodgates to 'junk science' – something which, so far at least, has yet to occur. Preprints may not be peer reviewed, but authors know full well that preprints are immediately opened up for critique and discussion by a worldwide community of reviewers. *line 45*

Tanya Elks, a psychology professor, recalls: 'My paper was a critique of a published paper – a scenario which isn't well handled by the conventional journals. Under their system of anonymous peer reviewing, either the authors of the original paper are chosen as reviewers and there is a risk that the unscrupulous ones might block a critical paper; or they're not chosen and may justifiably complain about misrepresentation. As we posted a preprint, the original authors had their say and we could take their points on board. All the commentary is out in the open so readers can evaluate the quality of the arguments. The possibility of rejection by journals is less of an issue too, given that we'll still have the preprint and comments out in the public domain, so our work won't be wasted.'

Preprint archives enable, on a global scale, the informal scientific discussions once confined to correspondence between individuals. They could also become an effective outlet for negative results – a vital aspect of the scientific process often overlooked by the journals' excessive preoccupation with new discoveries. Furthermore, presence on preprint archives significantly increases the number of times papers are read and cited by others; a potent demonstration of the efficacy of dissemination through preprint. By harnessing the web's culture of openness and accessibility and recalling the collaborative, amateur ethos still at large within the scientific community, preprints should help to refocus attention where it matters – on the work itself, not where it is published. *line 7* *line 7* *line 7* *line 7* *line 8* *line 8*

31 In the first paragraph, the writer expresses doubt regarding the part that peer review plays in

- **A** provoking changes in the process of scientific publishing.
- **B** affecting deadlines for publishing scientific papers.
- **C** ensuring the quality of scientific research.
- **D** reassuring the public about new research.

32 What does the writer feel that many scientists need to be reminded of?

- **A** the absence of peer reviewing with preprints
- **B** the original aim of publishing scientific findings
- **C** the ulterior motives which lie behind reviewers' comments
- **D** the prestige which can be gained by being published in a journal

33 What does the writer accuse scientific journals of doing?

- **A** encouraging scientists to compete against each other
- **B** trying to reduce costs in order to maintain their position in the market
- **C** relying too heavily on reviewers to decide whether to publish an article
- **D** choosing articles for their appeal rather than their scientific value

34 What does the writer admit may be an 'odd claim' in line 45?

- **A** the idea that it was fitting for biologist Ron Vale to argue his case in a preprint
- **B** the assertion that adopting preprints does not require a radical change of behaviour
- **C** the notion that too few scientists are pushing for a rethink of the peer review
- **D** the suggestion that preprints will be readily accepted by the scientific community

35 What point does Tanya Elks make about her experience of posting a preprint?

- **A** Her work is less likely to be rejected now since others have made positive comments about it in public.
- **B** She appreciated the fact that she could see what fellow scientists thought of her paper.
- **C** It was unfair to use the authors of the research she was evaluating to review her paper.
- **D** She chose a preprint because she feared her paper would not otherwise be published.

36 The phrase 'collaborative, amateur ethos' in the final paragraph refers back to the earlier phrase

- **A** 'correspondence between individuals' (lines 75–76).
- **B** 'effective outlet for negative results' (line 77).
- **C** 'preoccupation with new discoveries' (line 79).
- **D** 'efficacy of dissemination' (lines 82–83).

Part 6

You are going to read four commentaries on the subject of living in London. For questions **37–40**, choose from the commentaries **A–D**. The commentaries may be chosen more than once. Mark your answers **on the separate answer sheet**.

London

A Bridget Atkins

London is a cruel city. A quick walk from the steel and glass money temples of the financial district to one of the rundown estates fifteen minutes away shows you most of what you need to know about its harshness and problems. Depressing as that walk may be, I'd still recommend it more than struggling through the public transport network. It isn't just that the trains are overcrowded, overheated and unreliable – it's that you have to pay such an insulting amount for the privilege of travelling in such misery. Talking of contempt, I haven't even got on to landlords, rent, and the fact that a shoebox in London will cost you more than a palace outside London. That's not to say it's all bad though. I do rejoice in the internationalism of my city, the way I learn so much about different cultures and cuisines just by attending a local street party.

B Tim Christie

London is an endlessly inventive city. We've happily embraced using both the London Underground and Overground, cycling and walking, finding one-bed flats further away from the centre. Until now the trend has been to move further out to find a place to live, but it doesn't need to be like that. Some of the most interesting work going on in London now is around the politics of scarcity. We need to release spare space, as well as investigate new models for flexible living and co-housing. People talk about disparities between the haves and the have-nots, but I'd say there's no other place in the world where it's better to be an entrepreneur. You don't have to be born with a silver spoon in your mouth to make it here, and that's what I see – people who are in the process of making it or who already have – just in different places on a kaleidoscopic spectrum.

C Anna Fry

Aside from the fact that most people can no longer afford to live here, there also seems to be a sad conformity among those that do. The big beard, tight-trousered, hipster phenomenon, for instance, is essentially tribal and conservative. I do love the eclectic transport system though. You can make your way across the city by a multitude of transport modes; the whole city is pretty much anti car. Even if you're happy paying the congestion charge, you've still got to drive around in circles looking for a place to park. Get it wrong and there'll be one of London's finest parking attendants there to remind you with the much despised penalty charge notice. But I'm all in favour of that. We all have to breathe the air no matter if we're rich or poor, and that's what I love about the whole system. It's a great equaliser. Take it or leave it.

D Jon Bennett

I don't get the fascination with London's decrepit housing stock. It's overpriced and falling to pieces. All this talk of old-world charm, character and conservation areas, for what is essentially a totally dysfunctional stock of properties not fit for modern-day living. Unless you're a multi-millionaire that is, with money to burn on heating, only for it to go straight out the hundred-year-old windows. Because that's who's drawn here, unless we're talking about the run-down, gritty areas that attract outsiders from all walks of life. If it weren't for them, this would be a dull place to live. I love the way they colonise an area with pop-ups, cafés and art spaces, until they're priced out. The system seems to favour those living off their inheritance. Why else would you need to pay such a ridiculous sum just to get from A to B on a late-running, museum-piece transport system?

Which commentator

expresses a different view from the other three commentators regarding the housing situation in London?

37 ☐

shares C's opinion on London's public transport system?

38 ☐

has a different view from A on the multi-cultural nature of London's population?

39 ☐

shares A's opinion on the inequality of wealth prevalent in London?

40 ☐

Part 7

You are going to read a magazine article about the ecological importance of the semi-aquatic animal, the beaver. Six paragraphs have been removed from the article. Choose from the paragraphs **A–G** the one which fits each gap (**41–46**). There is one extra paragraph which you do not need to use.

Mark your answers **on the separate answer sheet**.

Beavers

Beavers play an important role in keeping Rhode Island's waters clean

There are an estimated 30 million beavers across North America. As a keystone species, beavers enrich ecosystems around them. By building dams, they control water moving through their habitat, retaining the flow during times of drought and slowing it down during heavy rain and floods. This also creates beaver ponds – areas several meters deep they use for sleeping and eating. However, a study by the American Society of Agronomy says beavers are doing something more: they are now helping to remove nitrogen that has moved its way through soil into ground water and lakes and streams.

| 41 | |

In time these plants die and decompose, consuming the oxygen from the waters, creating low oxygen levels that kill fish. While these dead zones are common in the Gulf of Mexico, they are also becoming a problem along northeastern U.S. coastlines. However, according to the study findings of Professor Arthur Gold and colleagues of the University of Rhode Island, this problem is less common where there are beavers.

| 42 | |

Thanks to a naturally occurring bacterium present in the soil of beaver ponds, 5% to 45% of nitrogen in the water can be removed, depending on the pond and the amount of nitrogen present, the study found. This bacterium is able to transform nitrogen in the water into nitrogen gas.

| 43 | |

This transformative power was tested by taking samples from the beds of beaver ponds, and adding nitrogen to them. These samples were large enough to incorporate the factors that generate the chemical and biological processes that take place in the pond.

| 44 | |

The experiments also found that 12% of the nitrogen gases created in the samples were nitrous oxide, a very potent greenhouse gas and air pollutant. To put this into perspective, considered over a 100-year period, nitrous oxide is calculated to have between 265 and 310 times more impact than carbon dioxide does. However, the scientists pointed out that the high amount was likely to be a result of some unique laboratory conditions and that it is unlikely these ponds would release that much of the gas in nature.

| 45 | |

Most of these semi-aquatic animals are in areas with small streams, rather than big rivers, and the beaver dams in these smaller streams are usually the first to be removed. They are considered a nuisance because they block the waterways. This causes a decrease in beaver populations. It is therefore important that these areas remain untouched so they can positively affect nitrogen levels downstream. Professor Gold now hopes to study the ponds over a longer period and to investigate abandoned ponds to see if the nitrogen-retaining qualities remain after the beavers have gone.

| 46 | |

In addition, these areas of water also attract other wildlife such as insects and birds which are vital to the ecosystem. Studies like the one carried out by Professor Gold may well give people a new-found appreciation for the beaver.

A These results have interesting implications. According to Julia Lazar, who was involved in conducting some of the work as part of her doctoral dissertation and is now working as an environmental consultant, it might change our attitude to beavers and their ponds.

B At the same time, the specimens were also sufficiently small to be easily replicated, managed and measured for numerous changes. The scientists then added a special type of nitrogen to the soil that allowed them to tell if the nitrogen levels were altered and how.

C 'Streamside wetlands are one example of such elements,' said Professor Gold, who studies these types of features in his research. But nobody had ever documented the role beaver ponds might play.

D Found in agricultural fertilizers, nitrogen is often introduced to such areas by runoff, eventually travelling to estuaries where rivers meet the sea. Once in the water system, it has been known to cause what is known as eutrophication. This is where a sudden increase in nutrients can cause blooms of algae to grow.

E This process is known as de-nitrification and means the nitrogen is no longer stored within the stream or pond, and thus can no longer degrade water quality further downstream. However, some of the nitrogen is not changed to gas, but instead is stored in organic soils.

F They are a species whose numbers crashed after widespread hunting 150 years ago, but with their return they are helping solve one of the major problems of the 21st century and that should not be underestimated. It is important to remember that those ponds would not be there without the beavers.

G When the team set out to conduct their research, they quickly realized the water retention time and organic matter build-up within beavers' ponds lead to the creation of ideal conditions for eliminating nitrogen. They then wanted to see how effectively this was done.

Part 8

You are going to read an article in which a squash player writes about the fact that his sport is not included in the Olympic Games. For questions **47–56**, choose from the sections (**A–D**). The sections may be chosen more than once.

Mark your answers **on the separate answer sheet**.

___

In which section does the writer

say that he's finding it difficult not to express his emotions?	**47**
express ignorance of certain sports?	**48**
outline the reasons behind particular decisions?	**49**
express admiration for some of his colleagues?	**50**
admit that it had seemed unlikely that his sport would be chosen?	**51**
acknowledge that he may be repeating a familiar argument?	**52**
show determination not to be put off his sport by the decision about the Olympics?	**53**
appear to be asking for advice from the reader?	**54**
express a fear that people are making fun of his sport?	**55**
suggest that squash players have had enough of trying to persuade the Olympic committee?	**56**

The Olympic Games and the sport of squash

Squash player Stuart Lee outlines his reaction to the decision not to include squash in the Olympic Games

A How should I and my fellow squash players react as our sport once again fails to earn a place at the next Olympic Games? With the increasing numbers of international competitions and the recent successful integration of women's and men's tours, one might be forgiven for thinking that the sport has arrived. Except, in Olympic terms, it hasn't. In fact, it's all over the place. For the umpteenth time, squash tried to sell itself and lost. We have pleaded for years and hoped to appeal to a very powerful governing committee responsible for the world's greatest sporting event, and were rejected again. Stop me if you've heard all this before, but over the years, we've dared to think (many times) that we were close to securing Olympic inclusion. Following our latest attempt, five sports were recommended as better options for the next Olympic Games.

B It was always going to be touch-and-go, as the host nation this time around has not traditionally been strong on squash. There was little surprise over the inclusion of baseball and softball – they'll fill arenas and put money in the bank. Surfing is also a fair choice: it's a tough sport, enjoyed by millions of people across the world. But then came sport climbing, and skateboarding. Judging by the reactions I've seen and heard, many people were unaware that such things even existed as sports. Climbing, yes, but what's 'sport climbing'? Do these sports have governing bodies and world titles? Are they televised? Are there rules? Do they have infrastructures and do millions of people do them? I'm not trying to be clever, just asking the questions. Any sport that encourages activity and participation is a great thing, I'm not here to denigrate anything that provides this outlet. I don't know enough about them to say what appeal they would give to the Olympics. Clearly more than squash.

C The official line from both the Professional Squash Association and the World Squash Federation has been extremely gracious, as always. Players have been told not to react negatively, criticise those in charge or lambast other sports, but we're struggling to stop ourselves at this stage. There's some feeling now that it's going to be very hard to keep responding peaceably, merely saying 'Oh well, maybe next time'. Everyone who asks us questions about the Olympics asks with disdain why other sports are selected before squash, and it now seems that disdain has turned to amusement. It was bad enough to play second fiddle to golf and rugby sevens, but at least people who asked for our reaction to those decisions understood that they are established and recognised entities. It has been back-breaking work for squash associations to lobby for inclusion year after year. We've produced swanky and expensive promotional videos with money we didn't have and we have enlisted every celebrity we could get our hands on to hold posters up saying things such as: 'Squash for the Olympics – I'm in – are you?'

D Nobody is quite sure why the sport has suffered these repeated failures. The Olympics is the biggest sporting event in the world. Of course we want to be there, we dearly want to be there but, with respect, all we ever do is try to justify ourselves. Our top players, who are by anyone's standards some of the greatest athletes alive, shouldn't need to do this. This is our sport, it is what it is, and it's getting better all the time. Take it or leave it. We want the Olympics and we hope the Olympics want us. When I heard the news of this latest rejection, I was in the US, playing in an international tournament, and all the players were comforted by the fact that the event had the crowds in raptures every night. It's a fine thing to play in front of such warm and enthusiastic people. The spectators may or may not have heard the news that was on all the players' minds, but squash goes on, Olympics or not.

WRITING (1 hour 30 minutes)

Part 1

You **must** answer this question. Write your answer in **220–260** words in an appropriate style **on the separate answer sheet**.

1   Your class has watched a studio discussion on the role of music in society. You have made the notes below:

The role of music in society:
- enriching people's lives
- uniting social groups
- educating young children

Some opinions expressed in the discussion:

"The purpose of music is to bring beauty to our lives."

"Music can help bring different people together."

"Music lessons at school can improve learning in other subjects."

Write an essay for your tutor discussing **two** of the roles of music in society in your notes. You should **explain which role is more significant, giving reasons** to support your opinion.

You may, if you wish, make use of the opinions expressed in the discussion, but you should use your own words as far as possible.

Part 2

Write an answer to **one** of the questions **2–4** in this part. Write your answer in **220–260** words in an appropriate style **on the separate answer sheet**. Put the question number in the box at the top of the page.

2   This is part of an email you have received from your friend Anna in New Zealand:

> …
>
> I'm doing a project about people's reading habits in different countries. Can you tell me about your country? Can you give me some idea about the situation in your country? What changes have there been in what people read and how they read? Is this the same for all age groups?

Write your **email**.

3   You have just helped organise a day of activities to welcome new students to the international college where you are a student. The principal has asked you for a report. In your report, you should briefly describe the day, comment on how effective the activities were in welcoming the new students and make recommendations for a similar event next year.

Write your **report**.

4   Your college website welcomes film reviews from students. You decide to write a review of a science fiction film. In your review, you should briefly describe the film, and consider whether other students would enjoy it. You should also explain how it differs from other popular science fiction films.

Write your **review**.

LISTENING (approximately 40 minutes)

Part 1

You will hear three different extracts. For questions **1–6**, choose the answer (**A**, **B** or **C**) which fits best according to what you hear. There are two questions for each extract.

Extract One

You hear two friends discussing an exhibition they have just visited, featuring a female sculptor called Sue Lin.

1   What does the woman think about the way the exhibition was set out?

    A   It enabled people to appreciate how innovative Sue's work was.

    B   It reflected Sue's original intentions for her sculptures.

    C   It placed too much emphasis on Sue's contemporaries.

2   The man says the decisions made about what to include in the exhibition have

    A   helped to increase visitor numbers.

    B   diminished his opinion of Sue's sculptures.

    C   disappointed admirers of Sue's talent.

Extract Two

You hear part of a discussion between two psychology students on the subject of laughter.

3   What is the man doing?

    A   describing different kinds of humour

    B   complaining about his tutor's attitude towards his work

    C   highlighting how surroundings can influence people

4   What do they both think about research into laughter?

    A   It is an effective way to find out about human behaviour.

    B   It should focus on the physical processes of the brain.

    C   It has become a popular field of study.

Extract Three

You hear two friends discussing their experiences of learning to play the piano.

5   The woman says that since starting to learn the piano, she's felt

    A more confident about facing challenges in general.

    B newly convinced of the value of perseverance.

    C better able to remember factual information.

6   Which research findings into playing an instrument does the man question?

    A that it improves abstract reasoning skills

    B that it fosters creative thinking

    C that it acts to relieve stress

Part 2

You will hear a book illustrator called Colin Rodgers talking about his work to a group of students. For questions **7–14**, complete the sentences with a word or short phrase.

Colin Rodgers – book illustrator

Colin finds that what particularly holds his attention is the **(7)** .... in

book illustrations.

He advises would-be artists to recognise the importance of continual

(8) .... when they are practising drawing an image.

He finds it hard to capture what he refers to as the **(9)** .... of

a story when he's illustrating it.

He says that children can be more **(10)** .... than adults when

looking at images.

He believes drawings of **(11)** .... in illustrations are readily

understood by everyone.

He gives the example of **(12)** .... as creatures that are easily

placed in any of his pictures.

He stresses the necessity of developing what he terms **(13)** .... in

today's world.

He thinks the quality of **(14)** .... is the most important one for illustrators.

Part 3

You will hear an interview in which a deep-sea map-maker called Sally Gordon and a marine biologist called Mark Tomkins are talking about making maps of the ocean floor. For questions **15–20**, choose the answer (**A**, **B**, **C** or **D**) which fits best according to what you hear.

15 How did Sally feel when she had completed her first mapping expedition?
    A anxious about the prospect of spending more time at sea
    B unsure whether she had made a good impression
    C keen to begin making a reputation as a leader
    D excited at the prospect of making further discoveries

16 Mark compares the ocean floor to the planets in order to
    A emphasise how under-explored it is.
    B reassess its geographical features.
    C challenge assumptions about the practical difficulties of researching it.
    D speculate about the extent of the area it covers.

17 How does Sally feel about attitudes towards deep-sea exploration?
    A glad that its importance is recognised
    B frustrated that it's not regarded with more enthusiasm
    C optimistic about the possibility of gaining support for it
    D disappointed by public misunderstanding of it

18 They agree that corporate funding of science projects
    A appeals to an idealistic kind of entrepreneur.
    B is now more popular than sports sponsorship.
    C generates a lot of positive publicity for companies.
    D leads to more accurate results than government funding.

19 When talking about the territorial ambitions of some island nations, Mark reveals his
    A irritation at their lack of scientific know-how.
    B support for their right to claim what's theirs.
    C scepticism about the legality of the process.
    D concern about the potential consequences.

20 Sally and Mark predict that future developments in deep-sea exploration will
    A result in a change in human behaviour.
    B help to raise the profile of marine biology.
    C enable a new form of tourism to come into being.
    D have a bigger impact than those in space exploration.

Part 4

You will hear five short extracts in which people are talking about going to live in another country.

TASK ONE

For questions **21–25**, choose from the list (**A–H**) what each speaker's main reason for moving to the new country.

TASK TWO

For questions **26–30**, choose from the list (**A–H**) what each speaker about the place where they are now living.

While you listen, you must complete both tasks.

A to satisfy a desire for change

A differences in language use

B to take the advice of a friend

Speaker 1 | 21

B a seasonal abnormality

Speaker 1 | 26

C to have a chance no longer possible at home

Speaker 2 | 22

C the national cuisine

Speaker 2 | 27

D to achieve a long-standing ambition

Speaker 3 | 23

D practical difficulties of daily life

Speaker 3 | 28

E to accompany someone else

Speaker 4 | 24

E the contrast in working cultures

Speaker 4 | 29

F to improve a particular skill

Speaker 5 | 25

F people's sense of humour

Speaker 5 | 30

G to be part of an important trend

G the attitude of local people

H to take advantage of an unexpected opportunity

H the authentic reconstructions

SPEAKING (15 minutes)

There are two examiners. One (the interlocutor) conducts the test, providing you with the necessary materials and explaining what you have to do. The other examiner (the assessor) is introduced to you, but then takes no further part in the interaction.

Part 1 (2 minutes)

The interlocutor first asks you and your partner for some information about yourselves, then widens the scope of the questions by asking about e.g. your leisure activities, studies, travel and daily life. You are expected to respond to the interlocutor's questions and listen to what your partner has to say.

Part 2 (a one-minute 'long turn' for each candidate, plus a 30-second response from the second candidate)

You are each given the opportunity to talk for about a minute, and to comment briefly after your partner has spoken.

The interlocutor gives you a set of three pictures and asks you to talk about two of them for about one minute. It is important to listen carefully to the interlocutor's instructions. The interlocutor then asks your partner a question about your pictures and your partner responds briefly.

You are then given another set of pictures to look at. Your partner talks about these pictures for about one minute. This time the interlocutor asks you a question about your partner's pictures and you respond briefly.

Part 3 (4 minutes)

In this part of the test, you and your partner are asked to talk together. The interlocutor places a question and some text prompts on the table between you. This stimulus provides the basis for a discussion, after which you will need to make a decision on the topic in question. The interlocutor explains what you have to do.

Part 4 (5 minutes)

The interlocutor asks some further questions, which leads to a more general discussion of the topic you have discussed in Part 3. You may comment on your partner's answers if you wish.

Test 2

READING AND USE OF ENGLISH (1 hour 30 minutes)

Part 1

For questions **1–8**, read the text below and decide which answer (**A**, **B**, **C** or **D**) best fits each gap. There is an example at the beginning (**0**).
Mark your answers **on the separate answer sheet**.

Example:

0 A crammed　　**B** crushed　　**C** massed　　**D** piled

0	A	B	C	D
	▬	▭	▭	▭

Reading the slow way

It's 7 pm and I'm sitting in a café I've never been in before. It's **(0)** …….. with people, but nobody's talking. Nothing **(1)** …….. about this in a big city, but we're not just sitting there ignoring each other. **(2)** …….. the opposite; we're all reading together, silently, in a 'Slow Reading Club', an idea from New Zealand. **(3)** …….. our lives, clearing some mental **(4)** …….. where our attention is not constantly divided between ten different things is the trend of the moment, but it's not easy to **(5)** …….. .

The Slow Reading Club aims to meet that challenge by encouraging people to apply the same discipline to reading as to going to the gym or completing a task at work. The rules are **(6)** …….. straightforward: bring a book and **(7)** …….. yourself in it the way you did as a child. I've brought a thriller which has lain **(8)** …….. on my bookshelves for years. At the end of our hour, we're told it's time to stop reading and it feels like emerging from a deep sleep. I'm off home to carry on reading.

1 **A** contrary   **B** abnormal   **C** variable   **D** disparate

2 **A** Fully   **B** Thoroughly   **C** Wholly   **D** Quite

3 **A** Simplifying   **B** Relieving   **C** Moderating   **D** Relaxing

4 **A** place   **B** span   **C** space   **D** area

5 **A** deliver   **B** attain   **C** perform   **D** acquire

6 **A** exactly   **B** rather   **C** thereby   **D** somewhat

7 **A** lose   **B** place   **C** concentrate   **D** free

8 **A** negated   **B** deserted   **C** declined   **D** neglected

Part 2

For questions **9–16**, read the text below and think of the word which best fits each gap. Use only **one** word in each gap. There is an example at the beginning (**0**).
Write your answers **IN CAPITAL LETTERS on the separate answer sheet**.

Example:

0		T	O															

Discovering new material

Vulcanised rubber, celluloid and plastic – these materials were, **(0)** …….. a certain degree, invented by accident. In fact, the history of materials can be described **(9)** …….. a history of accidents, but this is not as catastrophic as it sounds. **(10)** …….. the beginning of scientific investigation, scientists have stumbled across new and wonderful materials in **(11)** …….. course of exploring something completely different. But this chance discovery of useful materials **(12)** …….. undergoing a change.

Scientists sitting at their desks, now turn to computers to design materials and to work out their properties long **(13)** …….. they need to go anywhere near a laboratory. But the element of chance is still present as the ultimate application of these new materials remains tentative. **(14)** …….. scientists are confident about is that each has the potential to be revolutionary. The race is now on to make these materials reality. **(15)** …….. the history of materials is any guide, how we eventually use them will, **(16)** …….. part, be discovered accidentally.

Part 3

For questions **17–24**, read the text below. Use the word given in capitals at the end of some of the lines to form a word that fits in the gap **in the same line**. There is an example at the beginning (**0**). Write your answers **IN CAPITAL LETTERS on the separate answer sheet**.

Example:

0	A	P	P	R	E	N	T	I	C	E	S	H	I	P				

"Mouseman"

The furniture maker, Robert Thompson, was born in 1876. As a young

man he started an engineering **(0)** …….. . He described this time   **APPRENTICE**

as like a prison sentence with harsh,   **(17)** …….. conditions. This   **TOLERATE**

experience resulted in him taking the decision to work **(18)** …….. his   **ALONG**

father, who was making handcrafted oak furniture following traditional

methods. Following his father's death in 1895, Robert was left with full

(19) …….. for the family business.   **RESPONSE**

The company decided to include a **(20)** …….. of a mouse on all   **CARVE**

its items of furniture as a sort of logo. This gave Thompson the

nickname, "Mouseman", which remains the **(21)** …….. trademark of his   **DISTINCT**

company's furniture.

Time-honoured methods are still used for the **(22)** …….. of the furniture   **ASSEMBLE**

and any upholstery is always made of the highest quality leather,

(23) …….. to water and other stains. The company is still run by the   **RESIST**

Mouseman's **(24)** …….. , and now enjoys worldwide distribution of   **DESCEND**

its products.

Part 4

For questions **25–30**, complete the second sentence so that it has a similar meaning to the first sentence, using the word given. **Do not change the word given.** You must use between **three** and **six** words, including the word given. Here is an example (**0**).

Example:

0 James would only speak to the head of department alone.

ON

James ………………………………… to the head of department alone.

The gap can be filled with the words 'insisted on speaking', so you write:

Example:	0	INSISTED ON SPEAKING

Write **only** the missing words **IN CAPITAL LETTERS on the separate answer sheet**.

---

25 The tutors said we can't use the computers in the library for anything except assignments.

MEANT

The tutors said we ………………………………..... use the computers in the library for anything except assignments.

26 No other students apart from Martha were selected for the trip overseas.

BE

Martha was ………………………………..... selected for the trip overseas.

27 She loved the book, but she wondered whether the events were historically accurate.

ACCURACY

She loved the book, but she wasn't ………………………………..... the events.

28 Most people these days would be completely lost without their mobile phones.

IDEA

Most people these days would ………………………………... manage without their mobile phones.

29 Pat realised that trying to sleep before the neighbours' party ended was a waste of time.

POINT

Pat realised that ………………………………... trying to sleep before the neighbours' party ended.

30 If you hadn't taken me to the station, I wouldn't have caught my train.

GIVING

But ………………………………... to the station, I wouldn't have caught my train.

Part 5

You are going to read a newspaper article about food. For questions **31–36**, choose the answer (**A**, **B**, **C** or **D**) which you think fits best according to the text.
Mark your answers **on the separate answer sheet**.

The food scientist

Alice Baines meets the influential food scientist Charles Spence

Charles Spence will eat just about anything. 'We've got ice cream made from bee larvae at home,' says the Professor of Experimental Psychology in his office at Oxford
line 4 University in the UK. They may be maggoty in appearance, but they apparently have a 'slightly nutty, floral' flavour. How to make bug-eating acceptable is just one of the
line 7 many gustatory challenges that Spence and his team are tackling. Through his studies into how the senses interact to form our perception of flavour, Spence is influencing,
line 10 in a stealthy but not inconsiderable manner, what we eat
line 11 and drink, from the hefty output of food-industry giants (he sits on the scientific advisory board of one well-known multinational conglomerate, and receives funding from another), to the menus of leading restaurants.

Spence and his peers have, through a line of scientific inquiry that is informally referred to as gastro physics, studied in minute detail how we experience food and drink. Who we eat with; how food is arranged and described; the colour, texture and weight of plates and cutlery; background noise – all these things affect taste. Spence's book, *The Perfect Meal*, written with Betina Piqueras-Fiszman, is packed with insights that are fascinating to anyone in possession of an appetite.

Were you aware that the person in a group who orders first in a restaurant enjoys their food most? And did you realise that we consume about 35% more food when eating with one other person, rising to 75% more when dining with three others?

Spence's lab in Oxford is noticeably un-space-age. 'Low-tech, paper and drawing pin stuff,' he readily admits. There are soundproof booths that resemble human-sized safes ('most of my PhD was done in one of those,' he says fondly), along with stacks of ancient-looking audio-visual equipment. By keeping overheads low, he can afford to work more creatively with cooks who can't fund academic research themselves. Much of his work is funded by a major food multinational. Historically, he says, undertaking research which attracts industry funding has been seen in university circles as 'what you do if you can't do proper science'. But since the government insisted that universities demonstrate their work has an impact and that people are interested in it, this type of research has become a strategically good thing to do.

Spence is currently helping famous brands through (often government-imposed) reductions in salt and sugar. It is in their interests, he points out, to help loyal customers stay alive for longer. Perhaps surprisingly, many have been making these reductions furtively, behind closed doors. They do it gradually, so regular consumers don't notice the difference from one pack to the next. 'The research shows that when you tell people what you're doing, it makes them focus on the taste and for whatever reason they don't like it as much,' he says.

It was while working on a project for a major food producer that Spence was first introduced to Heston Blumenthal, the renowned experimental chef. 'At the time, people thought: "Science and food – that's horrible," although most food is scientific, in fact. Who better to change the mindset than Heston?' It was through Blumenthal's collaborations with Spence, who had been studying the effects of sound on flavour, that the 'Sound of the Sea' dish came about in Blumenthal's five-star restaurant. Interestingly, Spence says that members of the early-twentieth-century art movement, the Italian futurists, were 'doing sounds of croaking frogs with frogs' legs a century ago', but that it didn't catch on.

Now the food industry is applying Spence's sensory science to products left, right and centre. This includes his recent findings that higher-pitched music enhances sweetness, and lower-pitched and brassy sounds make food taste bitter. 'It's always surprising when shapes affect taste, or when a tune can impact on how you perceive a flavour,' he says. An airline will soon be matching music with food served to passengers. And last year, a well-known brand released a smartphone app that plays a concerto while your ice cream softens; they omitted to match the music to the taste, though, which is all too frequently the case according to Spence.

What, one wonders, are dinner parties like in the Spence household? There was the time they ate rabbit, with the fur wrapped around the cutlery. And the one at which they played with remote-controlled, multi-coloured light bulbs. 'We've had dinner parties with a tone generator, headphones and ten different drinks lined up to see whether they have different pitches.' Home, sweet shops, food conventions, international gastronomy conferences: they're all extensions of the lab to Spence.

31 Which word in the first paragraph is used to indicate distaste?

    A maggoty (line 4)
    B gustatory (line 7)
    C stealthy (line 10)
    D hefty (line 11)

32 What does the writer suggest about Spence's work in the fourth paragraph?

    A Small-scale projects have brought it most success.
    B It is less forward-looking than might be expected.
    C Perceptions of its value have changed.
    D It suffers from inadequate resources.

33 What point does Spence make about major food companies in the fifth paragraph?

    A They should pay less attention to public opinion.
    B They will benefit in the long term from selling healthier goods.
    C They are reluctant to invest in developing new products.
    D They have been too secretive about the way they work.

34 Spence's view of Heston Blumenthal is one of

    A enthusiasm for his links with innovators from the past.
    B admiration for his influence on ways of thinking about food.
    C fascination for his involvement with large food manufacturers.
    D respect for his thorough knowledge of science.

35 Spence is concerned that his ideas

    A are being developed in unexpected ways.
    B seem too challenging to be widely accepted.
    C appear to attract the wrong sort of organisations.
    D are often applied in a way that neglects some details.

36 What does the final paragraph highlight about Spence?

    A the commitment he shows to his research
    B the unpredictable nature of his character
    C the talent he has for entertaining people
    D the busy daily schedule he follows

Part 6

You are going to read four extracts from articles in which university professors give their views on choosing a degree subject. For questions **37–40**, choose from the extracts **A–D**. The professors may be chosen more than once.

Mark your answers **on the separate answer sheet**.

Choosing a degree subject: STEM (Science, Technology, Engineering and Maths) or the Arts?

A In recent years there has been a steady stream of industry bosses trying to persuade students to opt for STEM courses. This is presumably an attempt to suppress the wages of those already employed in the area as, in reality, there is no shortage of STEM graduates seeking employment. The biggest problem such graduates face is the fact that their qualifications point them exclusively in one direction. Many were no doubt attracted to their course by the promise of an enviable salary, despite the fact that a recent survey indicated that those who studied arts subjects make on average between one and two thousand pounds per annum more than their STEM counterparts. This is unsurprising, given that employees trained in the arts bring an alternative point of view in day-to-day decision making. The scientific way of looking at problems, with its emphasis on logic and reason, is valuable of course, but it can be limiting.

B Traditionally, students were told that maths and the sciences were just for those who wanted to go into a mathematical or scientific profession. Of course, now we know that couldn't be further from the truth. These are the courses that can unlock the doors to all sorts of jobs, and equip graduates to win the top positions and potentially reap the financial rewards, particularly at a time when politicians are promoting STEM as an engine for innovation and national defence. However, when HR managers are asked what kind of skills they look for when recruiting, the majority list critical thinking, complex problem-solving and written and oral communication – in other words, the skills gained from an arts education. That's why I advise those who are in doubt to go with their heart. It's worse than useless to push a student into a subject in which they have little talent or pleasure on the basis of a lifetime's extra earnings.

C The reason we've been hearing so much lately about the importance of STEM subjects is that our world is changing beyond recognition, and we need to ensure that our graduate workforce keeps up. The skills gained from these subjects come in useful in almost any area you care to name, from the creative industries to architecture, as well as the more obvious technical and scientific professions. I don't think it's an exaggeration to say that doing arts at university is a decision that will hold students back when it comes to seeking employment nowadays. It is pure indulgence to select a higher education course based simply on what you enjoy. Students need to acquire the skills and knowledge that will allow them to be competitive in the jobs market.

D Arts subjects train students to perform well in a world of subjectivity and ambiguity, a vital skill, since commercial decisions rarely involve a right or wrong answer. We've all heard stories about people who invest thousands in their arts-based education and then end up in a dead-end job, but when it comes to deciding on what to do at university, remember that those who are passionate about what they do are better placed to succeed in life. While it's true that a maths graduate may well take home extra over their working life compared to an English graduate, it's only about a thousand a year – little compensation if you're doing a job you loathe. In any case, it's becoming increasingly obvious that companies are looking for ways to avoid paying STEM professionals so much. An oversupply of such workers would be to their advantage, as it would push wages down, hence their constant call for more students with STEM degrees.

Which professor

has the same opinion as B on which degrees can lead to higher earnings?

| 37 | |

has a different opinion from the others on whether having studied for an arts degree is an advantage in the workplace?

| 38 | |

has a different opinion from D on how a student should choose a degree subject?

| 39 | |

has the same opinion as D on who or what is responsible for the current emphasis on STEM subjects?

| 40 | |

Part 7

You are going to read a newspaper article about a holiday in Costa Rica. Six paragraphs have been removed from the article. Choose from the paragraphs **A–G** the one which fits each gap (**41–46**). There is one extra paragraph which you do not need to use.

Mark your answers **on the separate answer sheet**.

Costa Rican holiday

Not again. It's the third morning in succession we've been woken by howler monkeys. The noise invades your consciousness like some distant wind and builds into a sustained roar until you fling off the sheets and sit up, cursing. Awake, you can hear the throaty rasp. The volume is astonishing: this is reputedly the loudest voice on the planet yet it comes from an animal no larger than a cat.

41	

Later on that morning, strapped into harness and helmet and slightly regretting my immense breakfast, I find myself standing on a narrow platform overlooking the forested gorge. A steel cable arcs down through the trees to some invisible point on the other side. This seems the last chance to voice my fears, were it not for the fact that my nine-year-old daughter is already clipped on ahead of me. The last thing I see as she launches into the void is her grin.

42	

As I zigzag down from platform to platform I can relax enough to appreciate the gurgle of the river and the chorus of birdsong. There is even time to spot a troop of howler monkeys in the crown of a fig tree. By the time we swing off the final platform, fun has definitely conquered fear.

43	

'They control our climate,' our guide Daniel Monge had told us on day one. He had showed us on our map how Costa Rica's peaks line up to form a barrier down the spine of the country. The eastern slopes, which fall away to the Caribbean, get most of the rainfall and are carpeted in lush tropical rainforest. The western Pacific slopes lie in the rain shadow, so their forests are more arid.

44	

By afternoon, the skies had cleared, giving us picture-book views of Turrialba, the next volcano on our route. An ominous plume of smoke rose from the summit, and the Lodge, our stop for the night, was directly below. 'Don't worry,' said Daniel, 'it's been doing that for three years.'

45	

From that experience to watching how sugar was made seemed a natural leap. We joined a group to watch as the estate's two oxen turned a huge mill wheel that crushed fresh cane to a sticky pulp. The children's eyes widened as the first fresh juice was boiled up into a slow-bubbling gloop of golden molasses, then the raw sugar was spread, chopped and sifted.

46	

For our last two days, we descended from Rincón de la Vieja to our hotel in Playa Panama. It turns out to be perfect: the lush grounds, the huge pool, the lavish breakfast and the warm ocean just beyond. How better to wind down before the flight home? There's only one problem, and it comes at 5.03 am on our final morning: a thunderous wake-up call courtesy of the planet's noisiest primates. I pull my pillow over my ears.

A Our next stop was on neither of these, however, but in the misty highlands that divide them. We drove up a hairpin ascent to Costa Rica's highest active volcano. On a good day, you can see both coasts from here. We had no such luck, but the swirling mist allowed glimpses into the flooded crater.

B Still, an early start is no bad thing. So far, we've needed every minute of daylight to get through our breathless itinerary, and our time at this guest house promises to be the most action-packed yet.

C That evening, inspired by what we'd seen, we cooked our own Costa Rican meal. Our hosts provided ingredients and instructions, and then kept a discreet distance as we sliced, mashed, drizzled and seasoned to produce our best shot at a traditional supper.

D But you don't need a guide to find Costa Rica's wildlife. In fact, you don't even need to go looking for it. So exuberant is nature in this part of the world that wild creatures form an unavoidable backdrop to whatever else you might get up to.

E The next morning, with these anxieties having proved unfounded, we wound further down through the coffee plantations in the sunshine to the estate of Tayutic. Here, my daughter helped to sort good macadamia nuts from bad as they rattled down the chute, then attempted to crush dried coffee beans in a stone mill.

F Admittedly, this would feel even more daunting if we hadn't done this already a few days ago, on the slopes of Arenal Volcano. Then, I found it terrifying, hurtling at unnatural speeds high above the canopy. Now I'm a little more confident.

G But before I can glory in my success, we're making our way to a hot springs resort, the penultimate stop on our two-week Costa Rican adventure tour. Like the other volcanoes we've seen in the country, the one near here belches sulphurous smoke.

Part 8

You are going to read an article about the difficulties associated with authenticating paintings by the 17th-century Dutch painter, Rembrandt. For questions **47–56**, choose from the sections (**A–D**). The sections may be chosen more than once.

Mark your answers **on the separate answer sheet**.

Which section mentions

a cumulative reaction?

| 47 | |

a lack of complaints among a particular group?

| 48 | |

a failed attempt to democratise a process?

| 49 | |

a common method for settling a debt?

| 50 | |

a shift in educational policy?

| 51 | |

a scientific process used to verify an opinion?

| 52 | |

a belief held where the negative aspects of a painting outweigh the positives on balance?

| 53 | |

a gesture attributed to a thought process?

| 54 | |

an opinion expressed to put an end to a trend?

| 55 | |

a false hypothesis devised with hindsight?

| 56 | |

How to identify a genuine Rembrandt

*Many of the Dutch painter's work are still disputed by art scholars – but why
are they so hard to authenticate?*

A When, in 1950, the 11th Duke of Devonshire was hit with a massive £7 million inheritance tax bill from the Collector of Taxes in the UK, he did what many stately homeowners do and gazed up at his walls to see what art might be sold. The Duke found that he had three Rembrandts, and suggested one of them in part-payment of the tax. Thus in 1957 a fine, signed Rembrandt, *Old Man in an Armchair*, went on display at the National Gallery in London. Barely a decade later, however, the picture was downgraded to being painted by 'a follower of Rembrandt'. 'Imposing as the mood is,' said the art historian Horst Gerson, 'the overall structure of the picture is very weak, even contradictory with divergences not to be found in Rembrandt's portraits from this great period'. Ever since, the picture has been largely ignored. Yet recently, Ernst van de Wetering, the world's leading authority on the artist, said the picture *was*, after all, by Rembrandt. 'It is a very important painting', he says, 'a painting about painting' that heralds reinvention in Rembrandt's technique in the 1650s. Van de Wetering believes Gerson made 'a vast mistake'.

B The fact that *Old Man in an Armchair* should not be treated as a portrait commissioned by a patron is crucial here. It's an observation of life, not intended as a likeness to the patron. To help depict this, Rembrandt allowed himself greater freedom with the brush than usual. We don't need to focus on the dress, so it is painted fluidly and rapidly. The right hand is beautifully weighted: we can be sure the sitter is not holding his head but absent-mindedly touching it, as one does in pensive moments. This different opinion, however, was greeted with indifference. What had happened? Put simply, Rembrandt connoisseurship – the ability to tell who painted what by close inspection – had imploded. The Rembrandt Research Project had been established with an admirable objective: namely, to say what was and what was not a genuine Rembrandt. But two key factors spelt doom for this approach. Firstly, it tried to make attributions by relying on a committee, thus allowing for indecision and group-think to reign. Secondly, connoisseurship itself became unfashionable and was seen as a redundant, elitist practice, no longer taught as a key skill in training art historians and curators.

C As the Project members began to cast doubt on the authenticity of some of Rembrandt's paintings, others joined in too, including major museum curators. Rembrandt experts became gripped with uncertainty – if opinion of picture X was no longer 'right', then surely pictures Y and Z, which were painted in a similar manner, must also be 'wrong'? Sometimes, rejections were made on the flimsiest of grounds: some paintings were downgraded, not because they didn't look like Rembrandt's late work, but because X-rays suggested that underneath the paintings there were signs of an unusual technique. And so it went on, until Van de Wetering saw that the madness had to stop. 'The Project had failed', he said, 'it was no good'. The latest 'official' number of Rembrandts is 340 which is believed by some still to be too few. It is pointed out that Van Dyck, not an especially rapid painter, is credited with about 750 works, and he died aged forty-two. Rembrandt lived until he was sixty-three.

D What then continues to hold back art historians and museum curators? Rembrandt scholars have convinced themselves that Rembrandt added his signature to works painted entirely by his many studio assistants in order to make money as quickly as possible. But there is no clear evidence for this; it is a theory that has been created. Rembrandt was more scrupulous than many scholars believe. It is known that Rembrandt was aware of how sensitive the matter of attribution was for patrons – at least twice Rembrandt was asked to adjudicate on work by other artists where it was suspected that they had added their signatures to work that was not their own. There is not a single case of one of Rembrandt's studio assistants grumbling about their master passing off their work as his own. Finally, it might be asked who were all these mysterious, supremely talented 'followers of Rembrandt' who have left no trace of any independent work: is it possible that they did not exist?

WRITING (1 hour 30 minutes)

Part 1

You **must** answer this question. Write your answer in **220–260** words in an appropriate style **on the separate answer sheet**.

---

1   Your class has listened to a radio discussion about the benefits of learning languages. You have made the notes below:

> **Benefits of learning languages:**
> - understanding other cultures
> - increasing job opportunities
> - providing intellectual challenge

> Some opinions expressed in the discussion:
>
> "When you learn a language you learn a lot more than just words."
>
> "You can apply for great jobs if you speak other languages."
>
> "Learning languages is good for the brain."

Write an essay for your tutor discussing **two** of the benefits of learning languages in your notes. You should **explain which benefit is more important, giving reasons** to support your opinion.

You may, if you wish, make use of the opinions expressed in the discussion, but you should use your own words as far as possible.

Part 2

Write an answer to **one** of the questions **2–4** in this part. Write your answer in **220–260** words in an appropriate style **on the separate answer sheet**. Put the question number in the box at the top of the page.

---

2   A TV company, FileView TV, is planning to produce a series 'The World's Greatest Sports Personalities of All Time'. They would like viewers to send in proposals suggesting someone to feature in the series. Say who you would suggest, describe that person's contribution to their sport, and explain whether or not the person is a good role model for today's young people.

    Write your **proposal**.

3   You are a student at an international college. You have decided to write to the college principal to suggest that the college should start a bus service for the college. In your letter, you should describe the problems of travelling to and from college, explain the reasons for your suggestion, and assess the benefits for the college and the local area.

    Write your **letter. You do not need to include postal addresses.**

4   You have just completed three months of unpaid work experience in a large company to learn about a career you are interested in. The company director has asked you to write a report. In your report, you should describe the new skills you acquired, comment on how well you were supported by the people you worked with, and evaluate how useful the experience will be for your future career.

    Write your **report**.

LISTENING (approximately 40 minutes)

Part 1

You will hear three different extracts. For questions **1–6**, choose the answer (**A**, **B** or **C**) which fits best according to what you hear. There are two questions for each extract.

Extract One

You hear two friends talking about people who were once famous but who are now relatively unknown.

1 What point does the man make about people who are no longer famous?

    A The public does not allow them to move on.

    B The probability of them being recognised is low.

    C The temptation for them not to let go of their celebrity status is great.

2 Why does the woman mention the example of the dancer?

    A to highlight the dancer's need for support from others

    B to express her admiration for the dancer's coping strategies

    C to suggest that the dancer's approach is by no means unusual

Extract Two

You hear two friends talking about swimming in rivers and lakes, a practice known as 'wild swimming'.

3 The woman decided to take up wild swimming because of

    A her desire to explore unfamiliar places.

    B the chance it offers to tackle a difficult challenge.

    C a feeling of boredom with existing hobbies.

4 Which aspect of communal swimming do they both particularly appreciate?

    A the variety of people they meet

    B the feeling of mutual support

    C the sharing of notable experiences

Extract Three

You hear two friends talking about installing solar electricity systems in private houses.

5   What aspect of solar power do the friends disagree about?

   A   the need for the government to support the industry

   B   the influence of the media on people's opinions

   C   the importance of price in the demand for green energy

6   In the man's opinion, what will happen in the future regarding energy?

   A   Vital resources will be scarce.

   B   People will be forced to accept major lifestyle changes.

   C   The current situation will continue for longer than expected.

Part 2

You will hear a sports nutritionist called Emily Anderson talking to a group of students about how she helps young athletes with their diet. For questions **7–14**, complete the sentences with a word or short phrase.

Working as a sports nutritionist

Emily's early passion for **(7)** .... influenced her choice of career.

After completing her education, Emily wanted to find employment in

(8) .... but there was a lack of opportunity.

Emily uses the word **(9)** .... to describe the stage youth

athletics has reached.

Emily often leads **(10)** .... , which she finds very rewarding.

Emily recommends doing a degree module in **(11)** .... to

increase work opportunities.

Emily explains that reading **(12)** .... the best way to keep

up with the latest developments.

Emily points out that what she calls the **(13)** .... can require

considerable investment.

Emily was surprised that one of the advantages of her job is the **(14)** ....

that she can use.

Part 3

You will hear part of an interview with two environmentalists, Carol Jones and James Wilson, who are talking about an approach to conservation called rewilding, and damaged environments. For questions **15–20**, choose the answer (**A**, **B**, **C** or **D**) which fits best according to what you hear.

---

15 Carol's view of rewilding as a form of conservation is that it
    A   is limited in its scope.
    B   enables native species to thrive.
    C   is often misunderstood by non-scientists.
    D   may be difficult to implement with some species.

16 James supports the presence of alien species because
    A   they have been shown to improve soil quality.
    B   they are part of the evolution of nature.
    C   the problem of removing them is too complex.
    D   most native species are too weak to survive.

17 Carol produced her report on the location of native species in order to
    A   contradict certain widely-held beliefs.
    B   criticise the way people neglect nature.
    C   provide support for her original hypothesis.
    D   enable research to be done into unusual habitats.

18 With conservation work, Carol and James both think that
    A   it's easy to learn from past mistakes made with ecosystems.
    B   most ecosystems today have undergone some improvement.
    C   it's necessary to understand that all ecosystems are dynamic.
    D   most people accept the idea that climate change affects ecosystems.

19 Why does Carol mention wildlife corridors?
    A   to illustrate what ordinary citizens can do
    B   to clarify a scientific term that is often misunderstood
    C   to describe the way animals behave in urban environments
    D   to show why open spaces have disappeared from cities

20 How does James feel about the attitude of some people towards the environment?
    A   worried about the way they ignore the problems
    B   annoyed that they are unwilling to listen to suggestions
    C   frustrated that they continue to plant non-native species
    D   disappointed that they are only concerned with their own interests

Part 4

You will hear five short extracts in which people are talking about leaving their previous jobs to work freelance from home.

TASK ONE

For questions **21–25**, choose from the list (**A–H**) the reason why each speaker decided to work freelance from home.

TASK TWO

For questions **26–30**, choose from the list (**A–H**) the aspect of working freelance from home which each speaker has found challenging.

While you listen, you must complete both tasks.

A resisting online distractions				

A to fulfil a greater variety of tasks		Speaker 1		21	
B to feel free of supervision		Speaker 2		22	
C to follow the example of a friend		Speaker 3		23	
D to develop their creativity		Speaker 4		24	
E to gain greater financial rewards		Speaker 5		25	
F to avoid travel difficulties					
G to be in control of their workload					
H to have more options for holidays					

A resisting online distractions		Speaker 1		26	
B having no colleagues to talk to		Speaker 2		27	
C stopping focussing on work at the end of the day		Speaker 3		28	
D feeling responsible for everything		Speaker 4		29	
E keeping up with professional developments		Speaker 5		30	
F organising the physical workspace					
G receiving no feedback from superiors					
H preventing interruptions from visitors					

SPEAKING (15 minutes)

There are two examiners. One (the interlocutor) conducts the test, providing you with the necessary materials and explaining what you have to do. The other examiner (the assessor) is introduced to you, but then takes no further part in the interaction.

Part 1 (2 minutes)

The interlocutor first asks you and your partner for some information about yourselves, then widens the scope of the questions by asking about e.g. your leisure activities, studies, travel and daily life. You are expected to respond to the interlocutor's questions and listen to what your partner has to say.

Part 2 (a one-minute 'long turn' for each candidate, plus a 30-second response from the second candidate)

You are each given the opportunity to talk for about a minute, and to comment briefly after your partner has spoken.

The interlocutor gives you a set of three pictures and asks you to talk about two of them for about one minute. It is important to listen carefully to the interlocutor's instructions. The interlocutor then asks your partner a question about your pictures and your partner responds briefly.

You are then given another set of pictures to look at. Your partner talks about these pictures for about one minute. This time the interlocutor asks you a question about your partner's pictures and you respond briefly.

Part 3 (4 minutes)

In this part of the test, you and your partner are asked to talk together. The interlocutor places a question and some text prompts on the table between you. This stimulus provides the basis for a discussion, after which you will need to make a decision on the topic in question. The interlocutor explains what you have to do.

Part 4 (5 minutes)

The interlocutor asks some further questions, which leads to a more general discussion of the topic you have discussed in Part 3. You may comment on your partner's answers if you wish.

Test 3

READING AND USE OF ENGLISH (1 hour 30 minutes)

Part 1

For questions **1–8**, read the text below and decide which answer (**A**, **B**, **C** or **D**) best fits each gap. There is an example at the beginning (**0**).
Mark your answers **on the separate answer sheet**.

Example:

0 A regard   **B** notice   **C** recognise   **D** watch

0	A	B	C	D
	⎯	⎯	⎯	▄

Glass

Over 400 years ago, the Italian inventor, Galileo, became the first person in history to use a telescope to **(0)** …….. the night sky and see the solar system in all its **(1)** …….. . This was possible because Europeans were already using glass, for example to make windows and elaborate chandeliers, and were well aware of its **(2)** …….. . So when Galileo decided he wanted a telescope, he had a **(3)** …….. tradition of glassmaking and highly skilled glassmakers who he could **(4)** …….. on to provide him with a lens.

Glass lenses were later **(5)** …….. to many other uses, not least the invention of eye glasses. It's hard to **(6)** …….. the impact of this technology on those who up to that point could only see a blurred world.

Yet for all its considerable importance in human history, glass is now taken for granted. When we go to the top of a skyscraper we **(7)** …….. the quality of the light but rarely the glass itself. Perhaps it's because we look through it, rather than at it, that glass fails to **(8)** …….. to our emotions.

1 **A** marvel   **B** glory   **C** magic   **D** triumph

2 **A** aspects   **B** means   **C** properties **D** resources

3 **A** fruitful   **B** deep   **C** plentiful   **D** rich

4 **A** catch   **B** hold   **C** call   **D** pick

5 **A** put   **B** taken   **C** set   **D** turned

6 **A** overcome   **B** overstate   **C** overtake   **D** overdo

7 **A** approve   **B** compliment **C** honour   **D** appreciate

8 **A** demand   **B** appeal   **C** claim   **D** attract

Part 2

For questions **9–16**, read the text below and think of the word which best fits each gap. Use only **one** word in each gap. There is an example at the beginning (**0**).
Write your answers **IN CAPITAL LETTERS on the separate answer sheet**.

Example:

0	A	R	O	U	N	D											

Handwriting is history

Handwriting has been (**0**) .... for about 6,000 years, just a small fraction of the time that humans have been on this earth, but its effects have been enormous. Writing doesn't come naturally to us; (**9**) .... seeing and hearing, it must be taught.

However, (**10**) .... that computers have taken over our world, the need to write anything by hand is becoming redundant. Some educationalists are therefore questioning why schools should teach joined-up writing at (**11**) .... It takes up a lot of teaching time that could otherwise be devoted (**12**) .... keyboard skills. But these experts admit that handwriting (**13**) .... indeed have a presence that is absent in typed prose.

Many of us rebel (**14**) .... the radical idea of abandoning writing by hand because we think that our personal identity shines through in our handwriting. It allows self-expression to grow and is regarded by many (**15**) .... the mark of a civilised society. So, are we really ready to enter a world (**16**) .... the artistic flow of handwritten script might be about to disappear?

Part 3

For questions **17–24**, read the text below. Use the word given in capitals at the end of some of the lines to form a word that fits in the gap **in the same line**. There is an example at the beginning (**0**). Write your answers **IN CAPITAL LETTERS on the separate answer sheet**.

Example: | **0** | B | E | N | E | F | I | C | I | A | L | | | | | | | |

Singing in a choir is good for you!

According to researchers, not only does singing in a choir make us feel good, it may also be **(0)** …….. to our health. **BENEFIT**

A recent online survey of people who sang in choirs, played team sports or took up dancing all yielded very high levels of **(17)** …….. **PSYCHOLOGY**
well-being. However, it was the choristers who stood out as feeling the most **(18)** ……… . Why is this? Singing in a choir was shown **LIFT**
to be **(19)** …….. more effective at improving the mood of its **SIGNIFY**
(20) …….. because of the synchronised moving and breathing with **PARTICIPATE**
other people. Alternatively, it could simply be the fact that being part of a **(21)** …….. group is particularly satisfying. Over the years, **MEAN**
researchers have found that choral singing has a number of health benefits as well, including boosting the immune system and lowering stress levels. One study has even suggested that it can increase life **(22)** …….. . **EXPECT**

Although researchers admit that some of their studies are still **(23)** …….. , they feel there does seem to be the **SPECULATE**
(24) …….. that singing in a group is more than just fun. **IMPLY**

Part 4

For questions **25–30**, complete the second sentence so that it has a similar meaning to the first sentence, using the word given. **Do not change the word given.** You must use between **three** and **six** words, including the word given. Here is an example (**0**).

Example:

0 James would only speak to the head of department alone.

ON

James ………………………………… to the head of department alone.

The gap can be filled with the words 'insisted on speaking', so you write:

Example: | **0** | INSISTED ON SPEAKING |

Write **only** the missing words **IN CAPITAL LETTERS on the separate answer sheet**.

---

25 I'm convinced that David is holding something back about his plans for moving.

HONEST

I'm convinced that David is ……………………………….... about his plans for moving.

26 John always trained hard, but he never succeeded in winning a gold medal.

HOW

No ……………………………….... trained, he never succeeded in winning a gold medal.

27 The manager assured me that she would order a replacement watch.

WORD

The manager ……………………………….... that she would order a replacement watch.

28 There was no money to allow the construction of the road to continue.

LACK

Construction of the road could not ………………………….….. money.

29 The manager never doubted that the latest model of the phone would be a great success.

MIND

There was never any ………………………………….... that the latest model of the phone would be a great success.

30 Gina found it impressive that her tutor was able to remember all his students' names.

ABILITY

Gina was ………………………………….... to remember all his students' names.

Part 5

You are going to read an article about philosophy. For questions **31–36**, choose the answer (**A**, **B**, **C** or **D**) which you think fits best according to the text.
Mark your answers **on the separate answer sheet**.

Philosophy needs to engage more with the world

Philosopher Adrian Small considers the role of philosophers in modern life

'What do you do for a living?' It's classic small talk – we define ourselves by our jobs. And it's a question usually answered in a few words. However, when you're a philosopher, as I am, it's slightly harder to deal with. For one thing, describing yourself as a philosopher sounds rather pretentious. Saying you study or teach the subject is fine, but to say you are a philosopher is, in the eyes of many, to claim access to some mystical truth or enlightenment above one's fellows. This is clearly nonsense; philosophers are no different from – indeed are part of – the masses, but the persistence of the notion makes me hesitate.

So why does this stereotype of a philosopher pervade? One reason is that philosophers have established themselves as people who judge the activities of others and celebrate intellectual life. The Greek philosopher Aristotle (384 – 322 BC) argued that a life lived in contemplation, i.e. a philosophical life, was the most virtuous of all. Few modern philosophers would agree, but there's still a cultural aura around philosophy that associates it, rightly, with the life of the mind. Another Greek philosopher, Socrates, remarked that 'the unexamined life is not worth living', meaning that a life that simply accepted prevailing cultural norms would be deeply unsatisfying. It's partly mankind's innate ability to reflect upon the world that allows us control over our lives, and therefore the ability to make our own decisions.

But the examined life doesn't require the wide reading of the philosophical classics, nor a life dedicated to intellectual reflection. It simply means looking more closely at the everyday experiences that define our lives to ensure they deserve their central role. It doesn't need to be the life of the sage, removed from society in order to evaluate it impartially. In fact, in order for the examined life to serve in guiding the experience of individuals, it's actually a deeply practical enterprise, and one in which knowledge should be shared, as it's an essential element of the good life.

This brings me to a second reason for the misconception about philosophers: in becoming a profession, academic philosophy has grown increasingly removed from lived experiences, especially those of people without formal training in the discipline. This isn't entirely the fault of philosophers: university funding, performance evaluations and esteem are tied to increasingly expensive and inaccessible academic journals. As a result, philosophers have little opportunity to explain their ideas to anyone other than the minute group of experts who populate their particular field of study. For the lay observer, the discipline can often seem far removed from reality.

If the bulk of philosophers once challenged this view of themselves as being remote, many have since ceased. Although the university system initiated the environment of privileged isolation, academics haven't shied away from supporting it. As thinking in some areas has grown increasingly concerned with very specific, technical debates, the process of interpreting them for philosophers working outside the specific subfield can be laborious enough, but trying to do so for the untrained mind becomes almost impossible. Philosophy, in some circles, has withdrawn from society altogether. This trend must be reversed.

I sometimes describe myself as an 'ethicist', because most of my work is in ethics, the field of philosophy concerned with evaluating human activity. More recently, though, I've begun to feel that title insufficient to capture my area of inquiry, because ethics is commonly asserted as being connected to formal codes, values and laws. This represents quite a new and largely unconsidered development in philosophical thinking: the field of ethics has colloquially come to refer to applied ethics – a subfield that explores the justice of particular social practices. The task of the ethicist, in modern thinking, is to determine whether or not a certain activity is 'ethical' or acceptable.

These are important questions, and ones I engage in regularly. However, there's more to philosophy than this. A typical discussion might, for example, begin by exploring whether illegally downloading films is unethical (it is) before moving to an exploration of how we think about responsibility, our attitudes towards art, and the influence of market consumerism. In this way, philosophy can help people look a little more closely at the practices and behaviours that define their lives. Sometimes this might reveal something we already know; at other times we might discover that our beliefs are hard to justify. Either way, merely by examining these ideas, we'll be doing something for the benefit of everyone.

31 How does the writer feel when he is asked about his job?

    A annoyed that people do not understand what he says
    B frustrated that people define themselves by their work
    C apprehensive about the reaction his response will cause
    D anxious to explain that he is no cleverer than anyone else

32 In the second paragraph, what does the writer say about human beings?

    A We all enjoy challenging the established cultural norms.
    B We are all capable of a certain degree of contemplation.
    C We are wary of those who stand in judgement of others.
    D We have lost the ability to learn from teachings of the past.

33 According to the third paragraph, an examined life is one in which a person

    A understands the practical application of their studies.
    B appreciates knowledge for its own sake.
    C considers their priorities.
    D lives apart from others.

34 The second reason the writer gives for the misconception about philosophers is that

    A few people ever find out about philosophical studies.
    B philosophers now work exclusively in universities.
    C philosophy has become less popular as a course of study.
    D the subjects which philosophers choose to focus on are obscure.

35 What does the writer say about the term 'ethicist' in the sixth paragraph?

    A He uses it to show he represents a new branch of philosophy.
    B The way in which it is used by philosophers has changed.
    C It makes clear his connection with the justice system.
    D It is too narrow to describe the work he does.

36 The writer uses the example of downloading films to show

    A the type of conversation that he thinks people should be having about philosophy.
    B how applied ethics can lead to considerations of more universal issues.
    C that the study of philosophy should play a greater role in modern life.
    D how people are able to ignore their own ethical failings.

Part 6

You are going to read four extracts from articles in which experts discuss Antarctica. For questions **37–40**, choose from the reviewers **A–D**. The reviewers may be chosen more than once.
Mark your answers **on the separate answer sheet**.

Antarctica

A Antarctica is a pristine and unspoilt continent. Not only is it unrivalled in its beauty but Antarctic science has revealed much about the impact of human activity on the natural world. For example, the discovery by scientists of the hole in the ozone layer above Antarctica revealed the damage done to the Earth's atmosphere by man-made chemicals. The fact that Antarctica is so vital for such scientific knowledge, to my mind, suggests that it must be left undisturbed in order to allow further scientific research on such critical international issues as climate change, long-range weather forecasting and the operation of marine eco-systems (crucial to sustainable fishing). If mines to exploit its natural resources were to be placed on the continent, these would undoubtedly affect the scientific readings. Only by having Antarctica completely untouched can we guarantee the level of accuracy we now have.

B Access to Antarctica should be restricted to those with a serious purpose. To suggest an example, almost 30,000 tourists are expected this year in what is, to my mind, a place of unparalleled charm in the universe. Most of them will be on cruise ships, which call at Antarctica's sites for just a few days. This number is, however, rising rapidly and some visitors are now undertaking adventurous activities such as ski-hiking, scuba-diving, snowboarding and mountaineering. Unchecked, this influx of people is greatly increasing the problems of waste management and their activities are having a negative impact on the coastal environment and its wildlife. Adventure tourists also need to be rescued by the authorities from time to time, diverting resources from science. The more vessels visiting the continent, the greater the chance of catastrophic oil spills or for rogue operators to neglect their environmental responsibilities.

C There may come a time when the need for resources calls into question the need for Antarctica to be left alone. However, continuing systematic investigation in Antarctica must, under no circumstances, be allowed to come to an end. Antarctica is a large continent, so it seems possible that mining for its resources could occur on one side of the continent, while the other could be maintained for investigative purposes. The distances between the bases would ensure there would be no adverse effect on either area of work. Furthermore, as the scientists worked, they would be able to notice any abnormalities caused by the exploitation of resources. If any were to come to light, scientists could promote discussions with governments and mining companies in order to address the issues involved. In this way, scientists would ensure that any negative impact on this most enchanting of environments would be kept to a minimum, thus eliminating cause for concern.

D The vast continent of Antarctica has been a major focus of scientific exploration for relatively few decades when compared to most areas on Planet Earth. Despite its remoteness, it has always attracted visitors, whether for adventure or leisure purposes. However, let's not lose sight of the fact that it's just one region and there are undoubtedly others which are equally stunning. Antarctica should be for all of humanity, not just for elite scientists who seek to deny others the right to go there while simultaneously demanding huge sums of money for their research projects. If the continent were opened up to tourism, revenues from this could be taxed as a way of offsetting the cost of scientific research. In order to prevent resulting damage to the environment, the International Association of Antarctica Tour Operators operates a strict code of practice. Therefore, I see no reason why we should be unduly alarmed about adverse effects on the landscape in Antarctica.

Which expert

shares an opinion with A on the value of carrying out scientific research in Antarctica?

37

has a different opinion to D on restrictions on visitors to Antarctica?

38

holds a different view from the other three on the subject of the beauty of Antarctica?

39

expresses a similar view to C regarding harm to Antarctica?

40

Part 7

You are going to read an article about the difficulties of being an environmentalist. Six paragraphs have been removed from the article. Choose from the paragraphs **A–G** the one which fits each gap (**41–46**). There is one extra paragraph which you do not need to use.
Mark your answers **on the separate answer sheet**.

The unbearable hypocrisy of being an environmentalist

Canadian environmentalist Rosa Sharp explores the contradictions
inherent in the lives of those who choose to live a greener life

I consider myself an environmentalist, yet last weekend I spent five hours in a car dealership going through the rigmarole of getting a new car – arguably one of the most polluting devices in modern-day life.

41	

In a similar vein, an environmental lawyer I know, who came to his profession amid a deep affinity for and desire to protect the environment, now works seventy hours a week in a city centre office, staring at his computer screen. The work in which he makes great strides to protect the natural world also prevents him from enjoying it, leaving him torn between the change he wants to create, and his ability to enjoy the countryside for more than the odd weekend between cases.

42	

This unbearable hypocrisy is a struggle for the individual and a delight for the critic, yet it seems both necessary and inescapable. All of us exist within the very system we hope to change. I use a laptop, a smartphone, internet, electricity. Most of the publications I write anti-consumerism articles for are paid for by advertisements for consumer products. This delicate balancing act epitomises the seemingly inescapable reality of the modern world which we've built and which now runs our lives.

43	

However, an escape of this kind also means losing priceless human connection and culture, as well as the chance to educate or inspire change in others.

The fear of navigating this intellectual conflict, as well as the fear of armchair critics declaring that you've failed is, I believe, at the heart of many people's reluctance to adopt more green practices.

44	

Apparently, a decision to live in a way which limits the damage you're causing to the environment means instantly opening yourself up to harsh criticism. You never committed to changing everything in your life, and yet, having made one or two changes, you're suddenly expected to be able to justify just about any aspect of your life that your attacker chooses.

45	

My own reluctant decision to continue running a car came about as a result of several carefully considered factors including the limited public transportation options in my city and six months of harsh Canadian winter. Yes it makes me feel bad, but choosing to try to be green means putting up with the fact that you'll fail, at least some of the time.

46	

I think environmentalist George Monbiot sums it up best: 'Hypocrisy is the gap between your aspirations and your actions. Environmentalists have high aspirations – they want to live more ethically – and they will always fall short. But the alternative to hypocrisy isn't moral purity (no one manages that), but cynicism. Give me hypocrisy any day.'

A After all, most of us would be put off to discover that, by deciding to start cycling to work or buying only locally produced food, we have tacitly branded ourselves and joined the often-mocked world of righteously indignant environmentalists who protest against energy companies while still availing themselves of heated homes and gas-powered transportation.

B It seems cruel that trying to safeguard what you love should mean you are unable to experience it first-hand. But such contrasts exist in the lives of most environmentalists. Some of us own cars; some still eat meat. The more famous regularly fly great distances to speak about the horrific impact of carbon emissions – such as that released by the airplanes they arrived on.

C And after all, why should anyone have to do this? There's an assumption that you'll have all the answers. 'Why bother recycling when you still drive?' 'Aren't those annual flights erasing the impact of anything else you do?' Well, of course in an ideal world, we environmentalists would live completely ethically, but this isn't an ideal world.

D Although I advocate buying second-hand, I chose to lease new. I encourage walking, cycling and public transportation, and I do take advantage of these options regularly, yet here I was, accepting the keys and setting off with a shiny new ride and a sinking sense of discomfort.

E They provide a perfect illustration of how being an environmentalist has always been about the need to make compromises. For most of us, leaving modern life behind just isn't an option. However, the fact that living a greener existence is challenging doesn't mean we shouldn't do what we can.

F In order to avoid it, one would need to go off the grid; abandon modern living for a hut in the woods. It's a move which, if you're brave enough to make it, enables you to subtract most of your environmental impact, and I think everyone, myself included, fantasises about it from time to time.

G And I've come to realise that it's a compromise I can live with. We can either accept the *status quo*, or work towards something better. Doing so often looks less like an off-grid hut in the woods and more like finding a way to exist in an uncomfortably unsustainable society whilst also trying to change it.

Part 8

You are going to read an article about an artist who made a film which shows her daughter Billie between the ages of eleven and eighteen. For questions **47–56**, choose from the sections (**A–D**). The sections may be chosen more than once.

Mark your answers **on the separate answer sheet**.

Which section mentions

speculation as to the motives behind the project?

| 47 | |

praise for the choice of medium used?

| 48 | |

a difference in attitudes towards the project?

| 49 | |

a recollection which remains very vivid?

| 50 | |

details about personal habits which have remained constant?

| 51 | |

something which the artist wishes to retain?

| 52 | |

an assertion that the film contains a narrative element?

| 53 | |

details of how content to be included was approved?

| 54 | |

a reference to Billie's increased reluctance to reveal true feelings?

| 55 | |

factors which made Billie feel limited by the project?

| 56 | |

Growing up on film

A When artist and film maker Melanie Manchot's daughter Billie was 11, Manchot had the idea of videoing her for just one minute every month until she turned 18. And when she proposed the idea to her daughter, the answer was an instant affirmative as Billie was familiar with the processes involved. 'She grasped the idea quickly,' Manchot says. 'To me, it was a commitment from the beginning. I wanted it to last for seven years. For Billie, it was much lighter – a "let's try it".' Starting as Billie began her last term of primary school, the project slipped seamlessly into their routine. 'It was always at the beginning of the month, Billie back from school, at the end of my working day,' says Manchot. 'We'd go downstairs into the studio. I marked the spot where Billie would stand and where the camera would be and it stayed the same for seven years.'

B How does Billie remember the process? She thought that overall it was not that bad though there were times when she was less keen. She says: 'You have to stay in the one spot and there's no sound, so you can't really do much. I think the fact that it was a film, not photos, made it more representative. You can pose for a quick photo but when you're standing there for a minute, it feels more like you. It wasn't digital, so I didn't really see it afterwards. We might film for a year and then it would be sent off to be developed. I didn't have a sense of what it would all be like.' Manchot was equally uncertain: 'I didn't see it for long periods and didn't know what it would become. Billie had veto rights all the way through. She could always tell me that she wanted something to stay private. Then that piece of film would become a portrait for us as a family.'

C Filming for the project finished as Billie turned 18. Shortly afterwards, Manchot was invited to exhibit it. It was as if the whole thing had been planned – the exhibition started five days before Billie was due to go away to university. 'I was looking back at all this film, seeing the years gone by, putting it into a sequence – and Billie was packing up her whole life, ready to leave,' recalls Manchot. The installation, *11/18*, is an 18-minute sequence, with a screen for each year. 'There's no story,' says Manchot. 'But in a way, there is. It's the story of growing up.' Billie at 11 looks more playful, more relaxed. She laughs and yawns and shows things to the camera. The older Billie is more still, more wary, more steady and composed. There's the sense of an interior, a holding back. But still there's continuity. Certain gestures – the way she pushes back her hair and looks up, for example – survive from 11 into adulthood. In the final minute, all the images appear at the same time – all the Billies are present together. And then they are gone.

D What's striking for a parent is how fast we can forget our children's younger selves, how completely they vanish. Has making *11/18* helped Manchot hold on to every age and stage? 'When I see young children now, it seems such a distance,' she says. 'I remember Billie being six clearly and poignantly – we spent a month in Ibiza and I can almost project myself back to that time and see her and feel her, the size, the dimensions. But there are lots of times between that have disappeared because that's what time does – you can't hold on to it. I remember filming Billie so well – some of those memories are so powerful, what she wore, how she rolled up her T-shirt. The marks of where we had to stand are still there on the studio floor and I'm going to keep them there for ever. Maybe part of making this was to allow me as a mother and as an artist to stay more in touch with the many small moments that slip away.'

WRITING (1 hour 30 minutes)

Part 1

You **must** answer this question. Write your answer in **220–260** words in an appropriate style **on the separate answer sheet**.

---

1   Your class has just watched an online discussion about factors which influence our consumer choices. You have made the notes below:

Factors which influence our consumer choices:

- celebrities
- peer pressure
- marketing

Some opinions expressed in the programme:

"People want to be like their favourite stars."

"No one wants to be different."

"Who takes any notice of all those adverts?"

Write an essay for your tutor discussing **two** of the factors which influence our consumer choices in your notes. You should **explain which factor is more significant, giving reasons** to support your opinion.

You may, if you wish, make use of the opinions expressed in the programme, but you should use your own words as far as possible.

Part 2

Write an answer to **one** of the questions **2–4** in this part. Write your answer in **220–260** words in an appropriate style **on the separate answer sheet**. Put the question number in the box at the top of the page.

---

2   You were recently sent on a training course by the company you work for, and your manager has asked you to write a report on the training you received. In your report, you should briefly describe the training, explain why it was useful for your current job, and say how the new skills may help you in the future.

Write your **report**.

3   You receive an email from a friend.

> ...
>
> I hear you ran a half-marathon – that sounds interesting. What organisation were you raising money for? Why didn't you just give them some money?
>
> I look forward to hearing from you.

Write an email to your friend describing your experience, explaining the work of the organisation you were raising money for and saying whether you think such events are an effective way to support charities.

Write your **email**.

4   A car-sharing scheme has been running in your area for six months. You decide to write a review of the scheme for an English-language magazine. You should briefly explain how the scheme works in your area, and evaluate the advantages and disadvantages of such schemes, in general.

Write your **review**.

LISTENING (approximately 40 minutes)

Part 1

You will hear three different extracts. For questions **1–6**, choose the answer (**A**, **B** or **C**) which fits best according to what you hear. There are two questions for each extract.

Extract One

You hear two newspaper journalists talking about their work to a group of students.

1   The man gives the example of social media sites to

    A   clarify how important they are in everyday life.

    B   compare their usefulness with that of newspapers.

    C   defend people's attitude to news nowadays.

2   What do they both think about their job?

    A   It can be stressful at times.

    B   It is important to be a team player.

    C   There are more negatives than positives.

Extract Two

You hear two language teachers discussing the use of emoticons, the pictures many people use to express emotion in text messages.

3   What is the woman doing?

    A   questioning the value of current research into emoticons

    B   proposing ideas for potential uses of emoticons

    C   identifying reasons for the popularity of emoticons

4   What do they both think about emoticons?

    A   They need to be used with caution.

    B   They are a lazy form of communication.

    C   They have universal appeal.

Extract Three

You hear two friends talking about a young professional tennis player.

5   The woman feels that the comments about the player in the media reflect

    A   how easy it is to take sport too seriously.

    B   a common misconception about sportspeople.

    C   a lack of understanding amongst sports journalists.

6   How does the man feel about the player's outbursts of anger?

    A   It's essential that they're kept in check.

    B   They're understandable in the circumstances.

    C   He's irritated about the way they'll be perceived.

Part 2

You will hear a woman called Jane Brooks talking about her work on various marine conservation projects. For questions **7–14**, complete the sentences with a word or short phrase.

Conservation work

When choosing her first volunteer job, Jane was undecided between marine conservation in

Thailand and a **(7)** .... scheme in Belize.

In Cambodia, Jane is employed as a **(8)** .... working with volunteers.

Jane went from diving at intermediate level to receiving her official

(9) .... in under six months.

Jane contrasts her present situation, living in the centre of a **(10)** .... ,

with her time in Thailand.

Jane uses the expression **(11)** .... to describe the way the local people

view her.

Something that Jane finds particularly upsetting is the number of

(12) .... that the volunteers recover from the sea.

As part of her current project's wider aims, Jane says they will be helping set up a

(13) .... scheme.

One of the things Jane enjoys most is watching new divers gain

(14) .... during the learning process.

Part 3

You will hear an interview with two college lecturers, Sarah Banks and Tom Weston, who are talking about working in clothes shops when they were students. For questions **15–20**, choose the answer (**A**, **B**, **C** or **D**) which fits best according to what you hear.

15   Regarding her choice of job in an expensive clothes store, Sarah
    A   wanted to develop her retail skills.
    B   accepted it because of a lack of alternatives.
    C   felt it would suit her interest in high-end fashion.
    D   hoped to meet influential clients.

16   Sarah says one aspect of the job she enjoyed was
    A   selecting the perfect clothes for demanding clients.
    B   creating an atmosphere in which clients felt comfortable.
    C   seeing how certain clothes could transform clients' appearance.
    D   observing how clients would often make inappropriate choices.

17   What was Sarah's approach to the staff dress code?
    A   She admits she turned her choice of clothes into a kind of protest.
    B   She took the opportunity to break the rules whenever possible.
    C   She was proud to wear the shop's clothes outside her workplace.
    D   She found it relatively easy to conform to what was required.

18   How did Tom feel about what he overheard while working in a boutique?
    A   sad that his suspicions about his boss were confirmed
    B   disappointed that colleagues had concealed things from him
    C   frustrated that his ideas were so readily rejected
    D   infuriated with himself for having been so naïve

19   In Tom's opinion, the students he teaches who have had work experience are
    A   less likely to require help in order to cope with academic life.
    B   inclined to take a healthy financial situation for granted.
    C   prepared to make sacrifices for the sake of their studies.
    D   more critical about the quality of the courses they're following.

20   What do Sarah and Tom agree that they learnt from their work experience as students?
    A   People tend to behave in the same way wherever they shop.
    B   Retail skills can be applied in a range of other contexts.
    C   Shop work presents a unique chance to develop people skills.
    D   Any kind of job can bring an improvement in self-esteem.

Part 4

You will hear five short extracts in which people are talking about their favourite series of travel guidebooks.

TASK ONE

For questions **21–25**, choose from the list (**A–H**) what each speaker particularly likes about the series of travel guidebooks.

TASK TWO

For questions **26–30**, choose from the list (**A–H**) one criticism each speaker has of the series of travel guidebooks.

While you listen, you must complete both tasks.

A	the coverage of cultural aspects	**A**	unnecessary information
B	their organisation into ready-made tour schedules	**B**	focus on popular destinations
C	their value as background research	**C**	lack of practical detail
D	the variety of the images	**D**	confusing visuals
E	the contributions from respected authors	**E**	lack of expressive language in parts
F	the enjoyable style of writing	**F**	inconvenient to carry
G	the environmentally-friendly format	**G**	old-fashioned feel
H	the linguistic support offered	**H**	out-of-date content

Speaker 1	21	Speaker 1	26
Speaker 2	22	Speaker 2	27
Speaker 3	23	Speaker 3	28
Speaker 4	24	Speaker 4	29
Speaker 5	25	Speaker 5	30

SPEAKING (15 minutes)

There are two examiners. One (the interlocutor) conducts the test, providing you with the necessary materials and explaining what you have to do. The other examiner (the assessor) is introduced to you, but then takes no further part in the interaction.

Part 1 (2 minutes)

The interlocutor first asks you and your partner for some information about yourselves, then widens the scope of the questions by asking about e.g. your leisure activities, studies, travel and daily life. You are expected to respond to the interlocutor's questions and listen to what your partner has to say.

Part 2 (a one-minute 'long turn' for each candidate, plus a 30-second response from the second candidate)

You are each given the opportunity to talk for about a minute, and to comment briefly after your partner has spoken.

The interlocutor gives you a set of three pictures and asks you to talk about two of them for about one minute. It is important to listen carefully to the interlocutor's instructions. The interlocutor then asks your partner a question about your pictures and your partner responds briefly.

You are then given another set of pictures to look at. Your partner talks about these pictures for about one minute. This time the interlocutor asks you a question about your partner's pictures and you respond briefly.

Part 3 (4 minutes)

In this part of the test, you and your partner are asked to talk together. The interlocutor places a question and some text prompts on the table between you. This stimulus provides the basis for a discussion, after which you will need to make a decision on the topic in question. The interlocutor explains what you have to do.

Part 4 (5 minutes)

The interlocutor asks some further questions, which leads to a more general discussion of the topic you have discussed in Part 3. You may comment on your partner's answers if you wish.

Test 4

READING AND USE OF ENGLISH (1 hour 30 minutes)

Part 1

For questions **1–8**, read the text below and decide which answer (**A**, **B**, **C** or **D**) best fits each gap. There is an example at the beginning (**0**).
Mark your answers **on the separate answer sheet**.

Example:

0 A provision **B** output **C** yield **D** supply

0	A	B	C	D
	▢	▬	▢	▢

A taste of the future

Experimental psychologists, who have influenced the **(0)** …….. of food industry giants by studying how our senses interact to form our perception of flavour, are turning their attention to the menus of leading restaurants. How to make bug-eating acceptable to westerners is just one of the problems they are **(1)** …….. .

Sensory testing has already been used to **(2)** …….. how consumers are affected by the colours in packaging. It was found that increasing the amount of yellow on cans of lemonade **(3)** …….. people they could taste more lemon. **(4)** …….. the researchers are also helping brands to produce healthier food by making reductions in the salt and sugar they contain. If this is done **(5)** …….. , customers don't notice the difference from one packet to the **(6)** …….. .

Their study of how we experience food has already provided some fascinating **(7)** …….. for chefs. The colour of crockery, the weight of cutlery, background noise – these all control taste, and people, not surprisingly perhaps, eat more when in the **(8)** …….. of friends.

1	**A**	tackling	**B**	grappling	**C**	cracking	**D**	managing
2	**A**	dictate	**B**	decide	**C**	direct	**D**	determine
3	**A**	tricked	**B**	convinced	**C**	swayed	**D**	influenced
4	**A**	Lately	**B**	Instantly	**C**	Currently	**D**	Shortly
5	**A**	repeatedly	**B**	cautiously	**C**	regularly	**D**	gradually
6	**A**	next	**B**	previous	**C**	second	**D**	following
7	**A**	insights	**B**	judgements	**C**	features	**D**	elements
8	**A**	party	**B**	crowd	**C**	group	**D**	company

Part 2

For questions **9–16**, read the text below and think of the word which best fits each gap. Use only **one** word in each gap. There is an example at the beginning (**0**).
Write your answers **IN CAPITAL LETTERS on the separate answer sheet**.

Example: | **0** | | T | H | E | | | | | | | | | | | | | | |

Safer cycling

Everyone is familiar with (**0**) .... workings of airbags in cars, designed to absorb the impact of a crash. But now an airbag for cyclists has been invented and it's being promoted (**9**) .... a helmet for people who don't like wearing helmets.

When I started cycling, I always wore a helmet but after many years without ever really needing its protection, I started to leave it behind – (**10**) .... because of vanity, rather because of the hassle of having to carry it once I'd parked my bike.

The cyclist's airbag fits round your neck a bit (**11**) .... a scarf. It's heavier than it looks, which I put down (**12**) .... the fact that it includes a device that stops it being activated unnecessarily. In order to test it, I had to throw myself (**13**) .... the bike, head first. In mid-air, moments (**14**) .... I landed on the ground, I heard a loud bang. Then, (**15**) .... I was, lying next to my bike, wrapped in a firm white balloon. It certainly worked well but I'm not sure if it's good value (**16**) .... money as it can only be used once. Maybe I should go back to my helmet.

Part 3

For questions **17–24**, read the text below. Use the word given in capitals at the end of some of the lines to form a word that fits in the gap **in the same line**. There is an example at the beginning (**0**). Write your answers **IN CAPITAL LETTERS on the separate answer sheet**.

Example: | 0 | F | O | R | T | U | N | A | T | E | L | Y | | | | | | | | |

Laughter

Laughter is the best medicine they say and **(0)** …….. it's contagious.   **FORTUNE**

You know the situation – someone laughs and we **(17)** …….. laugh   **MIND**

in turn, without knowing why we've joined in. It's a totally **(18)** ……..   **VOLUNTARY**

response – just the sound of a laugh is enough to prompt it spreading.

It's no surprise, therefore, that recorded laughter is added to

television sitcoms. This laugh track **(19)** …….. the programme, in   **COMPANY**

the absence of a live audience, to stimulate laughter among the

(20) …….. at home.   **VIEW**

Naturally, the likelihood of our laughing is much greater in social

situations. Laughing with people brings the **(21)** …….. of feeling   **PLEASE**

accepted by the group; the only thing we have to be careful of is not

to laugh **(22)** …….. as that would destroy the positive group feeling.   **APPROPRIATE**

Laughter can be a particularly informative measure of relationships

because it's largely **(23)** …….. and hard to fake. As it's also a good   **PLAN**

guide to people's innermost **(24)** …….. , learning how to 'read' these   **THINK**

would be a valuable life skill.

Part 4

For questions **25–30**, complete the second sentence so that it has a similar meaning to the first sentence, using the word given. **Do not change the word given.** You must use between **three** and **six** words, including the word given. Here is an example (**0**).

Example:

0 James would only speak to the head of department alone.

ON

James ………………………………… to the head of department alone.

The gap can be filled with the words 'insisted on speaking', so you write:

Example:	0	INSISTED ON SPEAKING

Write **only** the missing words **IN CAPITAL LETTERS on the separate answer sheet**.

___

25 'I've never given this presentation before,' Mary admitted.

   FIRST

   Mary admitted that it was …………………………….... given that presentation.

26 Jane knew she should arrive at the airport two hours early.

   MEANT

   Jane knew she …………………………….... up at the airport two hours early.

27 Lisa was a good candidate so not surprisingly she was offered the job.

   CAME

   Lisa was a good candidate so it …………………………….... that she was offered the job.

28 Sally completely ignored the advice I gave her and bought that awful car.

NOTICE

Sally ………………………….... the advice I gave her and bought that awful car.

29 The price of computers has come down over the last few years.

DROP

There ………………………….... the price of computers over the last few years.

30 It'll be sunny later, so it's a good idea to apply some sunscreen.

BETTER

It'll be sunny later, so you ………………………….... on some sunscreen.

Part 5

You are going to read a magazine article about whether or not animals have emotions. For questions **31–36**, choose the answer (**A**, **B**, **C** or **D**) which you think fits best according to the text. Mark your answers **on the separate answer sheet**.

Animal Emotions

Tom Whipple asks 'Do animals really have emotions? And what are the consequences if they do?'

In a Swedish zoo a chimpanzee called Santino spent his nights breaking up concrete into pieces to throw at visitors during the day. Was he being spiteful? In caves in the US, female bats help unrelated fruit bat mothers if they can't find the right birthing position. Are they being caring? Fifty years ago, these questions would have been largely seen as irrelevant. Animals had behaviours, the behaviours produced measurable outcomes, and science recorded those outcomes. The idea that animals have consciousness, feelings and moral systems was sloppy and sentimental.

But recently that has partially changed. Thanks to research into the behaviour of bats, chimps, not to mention rats, dolphins and chickens, emotions of animals have gone from being a taboo area of investigation to being tentatively explored. It is a change that has in recent years filtered through the scientific strata to a selection of popular science books, such as Mark Bekoff's *Wild Justice* and Victoria Braithwaite's *Do Fish Feel Pain*? And in the process it has started a debate that may never be solved by science: can animals be said to have consciousness?

This debate stimulates a second, much less abstract, one: not of consciousness, but conscience – a person's moral sense of right and wrong that guides their behaviour. In a recent experiment involving cows that had to open a locked gate in order to get food, it became apparent that those that successfully opened the gate themselves showed more pleasure – by jumping and kicking their legs – than those that had to have the gate opened for them. If, as this research seems to imply, cows enjoy problem-solving, what does it mean for the production and consumption of beef?

The observations may not be disputed, but the interpretation of them is. According to Dr Jonathan Balcombe, author of *Second Nature*, the only logically consistent response to the new research is to stop eating meat. For him, humanity is on the verge of the greatest revolution in ethics since the abolition of slavery. According to Aubrey Manning, Professor Emeritus at Edinburgh University, we should at the very least re-evaluate our view of animal cognition. For him, 'the only tenable hypothesis is that animals do have a theory of mind, but it's simpler than ours.' And according to Professor Euan MacPhail we should just stop anthropomorphising. The three may never be reconciled because the crux of the issue is not so much a scientific disagreement, or even a moral one, but a philosophical one. Given that even defining consciousness is near impossible, can we ever hope to know, in the words of the philosopher Thomas Nagel, what it is like to be a bat? Let alone a bat midwife.

Balcombe describes a landmark experiment he did that – in his interpretation – appears to show that starlings – a type of bird – can get depressed. In a study at Newcastle University, starlings were split into two groups. Half were housed in luxurious cages, with plenty of space and water. The other half were housed in small, barren cages. Initially both groups were fed with tasty worms from one box and unpleasant worms from another, and soon learned to take only from the tasty box. But subsequently when the birds were offered only unpleasant worms, only the ones housed in luxurious cages would eat. It seemed, or at least Balcombe concluded, that being in a nasty cage caused the starlings to be pessimistic about life in general.

Balcombe, who has worked with animal rights groups, has a clear bias. 'We look back with abhorrence on an era where there was racism,' he says. 'Our view about animals will someday be the same. We can't espouse animal rights between bites of a cheeseburger.' If he were the only advocate of this view of animal consciousness, it might be easy to dismiss him as an extremist. Unfortunately for those who might prefer to ignore Balcombe, Professor Aubrey Manning is in the same camp. Manning has written a textbook, *An Introduction to Animal Behaviour*. 'What we are seeing is a pendulum swing,' he says. 'At the turn of the 20th century there were people who made assumptions that animals thought just like us, and there was a reaction against that. Now we are going the other way. But it is a highly contentious subject and you really want to try to avoid the sound of academics with various personal grievances and strong personal opinions.'

31 In the first paragraph the writer suggests that

    A some older animal research would now be seen as unscientific.
    B some animals respond too unpredictably to be included in reliable study data.
    C some animal research has come to conclusions that are highly questionable.
    D some animal behaviour is difficult to explain through a traditional approach.

32 In the second paragraph, what point is the writer making about the idea that animals have emotions?

    A It has been confused by many with another issue.
    B It has moved beyond mere academic speculation.
    C It has been fully accepted by the scientific community.
    D It has contradicted another recent proposal on the topic.

33 When the writer mentions cows, he is saying that

    A scientists now believe that certain animals have a sense of morality.
    B some animals are fundamentally unsuited to being kept in captivity.
    C the question of how animals should be treated needs to be re-examined.
    D the number of animals demonstrating intelligence is higher than previously thought.

34 In the fourth paragraph, what conclusion does the writer draw about the differing views of experts?

    A Some of them verge on the ridiculous.
    B They are based on flawed evidence.
    C They do not warrant further investigation.
    D A consensus is unlikely ever to be reached.

35 In the fifth paragraph, it is clear that the writer

    A wishes to be seen as objectively reporting Balcombe's experiment.
    B intends to defend Balcombe against a possible criticism.
    C is questioning the details of Balcombe's methods.
    D agrees in principle with Balcombe's ideas.

36 What is said in the final paragraph about Balcombe's views?

    A They have been directly influenced by research from a previous era.
    B They are shared by an eminent authority on the subject.
    C They have been rejected as extreme by one opponent.
    D They are seen as objectionable in some quarters.

Part 6

You are going to read four extracts from articles in which sports experts discuss hosting the Olympic Games. For questions **37–40**, choose from the experts **A–D**. The experts may be chosen more than once.

Mark your answers **on the separate answer sheet**.

Is hosting the Olympic Games worthwhile?

Four sports experts look at the pros and cons of hosting the summer Olympic Games

A It's clear that, both just before and immediately after the Olympics, the number of people routinely doing physical activity rises in the host country. But the main reason cities bid to hold the Olympics is that, perhaps against the odds, it's wildly popular with the voters who foot the bill. I say 'against the odds' because there is strikingly little evidence to suggest that such events draw new investment. Spending lavishly on a short-lived event is, financially speaking, a dubious long-term strategy. Additionally, when a city hosts the Olympics, those who may have been considering visiting it turn to other destinations in order to avoid the crowds. I don't think the issue would be solved by spreading the Games over more than one city, as this wouldn't be popular. In Sydney, for example, as many sports as possible were crammed into a dedicated Olympic Park, and the concept was very well received.

B It's rarely the case that all Olympic events are held in a single city. Early-round soccer games, for example, take place in many different towns. Still, hosting the Olympics poses a high risk to the leaders of the city involved. While in some places initial negativity turns to more positive emotions once the Games begin, in others strong local support during the bidding process can sour as the level of spending necessary becomes clear. Such a change seems rather unjust to me as cities which host the Olympics clearly experience a significant increase in trade. The positive impact on numbers of travellers including the host city in their itinerary is also generally quite significant. On the other hand, my research shows no direct link between the profile and popularity of a sport at the elite level during the Olympics and its subsequent uptake at the grassroots level in host cities.

C I think it's significant that, in the most recent round of bidding to host the Olympics, several world-famous cities withdrew after failing to summon sufficient support among their own citizens. Their objections were almost exclusively based around the huge budgets involved. Supporters like to point to the commerce that the Olympics has supposedly brought to certain cities. But that commerce was going to spring up anyway. It was not directly connected to the Olympics. The Olympics have become too big and expensive to have in one place. In this age of instant communication, there's simply no need to condense the Games in one overburdened location. Better distribution would also spread the associated rise in demand for hotels and restaurants that is one noticeable benefit of hosting the Games. Another is the increase in the number of people who, for example, join teams or start running regularly following the Olympics. We see this in almost all host cities.

D Every time we've analysed it, the conclusion has been the same: there is no real monetary benefit in hosting the Olympic Games. Temporary surges in consumer spending associated with a spike in arrivals from overseas may help to offset the expense of hosting, but it's clear that hosting the Olympics has become a burden. The solution, however, is simple – choose a range of cities to host, not just one. Politicians bid for the Olympics hoping it will increase their popularity. However, even if the bid is successful, the politicians involved are seldom still around once the event starts seven years later. And as for the claim that hosting the Games leads to fitter citizens, well we only have to look at London. Since the Olympics there, the number of people taking exercise for a minimum of thirty minutes at least once a week has actually declined.

Which expert

expresses a different view from the other three regarding the effect that hosting the Olympics has on the economy of the host city?

37 [ ]

has a different opinion from B on whether hosting the Olympics increases tourism in the host city?

38 [ ]

shares an opinion with B about whether hosting the Olympics increases participation in sport among residents of the host city?

39 [ ]

shares an opinion with C regarding the idea that several cities should get together to host the Olympic Games?

40 [ ]

Part 7

You are going to read a newspaper article about editing the sound in movies. Six paragraphs have been removed from the article. Choose from the paragraphs **A–G** the one which fits each gap (**41–46**). There is one extra paragraph which you do not need to use.
Mark your answers **on the separate answer sheet**.

The art of sound in movies

The monstrous complexity of sound editing work – the quest to make films sound the way the world sounds – may not be immediately apparent. After a movie has been filmed, it enters the labyrinthine world of post-production, in which the best takes are selected and spliced together into roughly 20-minute segments of film. These are worked on and then stitched together at the end of post-production.

41	

The distinction between these processes is subtle: the first two have more to do with the creation and selection of the sounds that make up each scene, and the development of a cohesive aural aesthetic for a movie. The third involves taking sounds created by the designers and editors and integrating them in each scene so that everything comes across as 'natural'.

42	

First, editors remove the audio recordings taken during filming and break down each scene into distinct sonic elements, namely dialogue, effects, music and Foley. 'Foley' is the term used for everyday sounds such as squeaky shoes or cutlery jangling in a drawer.

43	

Consider a classic movie scene in which something important has just happened, for example a villain has just pulled up in his car. There are a few moments of what might be mistaken for stillness. Nothing moves – but the soundscape is deceptively layered There might be a mostly unnoticeable rustle of leaves in the trees periodically, so faint that almost no one would register it consciously. Or the sound of a vehicle rolling through an intersection a block or two over; off camera, a dog barks somewhere far away.

44	

All this requires a very particular and somewhat strange set of talents and fascinations. You need the ability not only to hear with an almost superhuman ear, but also the technical proficiency and saint-like patience to spend hours getting the sound of a kettle's hiss exactly the right length as well as the right pitch – and not only the right pitch but the right pitch considering that the camera moves across the scene during the shot.

45	

This is why there is something very slightly unnerving about spending time around people whose powers of perception suggest the existence of an entirely different layer of reality that you are missing. The way they work requires an entirely different – and, in some senses, unnatural – way of experiencing sound. The process reflects the fact that each sound is important enough to deserve its own consideration, so each gets edited separately before being put all together and checked for coherence.

46	

Consequently, the vast majority of people walk around not hearing most of what there is to hear. Not so, for most sound editors. It can be mildly excruciating to listen this hard, to hear so much, which is why some of the team wear earplugs when they walk around the city.

A Each of these components needs to be built and then edited separately for every scene before being assigned its own dedicated editor. Then, the top guys take the team's work and layer it to make scenes that sound like the real world sounds.

B The gesture had the studious flourish which a minor orchestral instrumentalist – say, the triangle player – might devote to his one entrance. But instead of being the work of the actor, likely as not, that was a moustachioed man standing in his socks in a warehouse somewhere.

C This is radically unlike the way the human brain is designed to hear. We are predisposed to heed the rhythms and pitch of people talking and noises that might indicate threat. Other sounds – like 'white noise' – are depressed so that the brain fires fewer responses and we automatically 'tune out'. This is how the brain converts sound into information.

D The viewer's ear will subconsciously anticipate hearing a maddeningly subtle, but critical, Doppler effect, which means that the tone it makes as it boils needs to shift downward at precisely the interval that a real one would if you happened to walk by at that speed.

E Each part goes through picture editing (for such things as visual continuity or colour) before being handed over to the sound supervisor, who oversees all the various elements of sound design, sound editing, and mixing.

F When the thud of his boot heel finally connects with the asphalt, his breathing is laboured, even the pads of his fingers creak as they make contact with the collar of his leather jacket as he straightens. None of these are there because some microphone picked them up. They're there because someone chose them and put them there, like every other sound in the film.

G In other words, it is important to make sure the sound of a butterfly landing on the hood of a car isn't louder than a car backfiring. Only a few people have an ear for these types of work.

Part 8

You are going to read an article in which a scientist discusses the mistaken ideas people have about his profession. For questions **47–56**, choose from the sections (**A–D**). The sections may be chosen more than once.

Mark your answers **on the separate answer sheet**.

In which section does the writer

speculate about the experiences of other professionals?	47
suggest motives for the actions of particular scientists?	48
explain why an individual cannot be familiar with all branches of science?	49
suggest that being famous can cause people to behave in a particular way?	50
admit that a common portrayal of scientists achieves its purpose?	51
use an example from another profession to support an observation about human nature?	52
admit to a personal bias?	53
mention the role of the team in the advancement of scientific knowledge?	54
admit to a minor wrongdoing?	55
mention that misunderstandings about science are rooted in curriculum design?	56

Why people think scientists know everything

Neuroscientist Dean Burnett considers the reasons why people often have the wrong idea about science and scientists.

A One unexpected aspect of being a scientist is the weird questions you get asked by non-scientists. Whilst publicising my latest book, I've been asked many. Among my favourites is: 'Which are smarter, tigers or wolves?' As a neuroscientist, I'm not trained to answer this (assuming an answer even exists). Obviously, if I'm going to put myself out there as an authority on things, then I should expect questions. However, this happened to me even before I became a public figure, and other scientists I've spoken to report similar, regular occurrences. It's just something people do, like meeting a doctor at a party and asking them about a rash. If you're a scientist, people assume you know all science, something which would require several lifetimes of study. In truth, most scientists are, just like experts in any other field, very specialist. If you meet a historian who specialises in 19th-century Britain, asking them about ancient Egyptians is illogical. Maybe this does happen to historians. I can't say. It happens to scientists though. So where does this 'scientists know all science' preconception come from?

B Because my area of interest is the human brain, I tend to blame it for many of life's problems. For example, the way in which it handles information could lead to this idea of the all-knowing scientist. Our brain has to deal with a lot of information, so it often uses short cuts. One of these is to clump information together. While functionally useful, you can see how this would lead to inaccuracies or even prejudices. If someone struggles to understand science, in their heads it all gets lumped together as 'stuff I don't understand'. The same goes for scientists, who may get labelled as 'people who understand things I don't'. Education also plays a role. The study of science gets more specific the further you progress, but at a young age you get taught what's called simply 'science'. So you begin with this notion that science is just one subject, and have to gradually figure out otherwise. Would it be surprising then, if many people never really move on from this perception due to a disinterest in science, and consequently continue to regard scientists as interchangeable?

C The way in which scientists are portrayed in the media doesn't help either. Any new discovery or development reported in the press invariably begins with 'Scientists have discovered...' or 'According to scientists...'. You seldom get this in any other field. The latest government initiative does not begin with 'Politicians have decided...'. If any study or finding worth mentioning is invariably attributed to all scientists everywhere, it's understandable if the average reader ends up thinking they're all one and the same. The press also love the idea of the 'lone genius'. The story of a scientific discovery typically focuses on a single, brilliant intellectual, changing the world via his or her all-encompassing genius. While this makes for an inspiring narrative and therefore sells newspapers, it's far from the collaborative effort which most science is the result of. In fiction too, we constantly encounter the stand-alone genius who knows everything about everything, usually in very helpful and plot-relevant ways. This is bound to rub off on some people in the real world.

D Of course, this whole thing would be easier if it weren't for actual scientists making matters worse. Some, maybe unintentionally, make declarations about other fields which don't agree with what the evidence says. I've even done it myself occasionally. In popular science books, it's not uncommon for the author to stray into areas that they aren't that familiar with but which need to be addressed in order to provide a coherent argument. Sadly, you also get the scientists who, having achieved influence and prestige, start to believe their own press and end up making declarations about fields beyond their own, using confidence instead of actual awareness of how things work. Because such people have a public platform, the public assumes they must be right. The fact is that if scientists really did know everything, they'd know how to put an end to the misconceptions about their professions. But they don't. So they don't.

WRITING (1 hour 30 minutes)

Part 1

You **must** answer this question. Write your answer in **220–260** words in an appropriate style on **the separate answer sheet**.

---

1   Your class has just watched a TV documentary on factors influencing social trends. You have made the notes below:

Factors influencing social trends:
- communications
- opportunities
- advertising

Some opinions expressed in the discussion:

"The smartphone has transformed social interaction."

"Education and travel can affect people's tastes."

"No one can escape the social pressures of advertising."

Write an essay for your tutor discussing **two** of the factors in your notes. You should **explain which factor you think has greater influence on social trends, giving reasons** to support your opinion.

You may, if you wish, make use of the opinions expressed in the discussion, but you should use your own words as far as possible.

Part 2

Write an answer to **one** of the questions **2–4** in this part. Write your answer in **220–260** words in an appropriate style **on the separate answer sheet**. Put the question number in the box at the top of the page.

---

2   Local businesses have set up a fund to pay for a community facility in the area where you live, for example, a theatre, a nature reserve or perhaps an ice rink. The organisers have asked residents to give their opinions about how the fund should be used. You decide to write a proposal suggesting a facility, justifying your choice and explaining why you think it would be beneficial for the community.

Write your **proposal**.

3   You receive this email from an English-speaking friend:

> ...
>
> I'm about to start a business course at college and I'm wondering whether it'd be a good idea to take on a part-time job at the same time – I know that's what you did. How difficult did you find it to balance your work and study time? Can you suggest the most suitable kind of job to look for? I'd be grateful for any ideas and suggestions.

Write your **email**.

4   An international college magazine has asked for reviews of television documentaries. You decide to write a review of a documentary you have seen on learning languages.

Your review should explain what you found out about different ways of learning languages and evaluate how interesting the documentary was.

Write your **review**.

LISTENING (approximately 40 minutes)

Part 1

You will hear three different extracts. For questions **1–6**, choose the answer (**A**, **B** or **C**) which fits best according to what you hear. There are two questions for each extract.

Extract One

You hear two friends talking about their children's reading habits.

1   The man says his daughter is motivated to read when

    A   she is attracted by a book's illustrations.

    B   she is allowed to choose which books to read.

    C   she is able to identify with the characters in books.

2   They both feel that children who don't read for pleasure

    A   tend to associate books with studying.

    B   have too many other leisure distractions.

    C   are following the pattern set by parents.

Extract Two

You hear part of an interview with a man who worked as a team leader with students doing voluntary work in the rainforest.

3   When talking about the volunteers, he reveals that he is

    A   admiring of how quickly they adapted to a new environment.

    B   proud of the way they developed as people whilst there.

    C   appreciative of their efforts to complete the project on time.

4   What does he feel he gained most from the experience of being a team leader?

    A   a stronger sense of his own potential

    B   the ability to deal with the unexpected

    C   greater understanding of how people behave in groups

Extract Three

You hear two students talking about fast food.

5   The man says his housemates choose to eat fast food because

   A they've been influenced by marketing campaigns.

   B the generous size of servings represents good value.

   C their lack of cooking skills makes it an attractive option.

6   What is the woman's attitude to fast food?

   A She criticises its unappetising flavours.

   B She welcomes the new options available.

   C She doubts whether improved labelling will affect its popularity.

Part 2

You will hear an architectural photographer called Jack Gollins talking about his work immediately after receiving a professional award. For questions **7–14**, complete the sentences with a word or short phrase.

Architectural photographer

Jack says it was a conversation with **(7)** .... that made him

aware of how much work he's done during his career.

One of Jack's personal rules is that, unlike other architectural photographers, he shoots

photos with a **(8)** .... lens.

Jack uses the expression **(9)** .... to refer to places containing

buildings that have had a strong impact on him.

Jack recalls the need for powerful **(10)** .... when working in India.

Jack refers to his visits overseas as **(11)** .... for developing his

professional skills.

Jack explains how collaborating with a particular **(12)** .... has

helped him take elevated shots.

By doing a number of fast **(13)** .... , Jack is able to shoot from

the sky without annoying people on the ground.

Jack explains that capturing what he calls the **(14)** .... can be

very important financially.

Part 3

You will hear part of an interview in which a science writer called Andy Hicks and a psychologist called Dr Karen Ferrigan are talking about how technology affects our brains. For questions **15–20**, choose the answer (**A**, **B**, **C** or **D**) which fits best according to what you hear.

15 What point does Andy make about multitasking?
    A   Few people have the ability to master it effectively.
    B   People fail to understand its implications for their lifestyle.
    C   The different interpretations of what it means are valid.
    D   The idea itself is a popular misconception.

16 When asked about the effect of unread emails on intelligence, Andy says
    A   it is purely temporary in nature.
    B   it suggests people are easily able to change focus.
    C   it has been over-simplified by researchers.
    D   it is less dramatic than previously supposed.

17 Andy mentions workplace studies in order to illustrate
    A   the advantages of letting people multitask.
    B   how common self-deception is.
    C   a personal experience he has had.
    D   the need for more directed research.

18 Karen feels that problems with remembering passwords are due to
    A   the way the brain organises data.
    B   issues with different types of memory.
    C   inconsistent rules that users have to follow.
    D   the information overload now imposed on people.

19 What does Karen see as a key issue with the human brain?
    A   the methods used to do research into its workings
    B   how it struggles to keep up with technological change
    C   the way it physically adapts to environmental changes
    D   how bad it is at making effective decisions

20 When asked about the benefits of the information age, Karen and Andy disagree about
    A   the accuracy of the information we can access.
    B   the risks of neglecting traditional sources of information.
    C   the effects on people's abilities to retain information.
    D   the priorities for helping people exploit the mass of information available.

Part 4

You will hear five short extracts in which people are talking about their experiences of doing volunteer work.

TASK ONE

For questions **21–25**, choose from the list (**A–H**) the reason each speaker gives for doing volunteer work.

TASK TWO

For questions **26–30**, choose from the list (**A–H**) the change each speaker identifies in themselves as a result of doing volunteer work.

While you listen, you must complete both tasks.

	TASK ONE		TASK TWO	
A	to overcome a fear	**A**	better time management	
B	to meet like-minded people	**B**	an ability to deal with difficult people	
C	to acquire practical skills	**C**	enhanced powers of concentration	
D	to clarify future options	**D**	an appreciation of family	
E	to make a significant impact	**E**	improved level of fitness	
F	to match friends' expectations	**F**	an understanding of ecological problems	
G	to fill time usefully	**G**	a stronger sense of indentity	
H	to learn about the natural world	**H**	a greater awareness of others	

Speaker 1	**21**		Speaker 1	**26**
Speaker 2	**22**		Speaker 2	**27**
Speaker 3	**23**		Speaker 3	**28**
Speaker 4	**24**		Speaker 4	**29**
Speaker 5	**25**		Speaker 5	**30**

SPEAKING (15 minutes)

There are two examiners. One (the interlocutor) conducts the test, providing you with the necessary materials and explaining what you have to do. The other examiner (the assessor) is introduced to you, but then takes no further part in the interaction.

Part 1 (2 minutes)

The interlocutor first asks you and your partner for some information about yourselves, then widens the scope of the questions by asking about e.g. your leisure activities, studies, travel and daily life. You are expected to respond to the interlocutor's questions and listen to what your partner has to say.

Part 2 (a one-minute 'long turn' for each candidate, plus a 30-second response from the second candidate)

You are each given the opportunity to talk for about a minute, and to comment briefly after your partner has spoken.

The interlocutor gives you a set of three pictures and asks you to talk about two of them for about one minute. It is important to listen carefully to the interlocutor's instructions. The interlocutor then asks your partner a question about your pictures and your partner responds briefly.

You are then given another set of pictures to look at. Your partner talks about these pictures for about one minute. This time the interlocutor asks you a question about your partner's pictures and you respond briefly.

Part 3 (4 minutes)

In this part of the test, you and your partner are asked to talk together. The interlocutor places a question and some text prompts on the table between you. This stimulus provides the basis for a discussion, after which you will need to make a decision on the topic in question.
The interlocutor explains what you have to do.

Part 4 (5 minutes)

The interlocutor asks some further questions, which leads to a more general discussion of the topic you have discussed in Part 3. You may comment on your partner's answers if you wish.

Frames for the Speaking Test

Test 1

Note: In the examination, there will be both an assessor and an interlocutor in the exam. The visual material for **Test 1** appears on pages C1 and C2 (Part 2) and C3 (Part 3).

Part 1   2 minutes (3 minutes for groups of three)

Interlocutor: Good morning/afternoon/evening. My name is ………… and this is my colleague, ………… .

And your names are?

Can I have your mark sheets, please?

Thank you.

First of all we'd like to know something about you.

Select one or two questions and ask candidates in turn, as appropriate.

- Where are you from?
- What do you do here/there?
- How long have you been studying English?
- What do you enjoy most about learning English?

Select one or more questions for each candidate, as appropriate.

- What do you think is the best way to relax? ….. (Why?)
- Would you like to be famous? ….. (Why?)
- Who would you say had the greatest influence on you when you were a child? ….. (Why?)
- Is there a festival in your country which is very popular? ….. (Why?)
- How important do you think it is to know what's happening in other countries? ….. (Why? / Why not?)
- Do you think it's a good idea to work for a large company or a small one? ….. (Why? / Why not?)
- What sort of job do you think you will do in the future? ….. (Why?)
- How important do you think it is for people to see their friends regularly? ….. (Why?)

Part 2   4 minutes (6 minutes for groups of three)

Reading together

Advice

Interlocutor:	In this part of the test, I'm going to give each of you three pictures. I'd like you to talk about **two** of them on your own for about a minute, and also to answer a question briefly about your partner's pictures.
	(Candidate A), it's your turn first. Here are your pictures. They show **people reading together, in different situations.**
	Indicate the pictures on page C1 to the candidates.
	I'd like you to compare **two** of the pictures, and say **why the people might be reading together, and what they might do next.**
	All right?
Candidate A:	[*1 minute*]
Interlocutor:	Thank you.
	(Candidate B), **which people do you think need to read the most carefully? ...... (Why?)**
Candidate B:	[*Approximately 30 seconds*]
Interlocutor:	Thank you.
	Now, *(Candidate B)*, here are your pictures. They show **people asking for advice in different situations.**
	Indicate the pictures on page C2 to the candidates.
	I'd like you to compare **two** of the pictures, and say **why the people might be getting advice, and how useful the advice might be.**
	All right?
Candidate B:	[*1 minute*]
Interlocutor:	Thank you.
	(Candidate A), **in which situation do you think it's most important to get the right advice? ...... (Why?)**
Candidate A:	[*Approximately 30 seconds*]
Interlocutor:	Thank you.

Part 3   4 minutes (6 minutes for groups of three)

Part 4   5 minutes (8 minutes for groups of three)

Moving

Part 3

Interlocutor:	Now, I'd like you to talk about something together for about two minutes *(3 minutes for groups of three)*.
	Here are some things that can affect a person's decision to move to another country and a question for you to discuss. First you have some time to look at the task.
	Indicate the text prompts on C3 to the candidates. Allow 15 seconds.
	Now, talk to each other about **how these things might affect a person's decision to move to another country.**
Candidates:	[*2 minutes (3 minutes for groups of three)*]
Interlocutor:	Thank you. Now you have about a minute *(2 minutes for groups of three)* to decide **which of these things might have the least influence on a person's decision to move to another country.**
Candidates:	[*1 minute (2 minutes for groups of three)*]
Interlocutor:	Thank you.

Part 4

Interlocutor: *Use the following questions, in order, as appropriate:*

- Do you think most people would like to experience life in another country? ...... (Why? / Why not?)
- Some people say there's a real difference between being in a country for a limited time and staying there permanently. What do you think? ...... (Why? / Why not?)
- Do you think it's a good idea to encourage young people to spend a few months living in another country? ...... (Why? / Why not?)
- Sometimes older people decide to move to another country when they retire. Why do you think this is? ...... (Why? / Why not?)
- How much can a person's character influence the decisions they make? ...... (Why? / Why not?)
- How easy do you think it is to make important decisions? ...... (Why? / Why not?)

> *Select any of the following prompts, as appropriate:*
> - What do you think?
> - Do you agree?
> - How about you?

Thank you. That is the end of the test.

Test 2

Note: In the examination, there will be both an assessor and an interlocutor in the exam. The visual material for **Test 2** appears on pages C4 and C5 (Part 2) and C6 (Part 3).

Part 1   2 minutes (3 minutes for groups of three)

Interlocutor: Good morning/afternoon/evening. My name is ………… and this is my colleague, ………… .

And your names are?

Can I have your mark sheets, please?

Thank you.

First of all we'd like to know something about you.

Select one or two questions and ask candidates in turn, as appropriate.

- Where are you from?
- What do you do here/there?
- How long have you been studying English?
- What do you enjoy most about learning English?

Select one or more questions for each candidate, as appropriate.

- What do you think is the best way to relax? ….. (Why?)
- Would you like to be famous? ….. (Why? / Why not?)
- Who would you say had the greatest influence on you when you were a child? ….. (Why?)
- Is there a festival in your country which is very popular? ….. (Why?)
- How important do you think it is to know what's happening in other countries? ….. (Why? / Why not?)
- Do you think it's a good idea to work for a large company or a small one? ….. (Why? / Why not?)
- What sort of job do you think you will do in the future? ….. (Why?)
- How important do you think it is for people to see their friends regularly? ….. (Why?)

Part 2   4 minutes (6 minutes for groups of three)

Water in different situations

Eating outside

Interlocutor:	In this part of the test, I'm going to give each of you three pictures. I'd like you to talk about **two** of them on your own for about a minute, and also to answer a question briefly about your partner's pictures.
	(Candidate A), it's your turn first. Here are your pictures. They show **some people with water in different situations.**
	Indicate the pictures on page C4 to the candidates.
	I'd like you to compare **two** of the pictures, and say **why water is important to the people in these different situations, and how they might be feeling.**
	All right?
Candidate A:	[*1 minute*]
Interlocutor:	Thank you.
	(Candidate B), **who do you think values the water most?** ...... (**Why?**)
Candidate B:	[*Approximately 30 seconds*]
Interlocutor:	Thank you.
	Now, *(Candidate B)*, here are your pictures. They show **people eating outside.**
	Indicate the pictures on page C5 to the candidates.
	I'd like you to compare **two** of the pictures, and say **why the people might be eating outside, and how memorable the experience might be.**
	All right?
Candidate B:	[*1 minute*]
Interlocutor:	Thank you.
	(Candidate A), **which people do you think are enjoying their food the most?** ...... (**Why?**)
Candidate A:	[*Approximately 30 seconds*]
Interlocutor:	Thank you.

Part 3   4 minutes (6 minutes for groups of three)

Part 4   5 minutes (8 minutes for groups of three)

Motivation

Part 3

Interlocutor:	Now, I'd like you to talk about something together for about two minutes *(3 minutes for groups of three)*.
	Here are some things people often need motivation to do and a question for you to discuss. First you have some time to look at the task.
	Indicate the text prompts on C6 to the candidates. Allow 15 seconds.
	Now, talk to each other about **how people can motivate themselves to do these different things.**
Candidates:	[*2 minutes (3 minutes for groups of three)*]
Interlocutor:	Thank you. Now you have about a minute *(2 minutes for groups of three)* to decide **which of these things requires the greatest amount of motivation.**
Candidates:	[*1 minute (2 minutes for groups of three)*]
Interlocutor:	Thank you.

Part 4

Interlocutor: *Use the following questions, in order, as appropriate:*

- Do you think it's easier to motivate yourself or someone else? ...... (Why?)
- How can parents motivate their children to make the best choices in life? ...... (Why? / Why not?)
- Do you think that teachers can play a role in motivating students? ..... (Why? / Why not?)
- How far do you agree that it's easier to work towards a goal as part of a team rather than on your own? ...... (Why? / Why not?)
- Some people say that money is the main motivation in today's society. What's your view? ...... (Why? / Why not?)
- How important is it to have personal goals in life? ...... (Why? / Why not?)

Select any of the following prompts, as appropriate:

- What do you think?
- Do you agree?
- How about you?

Thank you. That is the end of the test.

Test 3

Note: In the examination, there will be both an assessor and an interlocutor in the exam. The visual material for **Test 3** appears on pages C7 and C8 (Part 2) and C9 (Part 3).

Part 1   2 minutes (3 minutes for groups of three)

Interlocutor: Good morning/afternoon/evening. My name is ………… and this is my colleague, ………… .

And your names are?

Can I have your mark sheets, please?

Thank you.

First of all we'd like to know something about you.

Select one or two questions and ask candidates in turn, as appropriate.

- Where are you from?
- What do you do here/there?
- How long have you been studying English?
- What do you enjoy most about learning English?

Select one or more questions for each candidate, as appropriate.

- What do you think is the best way to relax? ….. (Why?)
- Would you like to be famous? ….. (Why? / Why not?)
- Who would you say had the greatest influence on you when you were a child? ….. (Why?)
- Is there a festival in your country which is very popular? ….. (Why?)
- How important do you think it is to know what's happening in other countries? ….. (Why? / Why not?)
- Do you think it's a good idea to work for a large company or a small one? ….. (Why? / Why not?)
- What sort of job do you think you will do in the future? ….. (Why?)
- How important do you think it is for people to see their friends regularly? ….. (Why?)

Part 2   4 minutes (6 minutes for groups of three)

Preparing a special meal

Customer complaints

Interlocutor:	In this part of the test, I'm going to give each of you three pictures. I'd like you to talk about **two** of them on your own for about a minute, and also to answer a question briefly about your partner's pictures.
	(Candidate A), it's your turn first. Here are your pictures. They show **people preparing a special meal in different situations.**
	Indicate the pictures on page C7 to the candidates.
	I'd like you to compare **two** of the pictures, and say **who the people could be preparing the meal for, and how they might be feeling.**
	All right?
Candidate A:	[*1 minute*]
Interlocutor:	Thank you.
	(Candidate B), **who do you think will spend the longest time preparing the meal?** ...... **(Why?)**
Candidate B:	[*Approximately 30 seconds*]
Interlocutor:	Thank you.
	Now, *(Candidate B)*, here are your pictures. They show **people making complaints.**
	Indicate the pictures on page C8 to the candidates.
	I'd like you to compare two of the pictures, and say **why these people might be making a complaint, and how their complaint could be dealt with.**
	All right?
Candidate B:	[*1 minute*]
Interlocutor:	Thank you.
	(Candidate A), **whose complaint do you think should be taken the most seriously?** ...... **(Why?)**
Candidate A:	[*Approximately 30 seconds*]
Interlocutor:	Thank you.

Part 3   4 minutes (6 minutes for groups of three)

Part 4   5 minutes (8 minutes for groups of three)

Doing adventurous activities

Part 3

Interlocutor:	Now, I'd like you to talk about something together for about two minutes *(3 minutes for groups of three)*.

Here are some things that can affect people's views on doing adventurous activities and a question for you to discuss. First you have some time to look at the task.

Indicate the text prompts on C9 to the candidates. Allow 15 seconds.

Now, talk to each other about **how these things can affect people's views on doing adventurous activities.**

Candidates:	[*2 minutes (3 minutes for groups of three)*]
Interlocutor:	Thank you. Now you have about a minute *(2 minutes for groups of three)* to decide **which of these things it is most important to think about carefully.**
Candidates:	[*1 minute (2 minutes for groups of three)*]
Interlocutor:	Thank you.

Part 4

Interlocutor:

Use the following questions, in order, as appropriate:

- What do you think people gain from doing adventurous activities?
- How important do you think it is for people to do different activities in their free time? ...... (Why?)
- Some people say it's better to do activities in groups rather than on your own? What do you think? ...... (Why?)
- Do you think people have to spend a lot of money to do interesting activities in their free time? ...... (Why? / Why not?)
- Are you the kind of person who prefers doing activities spontaneously? ...... (Why? / Why not?)
- Sometimes activities can take over people's lives and leave them no time for work and studies. Why do you think this is?

Thank you. That is the end of the test.

Select any of the following prompts, as appropriate:

- What do you think?
- Do you agree?
- How about you?

Test 4

Note: In the examination, there will be both an assessor and an interlocutor in the exam. The visual material for **Test 4** appears on pages C10 and C11 (Part 2) and C12 (Part 3).

Part 1　2 minutes (3 minutes for groups of three)

Interlocutor:　Good morning/afternoon/evening. My name is .... and this is my colleague, ...

And your names are?

Can I have your mark sheets, please?

Thank you.

First of all we'd like to know something about you.

Select one or two questions and ask candidates in turn, as appropriate.

- Where are you from?
- What do you do here/there?
- How long have you been studying English?
- What do you enjoy most about learning English?

Select one or more questions for each candidate, as appropriate.

- What do you think is the best way to relax? ..... (Why?)
- Would you like to be famous? ..... (Why? / Why not?)
- Who would you say had the greatest influence on you when you were a child? ..... (Why?)
- Is there a festival in your country which is very popular? ..... (Why?)
- How important do you think it is to know what's happening in other countries? ..... (Why? / Why not?)
- Do you think it's a good idea to work for a large company or a small one? ..... (Why? / Why not?)
- What sort of job do you think you will do in the future? ..... (Why?)
- How important do you think it is for people to see their friends regularly? ..... (Why?)

Part 2   4 minutes (6 minutes for groups of three)

Problem solving

Using cameras

Interlocutor:	In this part of the test, I'm going to give each of you three pictures. I'd like you to talk about **two** of them on your own for about a minute, and also to answer a question briefly about your partner's pictures.
	(Candidate A), it's your turn first. Here are your pictures. They show **people solving problems in different situations.**
	Indicate the pictures on page C10 to the candidates.
	I'd like you to compare **two** of the pictures, and say **what sort of skills are needed to solve the problems, and what difficulties the people may face.**
	All right?
Candidate A:	[*1 minute*]
Interlocutor:	Thank you.
	(Candidate B), **who do you think will learn the most from solving their problem? ...... (Why?)**
Candidate B:	[*Approximately 30 seconds*]
Interlocutor:	Thank you.
	Now, *(Candidate B)*, here are your pictures. They show **people taking photos in different situations.**
	Indicate the pictures on page C11 to the candidates.
	I'd like you to compare **two** of the pictures, and say **why the people might have decided to take photos in these situations, and how carefully they needed to prepare.**
	All right?
Candidate B:	[*1 minute*]
Interlocutor:	Thank you.
	(Candidate A), **which situation do you think would produce the best photo? ...... (Why?)**
Candidate A:	[*Approximately 30 seconds*]
Interlocutor:	Thank you.

Part 3   4 minutes (6 minutes for groups of three)

Part 4   5 minutes (8 minutes for groups of three)

Planning a holiday

Part 3

Interlocutor:	Now, I'd like you to talk about something together for about two minutes *(3 minutes for groups of three)*.
	Here are some things that people have to consider when planning a holiday and a question for you to discuss. First you have some time to look at the task.
	Indicate the text prompts on C12 to the candidates. Allow 15 seconds.
	Now, talk to each other about **why people might consider these things when planning a holiday.**
Candidates:	[*2 minutes (3 minutes for groups of three)*]
Interlocutor:	Thank you. Now you have about a minute *(2 minutes for groups of three)* to decide **which two things are most important for a successful holiday.**
Candidates:	[*1 minute (2 minutes for groups of three)*]
Interlocutor:	Thank you.

Part 4

Interlocutor: *Use the following questions, in order, as appropriate:*

- Do you think it's important to take regular holidays? ...... (Why? / Why not?)
- Some people say it's better to have lots of short breaks rather than one long holiday. What's your view? ...... (Why? / Why not?)
- What are the benefits of having a holiday in your own country compared with travelling abroad? ...... (Why? / Why not?)
- Some people return to the same place every year for their holiday. Why do you think this is?
- Some people say the journey to your holiday destination can be just as exciting as the holiday itself. Do you agree? (Why? / Why not?)
- Do you think it's a good idea for people to plan all the details of their holiday in advance? ...... (Why? / Why not?)
- How important is it for people to experience the culture of the place they are visiting? ...... (Why? / Why not?)
- In your opinion, does tourism always have a positive impact on a place? (Why? / Why not?)

> *Select any of the following prompts, as appropriate:*
>
> - What do you think?
> - Do you agree?
> - How about you?

Thank you. That is the end of the test.

107

Marks and results

Reading and Use of English

Candidates record their answers on a separate answer sheet. One mark is given for each correct answer in Parts 1, 2 and 3 and up to two marks are given for each correct answer in Part 4. For Parts 5, 6 and 7 two marks are given for each correct answer and in Part 8 one mark is given for each correct answer. Candidates will receive separate scores for Reading and for Use of English. The total marks candidates achieve for each section are converted into a score on the Cambridge English Scale. These are equally weighted when calculating the overall score on the scale (an average of the individual scores for the four skills and Use of English).

Writing

Examiners look at four aspects of a candidate's writing: Content, Communicative Achievement, Organisation and Language. The total mark is converted into a score on the Cambridge English Scale for the paper.

- **Content** focuses on how well the candidate has fulfilled the task; in other words if they have done what they were asked to do.
- **Communicative Achievement** focuses on how appropriate the writing is for the situation and whether the candidate has used the appropriate register.
- **Organisation** focuses on the way the piece of writing was put together; in other words if it is logical and ordered, and the punctuation is correct.
- **Language** focuses on the candidate's vocabulary and grammar. This includes the range of language as well as how accurate it is.

For each of the subscales, the examiner gives a maximum of 5 marks. Examiners use the following assessment scale:

C1	Content	Communicative Achievement	Organisation	Language
5	All content is relevant to the task. Target reader is fully informed.	Uses the conventions of the communicative task with sufficient flexibility to communicate complex ideas in an effective way, holding the target reader's attention with ease, fulfilling all communicative purposes.	Text is a well organised, coherent whole, using a variety of cohesive devices and organisational patterns with flexibility.	Uses a range of vocabulary, including less common lexis, effectively and precisely. Uses a wide range of simple and complex grammatical forms with full control, flexibility and sophistication. Errors, if present, are related to less common words and structures, or are slips.

4	*Performance shares features of Bands 3 and 5.*			
3	Minor irrelevances and/or omissions may be present. Target reader is, on the whole, informed.	Uses the conventions of the communicative task effectively to hold the target reader's attention and communicate straightforward and complex ideas, as appropriate.	Text is well organised and coherent, using a variety of cohesive devices and organisational patterns to generally good effect.	Uses a range of vocabulary, including less common lexis, appropriately. Uses a range of simple and complex grammatical forms with control and flexibility. Occasional errors may be present but do not impede communication.
2	*Performance shares features of Bands 1 and 3.*			
1	Irrelevances and misinterpretation of task may be present. Target reader is minimally informed.	Uses the conventions of the communicative task to hold the target reader's attention and communicate straightforward ideas.	Text is generally well organised and coherent, using a variety of linking words and cohesive devices.	Uses a range of everyday vocabulary appropriately, with occasional inappropriate use of less common lexis. Uses a range of simple and some complex grammatical forms with a good degree of control. Errors do not impede communication.
0	Content is totally irrelevant. Target reader is not informed.	Performance below Band 1.		

Length of responses

Candidates need to make sure that they write the correct number of words. Responses which are too short may not have an adequate range of language and may not provide all the information that is required. Responses which are too long may contain irrelevant content and have a negative effect on the reader.

Varieties of English

Candidates are expected to use a particular variety of English with some degree of consistency in areas such as spelling, and not for example switch from using a British spelling of a word to an American spelling of the same word.

Writing sample answers and examiner's comments

The following pieces of writing have been selected from students' answers. The samples relate to tasks in Tests 1–4. Explanatory notes have been added to show how the bands have been arrived at.

Sample A (Test 1, Question 1 – Essay)

> The Role of Music in Society
>
> Music is something of utmost importance in people's lives. It is said that society can't live without music and this statement is true. Music has various roles in life including enriching daily routine, uniting different social groups, educating, etc. But there is a major dilemma which is the most significant role. Should it be the unit of social groups or bringing beauty to our lives?
>
> First, I believe that music can help our society bring people from different social groups and cultures together. Not only does it give these people something in common but also improves their understanding to other points of view. Furthermore, gathering people who do not share the same way of thinking could make them learn many new things about other music styles, life, friendship, etc.
>
> Second, I think that one of the main aims of music is to give people something amazing. For instance, when somebody feels bad they listens to music and it improves one's mood. All people enjoy music because they are all looking for something extraordinary – something that music could offer to everyone. Last but not least, one could learn very important things only by listening carefully to the lyrics of some songs. I would say that without music the hectic life of 21st century would be grey and boring.
>
> In conclusion, music plays one of the most important roles in modern-people's lives. In my opinion, the most significant facet is that it gives people food for thought and brings colour to the busy life.

Scales	Mark	Commentary
Content	4	All content is relevant to the task. Two roles of music are discussed and a choice made as to which is more significant. However, the supporting reasons for the choice are not developed so the target reader is not quite fully informed.
Communicative Achievement	4	The conventions of the essay genre are used effectively to hold the target reader's attention, communicating both simple and complex ideas with success. There is a clear introduction to the topic which sets the tone for the rest of the piece and opinions and explanations are given (*It is said; Should it be the unit …?; I believe that; I would say that; In my opinion*). The register is consistent and appropriate.
Organisation	3	The text is well-organised and coherent using a variety of cohesive devices and organisational patterns (*But there is; including; Not only does it give … but also; Furthermore; Last but not least; In conclusion*). It is clearly paragraphed with links across and within sentences and ideas developed in a logical way. Punctuation is accurate.
Language	3	There is a range of vocabulary, including some less common lexis, used appropriately (*of utmost importance; enriching daily routine; something in common; improves one's mood; food for thought*). There is a range of simple and complex grammatical forms used with control (*gathering people who do not share … life, friendship, etc.; All people enjoy music because … could offer to everyone*). The occasional errors do not impede communication.

Sample B (Test 1, Question 3 – Report)

> **Subject:** New students' arrival at Cambridge University
>
> **To:** Principal Winterdown
>
> I am writing on this occasion to give you a report of today's activities which were centered around the arrival of the new students to our college and of which I was in charge.
>
> The day started off with a greeting of all the new members of our community in the central garden in which everybody presented themselves and the welcoming committee gave a brief information session about Cambridge University. This was followed by an extensive tour of the campus. To top it all off, we ended the afternoon with a series of team games (capture the flag, tug of war, races, etc) and every participant was given a medal of completion.
>
> I must say that everything went splendidly. Not only did we not have any problems with organization but at the end of the day there was a strong feeling of trust. Despite the fact that at the beginning of the day we were all practically strangers, there was a very clear sense of unity in all of us – It was clear to me that everyone had realized that they now had a common factor: Cambridge University. From my point of view, things could not have gone any better.
>
> As far as suggestions go, the only one that comes to mind is to have more people on board in the organization committee for next year so as to be able to plan even more and grander events!
>
> I hope I have been thorough in my report and that you are satisfied with the results.

Scales	Mark	Commentary
Content	5	All content is relevant to the task and the target reader is fully informed. The context is clear and the points are developed appropriately. The day is described, the activities evaluated in terms of their success in welcoming new students and a recommendation made for the following year.
Communicative Achievement	4	The conventions of report writing are used effectively and sometimes with flexibility to describe, assess and make suggestions. The register is slightly inconsistent but a very positive tone is created throughout and the reader's attention would be held with ease.
Organisation	4	The text is a well-organised, coherent whole using a variety of cohesive devices and organisational patterns to generally good effect. Each paragraph starts in a different way and clear connections within and across sentences are made (*and of which; in which; This was followed by; To top it off; Not only did we … but; Despite the fact that; so as to*). A heading for each section would help highlight the information contained in each one. The opening of the text (*Subject: New students' arrival at Cambridge University / To: Principal Winterdown*) is also not consistent with a report style, however, this does not impede comprehension.
Language	4	The writer uses a range of vocabulary appropriate to the task, effectively (*centered around; in charge; extensive tour; practically strangers; clear sense of unity; comes to mind; more people on board*). There is a range of simple and more complex grammatical forms (*things could not have gone any better; the one that comes to mind is … more and grander events*). Errors are minimal and non-impeding.

Sample C (Test 2, Question 1 – Essay)

Throughout the years, discussions about whether one should learn a foreign language or not lead to heated debates. In recent years, the popularity of learning languages has increased and in my opinion, knowing more than your mother tongue represents an open door to job opportunities and helps the learner understand other cultures better.

To begin with, one would be amazed at the wide range of job opportunities you could have if you studied more foreign languages. For example, a person who can speak three languages would have a major advantage in comparison to another that can only speak two. A translator or a guide would also be useful in a company for languages connect people and a person who knows more is one who creates that bond everybody needs in order to communicate. Therefore, we need these bonds between people, as communication is the key to success.

Secondly, learning a foreign language not only implies knowing the grammar or a wide range of sophisticated words, but also using them efficiently. Moreover, a country does not only have a specific feature, that makes it different from the others (the language), but also the culture, tradition and history make it special. Thus, it is important to study that information with curiosity and let yourself carried away by the fascinating culture of that specific country you learn about.

Learning a foreign language implies more than grammar and it offers you great opportunities, as well as knowledge. It seems to me that the most important is the fact that you can actually use it to interact with people and travel around the world, all because of your job.

Scales	Mark	Commentary
Content	5	All content is relevant to the task and the target reader is fully informed. Two benefits of learning languages are discussed and 'increasing job opportunities' is chosen as the more important. Supporting reasons are given.
Communicative Achievement	4	The conventions of the discursive essay genre are used effectively to hold the reader's attention with ease. Each paragraph has a clear purpose – introduction, consideration of one benefit, consideration of a second benefit, conclusion – and complex ideas are conveyed. Register and tone are consistently appropriate.
Organisation	3	The text is well-organised and coherent. The ideas are presented logically and there is a clear focus and development to each paragraph, showing links and connections between ideas. A variety of cohesive devices and organisational patterns is used to generally good effect (*Throughout the years; To begin with; For example; in order to; Therefore; not only … but also; Thus; as well as*).
Language	4	There is a range of vocabulary which is generally used effectively and precisely (*heated debates; an open door to job opportunities; the key to success; a major advantage; bonds between people*). A range of grammatical structures, both simple and complex, is used with control and flexibility (*the popularity of learning languages … understand other cultures better; one would be amazed … more foreign languages*). Occasional errors do not impede and are either slips or caused when attempting more ambitious language (*let yourself carried away*).

Sample D (Test 2, Question 2 – Proposal)

LIONEL MESSI

Introduction

Replying to your announcement in your magazine I would like to propose one of the most popular football players in the world: Lionel Messi, who plays for the Barça team.

His contribution to his sport

Leo Messi has contributed to their football team, because thanks to him, his team is winning a lot of competitions, and all the followers of the team are so grateful. What is more, he has received personnal awards too, like the "Best football player in the world" award.

Good role for today's young people

It has been suggested that young people need a good role model to follow, and nowadays teenagers search these models in the television, by way of illustration actors or sport people.

In my opinion Messi is a good role model because he is a hard working man, and he can give the advice that if people try hard, do their best to follow their dreams, they can success in their lives.

Moreover, I would like to say that, although he is one of the best football players in the world, he is not a selfish man. On the contrary, he is very polite and his behave is perfect.

Conclusion

To sum up, in my opinion Messi is the person that you are looking for and I would like that you take my recommendation into account.

Scales	Mark	Commentary
Content	5	The target reader is fully informed. All content is relevant to the task and the three elements specified in the rubric are included and developed as appropriate.
Communicative Achievement	3	Proposal conventions are used effectively to hold the reader's attention. The tone is positive and persuasive (*I would like to propose one of the most popular football players; in my opinion Messi is the person that you are looking for*) and the writer uses language of description, explanation and opinion to put forward his views. The register is appropriate and consistent.
Organisation	2	The text is well-organised overall with effective use of headings. A variety of linking words and cohesive devices is used to generally good effect (*because thanks to him; What is more; like; In my opinion; Moreover; although; On the contrary*). Punctuation is mostly accurate.
Language	2	There is a range of everyday vocabulary used appropriately and some attempt to include less common lexis (*do their best to follow their dreams*). Both simple and some more complex grammatical forms are used with control (*It has been suggested that young people need a good role model to follow*). Errors do not impede communication (*they can success; his behave is perfect*).

Sample E (Test 3, Question 1 – Essay)

Nowadays every human being is a consumer. There are a lot of possibilities to choose something which is suitable for you. In this essay I am going to discuss two of the factors which influance consumer choices.

The first factor which might influance consumer choices is celebrities. It is well-known that usually celebrities have got more money than for example office worker. Celebrities can buy whatever they want to, so they are under the influence of money. People really want to follow their idols, they change sometimes their apperance to look more similar to their idols. On the other hand they do not know that very often they may fail in many aspects of their lifes because they are trying to be like someone else.

The next factor could be marketing. People decide what to buy for instance what they see in magazines or hear in the radio. For sure exist people who do not even look at all of this adverts. They just buy what they need. People may also decide about their choices because of talking with other people. In this way they could be informed about new products as well.

In my opinion the factor: marketing has got stronger influence on consumer choices.

The reason why I chose this one factor is that I suppose that not every single person has got idol who they can follow. For instance I do not want to be like someone else. Marketing is everywhere. There is a great number of choices we can make being under the influance of marketing.

Scales	Mark	Commentary
Content	5	All content is relevant to the task. All the rubric elements are addressed and developed so the target reader is fully informed.
Communicative Achievement	3	Appropriate essay conventions are used. The opening paragraph introduces the topic and leads into opinions and explanations in the following sections (*In this essay; The first factor; Celebrities can buy … so …; The next factor; People decide what to buy; In my opinion; I suppose that*). Straightforward and some complex ideas are communicated and, apart from a slip with '*For sure*', the register is consistent.
Organisation	3	The text is well-organised and coherent making good use of paragraphs. Although some of the sentences are quite short, there is a variety of cohesive devices and organisational patterns used to generally good effect (*The first factor; It is well-known that; On the other hand; In this way*).
Language	2	A range of topic-related vocabulary is attempted, with some success (*under the influence of money; want to follow their idols; may fail in many aspects of their lifes; great number of choices we can make*). There is a range of simple and some complex grammatical forms (*they are trying to be like someone else; the reason why I chose … who they can follow*) generally used with control. There are some errors (use of articles, word order) but these do not impede communication.

Sample F (Test 3, Question 4 – Review)

You have just achieved your driver's license and cannot afford an own car, but you do not want to have to rely on public transportation on your night out in the best clubs of the city? Many young people who have not started working yet can definitely relate to this problem which is now tackled by the newly founded car-sharing business in Frankfurt. This scheme allows you to choose one of the fifty locations in the city where you can pick up your car after receiving the key in exchange for a fee that is paid according to the distance you are expecting to drive. After your trip you will return both your car and the keys.

The local car-sharing business certainly is a welcome change from public transportation to many people. Despite of not being able to afford their own car, they can alternatively rent a car for little money and therefore experience a greater flexibility.

However, when deciding to use this option, customers also face several serious and inevitable difficulties. Namely, the key has to be picked up in one of five offices located in the downtown and at the borders of the city area and afterwards a car that might not even be parked close by needs to be picked up, too. This involves greater costs in terms of both money and time than the customer might want to invest. Moreover, despite being comparably affordable, the car-sharing business is no constant solution for everyone and will probably only be used from time to time.

All in all, I would definitely recommend this experience to people who do not mind making this effort once in a while as it is a very affordable and comfortable service.

Scales	Mark	Commentary
Content	4	All content is relevant to the task. The writer describes a car-sharing scheme in their area and explains how it works. The advantages and disadvantages of this scheme are evaluated but, as the rubric asks for comments on 'such schemes, in general', the target reader is not fully informed.
Communicative Achievement	4	The conventions of review writing are used to convey simple and complex ideas effectively and flexibly. The opening sentence directly addresses the reader of the English-language magazine (*You have just achieved your driver's licence … best clubs of the city?*) and this sets the tone for the rest of the piece. A balanced explanation and evaluation of the scheme is given and the closing paragraph ends the review in an engaging way.
Organisation	4	A variety of cohesive devices and organisational patterns is used effectively to create a coherent text, although slightly long (288 words). Quite straightforward cohesive devices are used (*However; Moreover: All in all*) but the writer also makes use of more sophisticated ways of linking the text to connect ideas within and across sentences (*Namely, the key has to be picked up … and at … and afterwards … picked up, too; greater costs in terms of both money and time*).
Language	4	A range of topic-specific vocabulary is used effectively (*relate to this problem; tackled by the newly founded; a welcome change; greater flexibility; comparably affordable; from time to time; once in a while*). A wide range of complex grammatical forms is used with control (*you do not want to have to rely on; you can pick up your car after … you are expecting to drive*). The errors are slips or related to less common lexis.

Sample G (Test 4, Question 1 – Essay)

According to many, recent years have been marked by changes in social trends. In fact, aspects such as people's tastes, interactions and social pressures have been utterly transformed. Here, we shall see what factors are influencing social trends as well as the reasons why.

Firstly, we might think of the effects of communications on social trends. The recent technological revolution, with the creation of the Internet, implied a revolution in international social interactions. Nowadays, people can communicate on a broader scale since it is possible to communicate easily with people from all around the world. Not only is it fast, but it is also more pratical since the smartphone's upswing at the start of the century. This upswing provoked an upheaval in the way people interact with each other, as now many prefer sending text messages to interacting directly. Therefore, communications have both a positive and a more negative side in influencing social trends.

Then, advertising also transformed social trends since it influences people's behaviour in front of products. Because of advertising, people are often drawn towards liking and wanting the same products. Mass consumerising of the same product increases, and therefore, personnality is affected. In fact products are no longer made in order to meet the need but to create this need, conveyed by adverts and hence influencing social trends.

To conclude, in my opinion the factor which has a greater influence on social trends is the transformation of communications since its changes the way people interact with each other. This change , if we allow it to be, can be positive and influence social trends for the better.

Scales	Mark	Commentary
Content	5	Two factors that might influence social trends – communications and advertising – are discussed and the former is chosen as having greater influence, with supporting reasons. All content is relevant to the task. The target reader is fully informed.
Communicative Achievement	4	Essay conventions are used with sufficient flexibility to communicate straightforward and complex ideas in an effective way. The opening paragraph introduces the topic and leads the reader into the discussion section (*Here, we shall see what factors are … as well as the reasons why*). Points and opinions are presented in a logical way with each paragraph having a different focus, and a conclusion reached. The register is appropriate and consistent.
Organisation	4	A range of cohesive devices and organisational patterns is used effectively to link ideas within sentences and paragraphs, creating a coherent text (*According to many; In fact; as well as; since; Not only is it fast, but it is also; Because of; in order to; hence; To conclude*).
Language	4	There is a range of vocabulary, including less common lexis, which is generally used precisely and to good effect (*marked by changes in social trends; upheaval; conveyed by adverts; for the better*). A range of grammatical forms is used with control and flexibility (*In fact products are no longer made … social trends*). Where there are errors some are slips and none of them impedes communication.

Sample H (Test 4, Question 3 – Email)

Dear …

I think it would be a good idea to have a part-time job. When I was doing the business course, I did spend a lot of time studying, but I had a part-time job anyway. Some days I was very busy with studying and the job, but if you just plan the schoolwork and your job. It won't be a problem. I would definitely recommend taking a part-time job because you will probably need the money. I took a part-time job because I could not pay for the course without it.

So if you are planning to search for a job. I would look for a job where you can plan whenever you want to work, so you don't have to work when it's a bad time for you. It would be very nice if you can cancel on your work, and they don't depend on you very much. I took a job like that at the local supermarket. When I really could not work, I always could cancel pretty easily. But you can't do that too often of course, because your boss might not appreciate it. I really liked that job.

Maybe you can work at a supermarket too, or maybe another store. I also knew someone who worked at a place where they sold ice cream, milkshakes and frozen yoghurt. She loved working there.

Good luck with finding a job and with your business course!

Scales	Mark	Commentary
Content	5	All content is relevant to the task. The email answers the questions posed in the rubric, giving information on how difficult the writer found it to balance work and study time at college and giving suggestions about suitable jobs. The target reader is fully informed.
Communicative Achievement	3	The conventions of informal email writing are evident in the opening and closing sections of the text (*Dear …*; *I think it would be a good idea*; *Good luck with finding a job*; *Love*) and in the friendly, positive and supportive tone used throughout. Information and suggestions are effectively communicated to the reader, holding their attention.
Organisation	3	The email is well-organised and coherent. Each paragraph is concerned with one aspect, which is very clear. A variety of cohesive devices and organisational patterns suitable for linking ideas in informal writing is used in a natural way. Punctuation, especially commas, is generally used to good effect.
Language	2	There is a range of everyday vocabulary used accurately and an attempt is made to include some less common lexis (*don't depend on you*; *might not appreciate it*). There is also a range of simple and some complex grammatical forms used with control (*would definitely recommend taking a part-time job because you will probably need the money*; *if you are planning to search for a job, I would look for a job when you can plan whenever you want to work*). Errors do not impede communication.

Listening

One mark is given for each correct answer. The total mark is converted into a score on the Cambridge English Scale for the paper.

For security reasons, several versions of the Listening paper are used at each administration of the examination. Before grading, the performance of the candidates in each of the versions is compared and marks adjusted to compensate for any imbalance in levels of difficulty.

Speaking

Candidates are assessed on their own individual performance and not in relation to each other, according to the following five analytical criteria: grammatical resource, vocabulary resource, discourse management, pronunciation and interactive communication. Assessment is based on performance in the whole test and not in particular parts of the test.

Both examiners assess the candidates. The assessor applies detailed analytical scales, and the interlocutor applies a global achievement scale, which is based on the analytical scales.

Analytical scales

Grammatical resource

This refers to the accurate and appropriate use of a range of both simple and complex forms. Performance is viewed in terms of the overall effectiveness of the language used in spoken interaction.

Vocabulary resource

This refers to the candidate's ability to use a wide range of vocabulary to meet task requirements. At Advanced level, the tasks require candidates to speculate and exchange views on unfamiliar topics. Performance is viewed in terms of the overall effectiveness of the language used in spoken interaction.

Discourse management

This refers to the candidate's ability to link utterances together to form coherent speech, without undue hesitation. The utterances should be relevant to the tasks and should be arranged logically to develop the themes or arguments required by the tasks.

Pronunciation

This refers to the candidate's ability to produce intelligible utterances to fulfil the task requirements. This includes stress and intonation as well as individual sounds. Examiners put themselves in the position of the non-ESOL specialist and assess the overall impact of the pronunciation and the degree of effort required to understand the candidate.

Interactive communication

This refers to the candidate's ability to take an active part in the development of the discourse. This requires the ability to participate in the range of interactive situations in the test and to develop discussions on a range of topics by initiating and responding appropriately. This also refers to the deployment of strategies to maintain interaction at an appropriate level throughout the test so that the tasks can be fulfilled.

Global achievement

This refers to the candidate's overall effectiveness in dealing with the tasks in the four separate parts of the Advanced Speaking test. The global mark is an independent, impression mark which reflects the assessment of the candidate's performance from the interlocutor's perspective.

Marks

Marks for each of the criteria are awarded out of a five-point scale. Marks for the Speaking test are subsequently converted into a score on the Cambridge English Scale for the paper.

Advanced typical minimum adequate performance

The candidate develops the interaction with contributions which are mostly coherent and extended when dealing with the Advanced-level tasks. Grammar is mostly accurate and vocabulary appropriate. Utterances are understood with very little strain on the listener.

Test 1 Key

Reading and Use of English (1 hour 30 minutes)

Part 1

1 A   2 C   3 B   4 C   5 D   6 A   7 C   8 B

Part 2

9 as   10 not   11 over   12 with   13 on   14 having   15 may / might   16 there

Part 3

17 wisdom   18 characterised / characterized   19 surroundings   20 sight
21 undetectable / undetected   22 vibrations   23 comparison   24 mysterious

Part 4

25 DEPENDING on | the number
26 a /the RISK of | not being
27 MATTER when/what time | he sets; MATTER how early | he sets
28 is / 's in CHARGE | of making
29 to have changed | his MIND about
30 has not / hasn't OCCURRED to me | until / till / before; (has) never OCCURRED to me | until / till / before

Part 5

31 C   32 B   33 D   34 B   35 B   36 A

Part 6

37 B   38 B   39 C   40 D

Part 7

41 D   42 G   43 E   44 B   45 A   46 F

Part 8

47 C   48 B   49 B   50 D   51 B   52 A   53 D   54 A   55 C   56 D

Writing (1 hour 30 minutes)

Candidate responses are marked using the assessment scale on pages 108–109.

Listening (approximately 40 minutes)

Part 1

1 C   2 B   3 C   4 A   5 A   6 C

Part 2

7 detail(s)   8 correction(s)   9 essence   10 observant   11 animals
12 dragons   13 visual literacy   14 self-belief

Part 3

15 D   16 A   17 B   18 C   19 D   20 A

Part 4

21 D   22 H   23 A   24 C   25 E   26 B   27 E   28 G   29 D   30 A

Transcript	*This is the Cambridge English Advanced Listening Test. Test One.*
	I'm going to give you the instructions for this test.
	I'll introduce each part of the test and give you time to look at the questions.
	At the start of each piece, you'll hear this sound:
	tone
	You'll hear each piece twice.
	Remember, while you're listening, write your answers on the question paper. You'll have five minutes at the end of the test to copy your answers onto the separate answer sheet.
	There'll now be a pause. Please ask any questions now because you must not speak during the test.
	[pause]
	Now open your question paper and look at Part One.
	[pause]
PART 1	*You'll hear three different extracts. For questions 1–6, choose the answer (A, B, or C) which fits best according to what you hear. There are two questions for each extract.*
Extract One	*You hear two friends discussing an exhibition they've just visited, featuring a female sculptor called Sue Lin.*
	Now look at questions one and two.
	[pause]
	tone
Woman:	Sue Lin's work had obviously been displayed with the aim of bringing out the ground-breaking nature of her achievements. The thing was, she began to look less like a pioneer than a disciple of everyone around her, surrounded

as she was by the work of her fellow artists. To me, her carvings recalled the aesthetics of other sculptors, too – although more as a passing tribute to them than deliberate copying. And she'd created all those sculptures in the open air, surrounded by the wild landscape of the coast, so I do wonder if something was lost by transposing them into the confines of a gallery.

Man: Mmm ... there was more of other sculptors' work included than I'd anticipated, given the exhibition was advertised as her work. I'd never really seen the work of all these artists exhibited side by side before, even though I've been an avid follower of their careers. Seeing what Sue's contemporaries were up to was enlightening for me – and in fact, the work I instinctively gravitated to was actually not hers, but another artist's, which put her work in the shade a bit for me. His animal figures were captivating.

Woman: Mmm ... interesting.

[pause]

tone

[The recording is repeated.]

[pause]

Extract Two   *You hear part of a discussion between two psychology students on the subject of laughter.*

Now look at questions three and four.

[pause]

tone

Man: It's strange that more research is done into negative emotions than into laughter – maybe researchers expect to learn more about people that way. Plus, some academics think laughter isn't a heavyweight enough topic for research.

Woman: Yet it's actually a rather fruitful area as laughter is essentially social – people laugh more in a group than on their own. Maybe that's why warm-up comedians appear before a live TV show is recorded – it's easier to make an audience laugh later on if they've already laughed together.

Man: Research also shows that physical environment plays a part – people laugh more easily if they're crowded together in rows. Apparently, sitting around tables shifts people's attention away from the person on stage. It tells us a lot about interaction. But there again, in one experiment, a joke that made one group laugh left another cold, although they were in the same room.

Woman: The areas of the brain responsible for basic behaviour like reflex actions and breathing also control laughing. Other brain functions are situated in different areas. Perhaps because laughter is a basic behaviour, that's why once a laugh has been triggered it can't be stopped.

[pause]

tone

[The recording is repeated.]

[pause]

Extract Three   *You hear two friends discussing their experiences of learning to play the piano.*

Now look at questions five and six.

[pause]

tone

Man: Hey, Jan – how're the piano lessons going?

Woman: Oh … early days yet, really – just ten months. I wonder sometimes how I've stuck at it this far, to be honest, but it's never felt boring, and I'd been warned even before starting that progress wouldn't happen overnight. I do find my early pieces quite simple now, though, and I'm taking the later, harder stuff in my stride, something which has spilt over into everyday life – things that seemed insurmountable don't any more. There's a heavy memory load, isn't there, especially initially when you're consciously thinking of every note, but I'm playing more naturally now, which is a real breakthrough.

Man: Great! You might find other things kicking in, too – well, according to the latest research that is. Daily practice is meant to lower heart rate and blood pressure, making you more relaxed, as well as encouraging innovation and lateral ways of thinking. The health claims don't seem to be borne out by my experience. I get pretty anxious when learning something new, I'm so aware of my errors! Studies also say learning an instrument makes you smarter – applying the theory uses similar processing skills to maths, I reckon though, judging from your expression, I clearly haven't convinced you of the link ...

[pause]

tone

[The recording is repeated.]

[pause]

That's the end of Part One.

Now turn to Part Two.

[pause]

PART 2   *You'll hear a book illustrator called Colin Rodgers talking about his work to a group of students. For questions 7–14, complete the sentences with a word or short phrase.*

You now have 45 seconds to look at Part Two.

[pause]

tone

Colin: Hi, I'm Colin Rodgers, and I'm a children's book illustrator. Drawing's always been important in my life, and as a reader, I've always been attracted to books featuring drawings. The more activity there is in them, and the greater the amount of colour, the more I like them. But it's the detail that always gets me poring over them endlessly! That's very much the style I've adopted in my work, too.

If you want a career in art, drawing skills are essential – so it's vital to do some drawing every single day. Draw whatever your imagination generates – and don't be put off when you go wrong. In fact, correction is something to value when you're drawing – if something's not right, keep drawing those lines over and over again rather than rubbing everything out, until you're happy with it. You'll learn a lot from that process!

But mastering technique is only one aspect of story illustrating. You'll also need a sort of 'inner eye' to help you judge your approach. And the challenge for me is always to comprehend the essence of what the text is about. But once I've eventually managed to do that, I know I'll come up with something wonderful. Then I'll consider how the text will fit with my images, and complement the author's ideas.

Drawing for children, as I do, may sound easy – but it's tricky! Adults can be negative about your work – how realistic it is, how successful it is in engaging readers. But children have a wonderfully observant quality that their parents seem to have lost, somehow. Of course, it's important to be appreciative of any feedback, because whether it's from adults or children, it can be constructive.

In my quest for realism, I often go and draw things in situ, whether it's trees in dark woods for a nature book, or clothes for a children's historical guide. And if I want to present universally recognisable images that transcend culture and gender, then animals seem to work particularly well. I've even substituted them for humans as the characters in some stories I've illustrated.

I also love drawing mythical creatures. I've done several stories about fairies – requiring a delicate hand – and monsters, where my imagination's run riot. And I'll always slip in dragons somewhere if possible, as you can represent them and arrange them however you like on the page.

There's a popular misconception nowadays, I think, that illustrated books aren't as serious as those with only text. Yet to me these books help readers improve what I call visual literacy. In an age where the interpretation of images, whether diagrams, photos or drawings, is taken for granted, this is a vital ability.

So finally – what's needed to become a good illustrator? Well, most people deal with rejection at some point, so resilience is always useful, not to mention dedication when you're not feeling inspired to draw! But never underestimate self-belief. Publishers can be challenging to work with, so use criticism to develop your ideas – but don't take it personally.

[pause]

Now you'll hear Part Two again.

tone

[The recording is repeated.]

[pause]

That's the end of Part Two.

Now turn to Part Three.

[pause]

PART 3   *You'll hear an interview in which a deep-sea map-maker called Sally Gordon and a marine biologist called Mark Tomkins are talking about making maps of the ocean floor. For questions 15–20, choose the answer (A, B, C or D) which fits best according to what you hear.*

You now have 70 seconds to look at Part Three.

[pause]

tone

Interviewer: Tonight we're talking to map-maker Sally Gordon, and marine biologist Mark Tomkins, about making maps of the ocean floor. Sally, how did you get started on your career? Tell us about your first expedition.

Sally: As a recent graduate, I was fortunate to receive a full-paid internship aboard an exploration vessel to participate in sonar mapping. I was delighted to be selected, but I was extremely nervous about living at sea for three weeks. Fortunately, everyone was really friendly and helpful to me as the new kid on board. On my very first mapping expedition, we collected some data which really changed the way that they thought about geology in that area, and from then on I was completely hooked, and inspired by the thought of repeating the success. Now a lot of my shipmates call me the Mapping Queen!

Interviewer: Mark, how far have we progressed in terms of researching the ocean floor?

Mark: Here's a troubling fact: most of us know more about planets than we do about the depths of the ocean. And yet with volcanoes, deep valleys, mountain peaks and vast plains, the landscape of the ocean floor is as varied and magnificent as it is on the surface of some astronomical body. Ninety-five percent of the ocean floor remains unexplored – which is nothing compared to how small a part of space we have reached, of course. But mapping the ocean floor is very technologically challenging and is progressing much more slowly than space exploration.

Interviewer: Sally, I know you were wanting to make a point about public attitudes towards deep-sea exploration.

Sally: Yes … thanks. I do think it's challenging to get the public engaged about deep-sea exploration. I think you can get people excited about some parts of marine science. People love to see footage of coral reefs, for example. These are bright, well-lit portions of the ocean, but really just its skin. But the depths are so far removed from people physically, so it's a case of out of sight and out of mind, I suppose, which is a shame and so unnecessary.

Interviewer: Here's a question for both of you. Where does the funding for these projects come from?

Mark: The government funding has tended to dry up in recent years, and a lot of corporations have really taken up some of the slack. Our project is financed by Alinson Insurance. It's a very interesting model for ocean science because it's like instead of sponsoring a football team, you're sponsoring a very important scientific mission that really can make a difference – and people notice that.

Sally: It's an interesting development. I think corporates are starting to see the opportunity here for getting massive brand exposure in an area that there aren't too many competitors. And I don't think a government funded project could've worked at the speed that we've been working at.

Interviewer: There are a lot of mineral resources under the sea. Mark, aren't some nations – particularly island nations – rushing in to exploit this?

Mark: Some are. Though, of course, without knowing the shape of the ocean floor, we'll never realise the economic viability of these resources. Some island nations have been trying to extend their territorial sea claims further under one interpretation of maritime law. I think who owns these resources is a huge issue, and particularly who might be responsible for any damage done to the ocean if these resources are mined – who would be liable.

Interviewer: With all the new technology, our knowledge of the oceans is increasing. Where do you both see this leading?

Sally: More awareness leads to more engagement and – I hope – more responsibility. People would be seeing landscapes everywhere, as gorgeous as the Himalayas or the Grand Canyon, and they'd be seeing them for the first time because these are places that no human had ever seen before. We've already witnessed this with photos of galaxies coming back from the latest space probes.

Mark: I think the only reason we haven't seen these places is we haven't had the will to go find them. It'll make people think before they're careless about pollution, or eating seafood unsustainably, because they'd really know how beautiful the ocean is, and that it's not just a big dumping ground. It's our planet, not some distant galaxy we're talking about here after all.

[pause]

Now you'll hear Part Three again.

tone

[The recording is repeated.]

[pause]

That's the end of Part Three.

Now turn to Part Four.

[pause]

PART 4   *Part Four consists of two tasks.*

You'll hear five short extracts in which people are talking about going to live in another country.

Look at Task One. For questions 21–25, choose from the list (A–H) each speaker's main reason for moving to the new country.

Now look at Task Two. For questions 26–30, choose from the list (A–H) what surprised each speaker about the place where they are now living.

While you listen, you must complete both tasks.

You now have 45 seconds to look at Part Four.

[pause]

tone

Speaker One: While I was happy back home in the UK, I love travelling, meeting local people, and experiencing new cultures, and I'd always wanted to see Australia so I needed no convincing when the chance to study there came up. It wasn't a complete surprise – after all, I'd been chasing this opportunity for months – but I was overjoyed when they said 'yes'. Life's great. I can afford to live pretty well and communication's no problem of course, but I did think the winter would be milder. Last year's just happened to be the worst in 26 years! Even my neighbours found it hard to bear and complained about it every time we met.

[pause]

Speaker Two: Don't get me wrong. The people here are great. We laugh at the same things. The food is as good as they say, but, well, when I arrived I was ambitious to make my mark on the company, pass on my skills and shake things up with my fresh ideas. Turns out this isn't how things are done here. I soon felt I was getting nowhere. It's disappointing. You know, there're many things that might push someone to seek new openings abroad. Maybe a painful break-up, maybe a dead-end career. With me, out of the blue I was offered a job that sounded perfect. Looking back, I should perhaps have done more research before I signed up.

[pause]

Speaker Three: Four years ago, we started a new life in the Italian countryside. We'd been working in TV, in Hollywood, like most people there, but an uncontrollable itch to do something different had surfaced. We knew nobody in Italy, had never lived in the countryside before – had no farming experience – we weren't even skilled gardeners but we loved every minute of it! We spoke basic Italian; that was about it. We couldn't get over how puzzled the villagers were about our decision. They kept saying, 'What are you doing here? Why give up good jobs to come here?' How funny, we thought. They just don't understand. Well, four years later, we certainly do!

[pause]

Speaker Four: I felt I was taking a risk staying where I was. Opportunities for young journalists had vanished really. One or two colleagues I knew had gone to Europe and prospered, so why not join them? Before leaving, I imagined my new life, sipping coffee in a beautiful sunlit old flat, or popping to the stores or travelling around by effortlessly hopping on the bus. It turns out old flats aren't very nice. Even the more expensive ones. Instead, my sunlit living room was built in 2007, the shops are two bus rides away … and as for the buses … slow, no climate control, and diversions mean it's less "effortless" than I'd reckoned.

[pause]

Speaker Five: From the minute we arrived and climbed into the taxi, on what felt like the wrong side of the road, the differences kept coming. I'd say most of the ones we've encountered here, we've accepted with good humour. I live with the fact that 50% of the time I'll have no idea what someone is saying to me – which is still something of a shock as we're both speaking English – and I smile even more at strangers than I did back home. It's been harder for my husband – he was learning the new job that had dragged us here in the first place. But if I'm honest with myself, I'm already longing for another change.

[pause]

Now you'll hear Part Four again.

tone

[The recording is repeated.]

[pause]

That's the end of Part Four.

There'll now be a pause of five minutes for you to copy your answers onto the separate answer sheet. Be sure to follow the numbering of all the questions. I'll remind you when there's one minute left, so that you're sure to finish in time.

[Teacher, pause the recording here for five minutes. Remind students when they have one minute left.]

That's the end of the test. Please stop now. Your supervisor will now collect all the question papers and answer sheets.

Test 2 Key

Reading and Use of English (1 hour 30 minutes)

Part 1

1 B   2 D   3 A   4 C   5 B   6 B   7 A   8 D

Part 2

9 as   10 Since / From   11 the   12 is   13 before   14 What   15 If   16 in

Part 3

17 intolerable   18 alongside   19 responsibility   20 carving   21 distinctive
22 assembly / assembling   23 resistant   24 descendant(s)

Part 4

25 are not / aren't | MEANT to; were not / weren't | MEANT to
26 the only student / one | to BE
27 sure / convinced / certain of / about | the (historical) ACCURACY of
28 have no IDEA | how to
29 there was | no POINT (in) (his / her)
30 for you / your GIVING | me a lift / ride

Part 5

31 A   32 C   33 B   34 B   35 D   36 A

Part 6

37 D   38 C   39 C   40 A

Part 7

41 B   42 F   43 G   44 A   45 E   46 C

Part 8

47 C   48 D   49 B   50 A   51 B   52 C   53 A   54 B   55 C   56 D

Writing (1 hour 30 minutes)

Candidate responses are marked using the assessment scale on pages 108–109.

Listening (approximately 40 minutes)

Part 1

1 A   2 B   3 A   4 B   5 A   6 C

Part 2

7 (playing) tennis   8 schools / a school   9 (an) emerging (field)
10 cooking / cookery workshops   11 journalism   12 scientific papers
13 hardware   14 hospitality tickets

Part 3

15 B   16 B   17 A   18 C   19 A   20 D

Part 4

21 H   22 G   23 F   24 B   25 A   26 G   27 H   28 C   29 B   30 E

Transcript	*This is the Cambridge English Advanced Listening Test. Test Two.*
	I'm going to give you the instructions for this test.
	I'll introduce each part of the test and give you time to look at the questions.
	At the start of each piece you'll hear this sound:
	tone
	You'll hear each piece twice.
	Remember, while you're listening, write your answers on the question paper. You'll have five minutes at the end of the test to copy your answers onto the separate answer sheet.
	There'll now be a pause. Please ask any questions now because you must not speak during the test.
	[pause]
	Now open your question paper and look at Part One.
	[pause]
PART 1	*You'll hear three different extracts. For questions 1–6, choose the answer (A, B, or C) which fits best according to what you hear. There are two questions for each extract.*
Extract One	*You hear two friends talking about people who were once famous but who are now relatively unknown.*
	Now look at questions one and two.
	[pause]
	tone

Man: Have you read this magazine article? It's about people that were once internationally famous, like astronauts and sports people, but who now live in relative obscurity, having retired or just given up doing whatever made them famous.

Woman: I imagine that can be really tough – having to recreate a completely new existence away from the spotlight.

Man: Well, in people's minds, they had their metaphorical 15 minutes of fame but after that they sort of cease to exist. I mean, we have this odd approach, we reduce famous people to being identified only through the most pivotal thing they ever did. But that may have occurred very early in their life. But when they're recognised much later on, and that happens all the time, it means they can't forget that thing – and settle into a 'normal life' and that's hard.

Woman: Mmm, I read about one dancer who suffered a profound sense of anti-climax after her career was over, but amazingly set about channelling her energies into other activities, refusing to accept that her life would be defined only by her work – which I guess is a lesson we could all take on board.

Man: Absolutely.

[pause]

tone

[The recording is repeated.]

[pause]

Extract Two   *You hear two friends talking about swimming in rivers and lakes, a practice known as wild swimming.*

Now look at questions three and four.

[pause]

tone

Man: Hey, Sarah – how've you found your first year in our wild swimming group? What got you started, anyway?

Woman: Well, I've been into water sports since I was a kid, but when I first heard about your group, it struck me as mad, if I'm honest – just too daring. I reckoned it'd push my boundaries too far. The thought of untried environments was irresistible, though – all those rivers and lakes out there, just waiting to be discovered. And the unexpected bonus is the fresh dimension it brings to the activity itself – swimming feels much more exciting, and I love doing it with others.

Man: Yeah – it's great for morale, swimming as a group. You positively feel others urging you on. And I also love the fact that it attracts people who wouldn't normally get together – we're a real mix, aren't we? The power of a joint passion, I guess.

Woman: And you build up a sort of collective memory bank, swimming regularly together, despite different interests away from the water. I mean, witnessing the sunrise on dawn swims wouldn't be half as good alone. And you look out for one other, too – you can't overestimate the importance of that. I've made lasting friendships as well.

[pause]

tone

[The recording is repeated.]

[pause]

Extract Three   *You hear two friends talking about installing solar electricity systems in private houses.*

Now look at questions five and six.

[pause]

tone

Man: I noticed you've had solar electricity panels fitted on the roof of your house. How's that going?

Woman: Good. It's lucky really. The government's just ended subsidies for solar electricity in private homes, but we just squeezed in and got 30% off the cost of installation. Scrapping subsidies is such a short-sighted idea. Now they expect people to cover the full cost! I tell you, it's no way to get people thinking green. And the press don't help, do they? All those scare stories about what a waste of money renewable energy is.

Man: No, they don't. But is it really a good idea for the state to get mixed up in it? It kills off competition I reckon, and that's what's keeping costs so high. Perhaps now, the market will open up.

Woman: Well, we'll soon find out. Either way, we'll all have to accept things like solar power at some point.

Man: Because oil's going to run out you mean? We've been hearing that for years now – everyone's going to have to stop driving and flying, live in eco houses, all that – but it's still with us and technology seems to be helping us keep things the way they are. Don't hold your breath, in other words.

[pause]

tone

[The recording is repeated.]

[pause]

That's the end of Part One.

Now turn to Part Two.

[pause]

PART 2   *You'll hear a sports nutritionist called Emily Anderson talking to a group of students about how she helps young athletes with their diet. For questions 7–14, complete the sentences with a word or short phrase.*

You now have 45 seconds to look at Part Two.

[pause]

tone

Emily: My name is Emily Anderson and I'm the founder of Move Nutrition and Fitness. I've been giving advice on sports nutrition for around 15 years now. And I can tell you exactly how I got into this career. It all started because my family really liked eating meals together and, because I loved playing tennis, I gradually developed a keen personal interest in the way I'd perform differently if I ate differently, not just physiologically speaking but also psychologically, the mental gain you might say.

So, I did my degree and I started by volunteering as a nutritionist for a local football team while doing other jobs to pay the bills. Although a few professional teams employed them, schools – which is where I hoped to be working – just didn't take on sports nutritionists back then. But after a few years building up experience, I finally landed my dream job.

However, my specialisation, youth athletics, is still an emerging field rather than an established discipline because historically, there wasn't much thought given to nutrition in young athletes. Nowadays, though, the pressure's on to perform well and young athletes increasingly need nutritional advice as they advance.

As part of my work I regularly run cooking workshops – I get a real kick out of that. And a small but growing part of what I do involves providing personal consultations.

In many countries, becoming a sports nutritionist requires little more than a diploma in basic nutrition, but if you want more professional scope, my advice would be to take an option in journalism as part of your degree, for instance – there are always plenty of chances to do media work when it comes to sports. After all, a sports nutritionist is required to be an excellent communicator and have good people skills. Other skills which are advantageous include marketing know-how, time management and other such business skills. You also need to be aware of the latest trends and while loads of people find blogs interesting, it's scientific papers that'll give you what you really need. I sometimes contribute to discussion forums which can be great fun.

If you're thinking of becoming a sports nutritionist, there are a couple of things to be aware of. If you're self-employed as a consultant, you charge an hourly rate. This can vary from $60 to $150 per hour depending on the client, however, remember that when you set up you'll need to spend a lot on what I refer to as the hardware – all the stuff you need to get your business off the ground. If you work in-house for an organisation though, you don't need to worry about overheads like lighting or heating. If financial rewards are what you're interested in, you could be disappointed. But there are a lot of perks that make it worthwhile – although it's awesome working with athletes, what I hadn't reckoned on is the hospitality tickets I get. And of course, you'll be in fantastic shape too.

[pause]

Now you'll hear Part Two again.

tone

[The recording is repeated.]

[pause]

That's the end of Part Two.

Now turn to Part Three.

[pause]

PART 3   *You'll hear part of an interview with two environmentalists, Carol Jones and James Wilson, who are talking about an approach to conservation called rewilding, and damaged environments.*

For questions 15–20, choose the answer (A, B, C or D) which fits best according to what you hear.

You now have 70 seconds to look at Part Three.

[pause]

tone

Interviewer: I'm talking to Carol Jones and James Wilson, environmentalists working with damaged environments. Carol, you're in favour of rewilding to deal with damaged ecosystems. For our listeners, rewilding is a large-scale approach to conservation which aims to restore and protect natural processes in wilderness areas. Tell us why you're in favour of this.

Carol: Rewilding involves both the re-introduction of key species that may have been lost due to eco-damage, and also the eradication of species that are not naturally found in an area. I often explain it to non-specialists as returning an environment to its natural state. Rewilding allows the original types of animals and plants to find food and flourish.

Interviewer: James, you have a different view.

James: Rewilding has its place, but I'd rather support alien species than get rid of them – by alien, I mean species not native to the area they're living in. On the whole, alien species are good for the environment; they usually increase biodiversity and don't often cause extinctions, because they're to do with the environment's own response to the damage people have done. They tend to be more resilient than native species, so prosper more easily, whether it's in soils that have been made salty or forests that have been cut down.

Interviewer: You've produced a report identifying places where native species once lived. Why was that, Carol?

Carol: People think they know about species that lived in Britain, like beavers and wolves, but imagine this was thousands of years ago – whereas actually the last wolf was killed in the seventeenth century. It seems unbelievable that elephants, hippo – even lions – once lived here – but bones found in London prove it. Armed with this information, we could bring some back – maybe not elephants but other wildlife. The idea appeals not only because it could reverse destruction caused by humans, but also because it seems rather magical.

Interviewer: In terms of conservation work, do you think we should look to the past?

Carol: Yes, it's essential to study the past to understand today's ecosystems. I don't see rewilding as backward-looking. The ecosystems that would emerge on rewilded land wouldn't be identical to those that were there before – partly because we've irredeemably lost a lot of species, and of course most scientists think the physical environment has changed through things like climate change, whatever its cause. We've learned that there can't be a fixed ecosystem or group of species.

James: There really isn't a 'native' ecosystem anywhere, and if there is, it's been messed up by humans. But I think it's the wrong way to look at ecosystems. They're constantly evolving, species are moving in and out all the time. So the whole idea of a stable, natural ecosystem is a misunderstanding of nature. It's not as fragile as we often think.

Interviewer: Does rewilding have to be an organised large-scale response to damaged ecosystems?

Carol: I don't think there's one right way of rewilding – there are many, like introducing wildlife corridors – you know – pathways that connect wildlife areas. You see, the biggest problem many species face is what scientists call 'habitat fragmentation' – we've built over areas where previously animals moved around looking for food. Everyone can help with this. I'd like to see people who have individual gardens joining them up to create these wildlife corridors, which could mean planting native trees to create a continuous run from one garden to another, linking them up with existing patches of forest. Species which otherwise wouldn't be able to enter that area could then pass through, and use that as their habitat.

Interviewer: People have different attitudes to environmental problems – how do you feel about that?

James: There are undoubtedly occasions where alien species cause a short-term problem for nature and humans – like weeds on farms. On the whole, though, such things are only inconvenient for people economically, but sadly, people can't see beyond that. Where alien species have caused actual harm, it's usually because humans have already messed up the environment – like the water hyacinth, which is clogging up ponds and rivers in some countries, but the plants only do that because the water's already been polluted by sewage and other things.

Interviewer: So how do you both feel about …

[pause]

Now you'll hear Part Three again.

tone

[The recording is repeated.]

[pause]

That's the end of Part Three.

Now turn to Part Four.

[pause]

PART 4   *Part Four consists of two tasks.*

You'll hear five short extracts in which people are talking about leaving their previous jobs to work freelance from home.

Look at Task One. For questions 21–25, choose from the list (A–H) the reason why each speaker decided to work freelance from home.

Now look at Task Two. For questions 26–30, choose from the list (A–H) the aspect of working freelance from home which each speaker has found challenging.

While you listen, you must complete both tasks.

You now have 45 seconds to look at Part Four.

[pause]

tone

Speaker One: I enjoyed my last job in a small manufacturing firm. The managers took everyone's opinion into account and trusted people to use their own ideas wherever possible. That helped prepare me for going freelance and being in sole charge of all decisions concerning the work I do for various electronics businesses. What I'd give, though, to get a 'well done' now from those same people – or even just a bit of constructive criticism. I guess the flexibility helps to compensate, though. That's what finally did it for me previously – my requests for leave never got a look-in as the bosses always took priority on the rota. I love looking online for cheap deals now – there are some real low-season bargains.

[pause]

Speaker Two: I went freelance three months ago and love it! I've had loads of emotional support from friends and family, which has been great – though I'm going to have to ask them to stop coming round to help out with what they wrongly reckon is too heavy a burden for me alone. They end up making coffees and conversation, which'd be lovely if I had time for it! I need 100% focus just now if I'm to make a success of things. Mind you, being selective about what I do is what lay behind my move towards independence. In my last place, my bosses were constantly giving me more and more to do, which finally got overwhelming.

[pause]

Speaker Three: I used to work as a technical writer in a multinational company where things were quite pressured at times, though, I must admit, anything but dull. I was on pretty decent pay but the daily commute started to get to me – all those cancelled trains and delays - and it struck me I could make better use of the hours I was losing either side of a long working day. Six months on, I've no regrets. There's no problem motivating myself – in fact, I have trouble switching off. I'm relieved, to be honest, when friends call round unexpectedly in the evening – it forces me to disconnect mentally, which isn't a bad thing.

[pause]

Speaker Four: In my last job, I always wondered about going freelance. One of my mates did it a few years ago, and reckoned it was brilliant, though the hours he was working put me off a bit. But I eventually reached the stage when I could no longer stand my manager constantly breathing down my neck. It was the same old story on every project I was involved in – suffocating. Being self-reliant now is liberating – even the fact that I've got no-one to blame but myself if anything goes wrong! I really miss the break-time natters with my team-mates though, but I'm gradually learning to adapt, and realise I've actually accomplished a great deal on my own.

[pause]

Speaker Five: Initially, my last job was exciting – despite an overwhelming amount of work – I never knew what each day would hold. After company restructuring, though, my range of duties narrowed right down and I longed for how things had been. It dawned on me that by setting up independently, I could recapture that initial feeling. So, I struck out on my own and I haven't looked back – and my earnings have increased. It's all too easy to fall behind in my specialism though, and I struggle a bit with staying on top of changes in my field. But I'm proud to say my home's my business base now, even if stuff tends to spill over into every room – it's great.

[pause]

Now you'll hear Part Four again.

tone

[The recording is repeated.]

[pause]

That's the end of Part Four.

There'll now be a pause of five minutes for you to copy your answers onto the separate answer sheet. Be sure to follow the numbering of all the questions. I'll remind you when there's one minute left, so that you're sure to finish in time.

[Teacher, pause the recording here for five minutes. Remind students when they have one minute left.]

That's the end of the test. Please stop now. Your supervisor will now collect all the question papers and answer sheets.

Test 3 Key

Reading and Use of English (1 hour 30 minutes)

Part 1

1 B   2 C   3 D   4 C   5 A   6 B   7 D   8 B

Part 2

9 unlike   10 now / given   11 all   12 to   13 does / can / may / might
14 against / at   15 as   16 where

Part 3

17 psychological   18 uplifted   19 significantly   20 participants   21 meaningful
22 expectancy   23 speculative   24 implication

Part 4

25 not | being (entirely / totally / completely) HONEST

26 matter | HOW hard John

27 gave me | her WORD

28 continue due / owing to / because of | (a / the) LACK of be continued; due / owing to / because of | LACK of

29 doubt in | the manager's MIND

30 impressed by / at her | tutor's ABILITY

Part 5

31 C   32 B   33 C   34 A   35 D   36 B

Part 6

37 C   38 B   39 D   40 D

Part 7

41 D   42 B   43 F   44 A   45 C   46 G

Part 8

47 D   48 B   49 A   50 D   51 C   52 D   53 C   54 B   55 C   56 B

Writing (1 hour 30 minutes)

Candidate responses are marked using the assessment scale on pages 108–109.

Listening (approximately 40 minutes)

Part 1

1 B   2 A   3 B   4 A   5 C   6 B

Part 2

7 rainforest (protection)   8 training manager   9 instructor('s) licence/license
10 peaceful (fishing) village   11 (a) familiar face   12 plastic bottles   13 recycling
14 confidence

Part 3

15 B   16 C   17 A   18 D   19 A   20 B

Part 4

21 H   22 A   23 F   24 C   25 E   26 A   27 D   28 H   29 C   30 E

Transcript	*This is the Cambridge English Advanced Listening Test. Test Three.*
	I'm going to give you the instructions for this test.
	I'll introduce each part of the test and give you time to look at the questions.
	At the start of each piece you'll hear this sound:
	tone
	You'll hear each piece twice.
	Remember, while you're listening, write your answers on the question paper. You'll have five minutes at the end of the test to copy your answers onto the separate answer sheet.
	There'll now be a pause. Please ask any questions now, because you must not speak during the test.
	[pause]
	Now open your question paper and look at Part One.
	[pause]
PART 1	*You'll hear three different extracts. For questions 1–6, choose the answer (A, B, or C) which fits best according to what you hear. There are two questions for each extract.*
Extract One	*You hear two newspaper journalists talking about their work to a group of students.*
	Now look at questions one and two.
	[pause]
	tone

Woman: My first job was on a fashion website, doing blogs and sound bites – it was good to work with other people but I found it unsatisfying and transitory. People kept telling me print journalism was dead, but I wouldn't have forgiven myself if I hadn't given it a go.

Man: There's still an appetite for commentary, but people's attention spans are short – they want bite-sized clips and breaking news delivered instantly in accessible chunks. I do use social media but 140 characters can't replace my in-depth interviews in a newspaper – it's my responsibility to present full facts and balanced opinions clearly.

Woman: I find chasing people for information puts me under pressure – you have to be persistent and meticulous in checking facts, and surfing the internet doesn't cut it. It's long hours, too.

Man: You have to engage your readers. And to know how to package an article well you have to work with editors to choose pictures and write headlines. On the downside, there are constant deadlines and that's difficult to deal with.

Woman: At least we don't get bored!

[pause]

tone

[The recording is repeated.]

[pause]

Extract Two   *You hear two language teachers discussing the use of emoticons, the pictures many people use to express emotion in text messages.*

Now look at questions three and four.

[pause]

tone

Man: Humans have communicated through pictures for thousands of years – think about cave paintings; emoticons just seem to be a natural development.

Woman: I do consider carefully before using them though because they can be interpreted in a different way from words. Science tells us that pictures activate the right side of the brain, whereas words activate the left, so an emoticon may produce a different response because of this. You can send messages using strings of emoticons instead of words, and a system like that – maybe with its own grammar – could lend itself to being a universal system of communication. It could transcend boundaries!

Man: Yet some people regard emoticons as frivolous. They're concerned about the dumbing-down of communication, well, it's true, emoticons don't belong in the workplace so you have to be aware of when they're appropriate. Personally, I think people who use them are perfectly capable of expressing themselves with words, but people do appreciate the fact that emoticons give them a different form of expression – something almost poetic that complements written language, even if it doesn't have a grammatical structure.

Woman: Emoticons may not be suitable for genuine deep grief or real anger, though – imagine Shakespeare's plays written using them!

[pause]

tone

[The recording is repeated.]

[pause]

Extract Three *You hear two friends talking about a young professional tennis player.*

Now look at questions five and six.

[pause]

tone

Woman: It amused me to read in the papers last week that he is, and I quote: 'charmless in character, and not a cultural individual'. OK, so he's not the sort of person you might wish to sit next to at a dinner party. So what do you think? He's not competing in the Charm and Personality Championships. More to the point, the obsessiveness and tunnel vision which seems to irritate commentators is the very source of his greatness as a tennis player.

Man: But he seems angry so much of the time – will he be able to control this as he gets more mature, as many great players have done in the past? Possibly yes, but it's not a prerequisite of success that he should do so, nor that he should be universally adored by the public. What's significant is that he possesses a burning desire to succeed and a competitiveness of equally fierce intensity – so is it any wonder that such a person will howl with rage at an error, either on his own part or by an official? And, of course, that will land him in a spot of bother with the authorities.

[pause]

tone

[The recording is repeated.]

[pause]

That's the end of Part One.

Now turn to Part Two.

[pause]

PART 2   *You'll hear a woman called Jane Brooks talking about her work on various marine conservation projects.*

For questions 7–14, complete the sentences with a word or short phrase.

You now have 45 seconds to look at Part Two.

[pause]

tone

Jane: Hello. My name's Jane Brooks and I'm going to tell you about my work as both a volunteer and an employee on various marine conservation projects all over the world.

After university, I was interested in doing some volunteer conservation work and a friend of mine recommended a useful website. When I looked, I found myself torn between two projects: volunteering on rainforest protection in Belize or marine conservation in Thailand.

I'd never done any diving before, but I've always been fascinated by the ocean, so I decided that the Thai project was the one for me. I started out there as an ordinary volunteer and, two years later I became Volunteer Co-ordinator. Then, I moved here to Cambodia for a paid job helping volunteers. My title is Training Manager, and I can honestly say I've never looked back.

Learning to dive ignited a passion for it. So after getting my intermediate diving certificate, I continued my dive education in Thailand right after finishing on the project there. I decided to stay on in the country, and after diving there daily for nearly half a year, I obtained my instructor licence, which was a very proud moment.

When I first arrived here in Cambodia, I was expecting something very similar to Thailand. Boy was I wrong! Unlike Thailand, where I was located in a busy harbour and everything was based on tourism, here I'm living in the heart of a fishing village but it's really peaceful and there's almost no foreigners. It's like another planet!

Everything takes time here, and if I need something special, I can't just go out the door and get it. There's a much more intimate feel to things, and I've become a real part of the community. The locals have accepted me as a familiar face. And it's wonderful that I don't feel like an outsider.

After starting or continuing their dive education with me, volunteers will study local marine life and its identification and assessment and, after some training, they start conducting environmental surveys. Another thing they do is cleaning up coral reefs, getting rid of the rubbish, like empty cans and stuff. And it breaks my heart to see all the plastic bottles floating around – it's so unnecessary! This is something we all have to address.

The project is still young. The ultimate goal is to make the archipelago into a marine reserve, but there's a lot to do before that happens. Our next step is to help local people establish a recycling system for waste.

Every day is different, but my favourite part is when you're teaching someone to dive and you see fear turn into confidence. Seeing smiling faces returning to the surface after that initial dive gives me a real sense of pride!

If you're interested in the environment and looking for an adventure, then sign up. We're here waiting to welcome you!

[pause]

Now you'll hear Part Two again.

tone

[The recording is repeated.]

[pause]

That's the end of Part Two.

Now turn to Part Three.

[pause]

PART 3   *You'll hear an interview with two college lecturers, Sarah Banks and Tom Weston, who are talking about working in clothes shops when they were students.*

For questions 15–20, choose the answer (A, B, C or D) which fits best according to what you hear.

You now have 70 seconds to look at Part Three.

[pause]

tone

Interviewer: With me today are Sarah Banks and Tom Weston, two college lecturers who both worked while they were students. Welcome!

Sarah: Thanks.

Tom: Thank you.

Interviewer: Sarah, tell us first about the job you had – in an expensive clothes shop?

Sarah: Mmm … it was in a fancy women's boutique. I'd like to say I got the job because of my fashionable appearance – I was studying fashion, so I always wore the latest stuff. But I think the manager just liked my outgoing manner. I was aware even then, though, that a shop job wasn't my thing, but there was little else around where I could get any experience, so off I went. It was in an affluent area, full of creative types. And the price tags were high, so we didn't need many sales for a good day's takings.

Interviewer: And was it enjoyable?

Sarah: Well, some customers could be difficult, and they all expected something special – soft fabrics, low lights, chic private changing rooms. They weren't just looking for clothes – they were after a whole experience. And often they'd pick out totally unsuitable things, but insist they were the right choice.

So I really appreciated it when a woman would finally step out of the changing room in the dress that completely altered her whole posture – head up, shoulders back. It demonstrated the magic of the perfect outfit – and fed into my later design work.

Interviewer: How easy was it to fit in at the shop?

Sarah: There was a strict dress code for staff; we had to wear stuff from the shop's range – I did fall into line with this, but only just. I remember feeling a distinct sense of rebellion when I realised how limited the choice was, as I felt – and still feel – people should express themselves through their clothes. So I deliberately chose the only two things that were comfortable – but they looked hideous together. No-one commented, but I felt I'd made my point – being so strict wasn't in the shop's best interest. Luckily, none of my friends saw me wearing the clothes – although I did eventually show them off at home.

Interviewer: And Tom, you also worked in a clothes boutique.

Tom: Yeah – I was a business student and the boutique really inspired me. The owner had become famous by making amazing clothes out of recycled stuff, but never seemed that interested in big profits, so I was intrigued by him. Then, I overheard staff talking about how he'd ring round his branches every day, demanding to know how much money they'd made. It was a real eye-opener – the fashion world clearly didn't survive on charisma and big ideas alone. I was really mad when I realised how stupid I'd been – I just wasn't worldly-wise enough then to see the reality. It taught me that things aren't always what they seem.

Interviewer: And you both teach students now. Tom, can you spot those that've had experience of work?

Tom: They're the ones who understand the importance of getting to classes, even for parts of the course they find less inspiring. They'll still manage to get something out of them. And they'll come over as fully functioning grown-ups, able to take responsibility for their lives without much assistance. They'll have learnt the basics of time management, and have an appreciation of whatever money they've got, too, although as students they usually don't have much, of course.

Interviewer: So finally, what did you learn from working while you were students? Sarah?

Sarah: Well, any job you do has its moments of tedium – but also work is great for boosting your confidence. And through working in a shop, I acquired expertise in several areas that's served me well across the board. I'm still an avid observer of customer behaviour. I often notice how little they change from shop to shop.

Interviewer: Tom?

Tom: I enjoyed learning how to interact with people. In fact, I'd dish out advice with no real idea what I was talking about – that comes in handy! And as an academic now, I'm grateful that I was trained in how to sell things, as even us bookish types have to market ourselves nowadays.

[pause]

Now you'll hear Part Three again.

tone

[The recording is repeated.]

[pause]

That's the end of Part Three.

Now turn to Part Four.

[pause]

PART 4

Part Four consists of two tasks.

You'll hear five short extracts in which people are talking about their favourite series of travel guidebooks.

Look at Task One. For questions 21–25, choose from the list (A–H) what each speaker particularly likes about the series of travel guidebooks.

Now look at Task Two. For questions 26–30, choose from the list (A–H) the one criticism each speaker has of the series of travel guidebooks.

While you listen, you must complete both tasks.

You now have 45 seconds to look at Part Four.

[pause]

tone

Speaker One: *Travel Easy* is the granddaddy of guidebooks series and there are few places they don't cover, often in too much painful detail. I find them best for dipping into. Most of these guides cover a specific place – continent, country, or city so there's something for everyone depending on how ambitious your plans are geographically. There's some downloadable material, but you'll miss out quite a bit if you try to go green and rely on that alone. What stands out for me are the sections covering the kind of phrases and basic vocabulary you need to get around. The photography leaves a little to be desired, but their hand-drawn maps are handy when exploring somewhere new.

[pause]

Speaker Two: I know the *Backpacking Basics* series have a bit less than others about times and prices, but for backpacking women like me, they're hard to beat. They more than make up for these shortcomings with their in-depth treatment of things like the local music, literature and food – they go way beyond just travel so they're better than many speciality guides. You're probably better off using your smartphone if you're trying to navigate your way around rather than try to make sense of the street plans in these guides though! A bit of help with the local language would be an idea for the future, but I have a soft spot for *Backpacking Basics* – there's something friendly about them.

[pause]

Speaker Three: *Bradley Guides* are my favourites – they were publishing entire books on offbeat destinations when others provided barely a page. I appreciate the 'single voice' that shines through, making them more of a pleasure to read than those that feel like they've been written by a committee.

I've used their no-nonsense guides all over and found information unavailable anywhere else. You do need to check when they were published as they have a smaller range of writers than the bigger-selling guides, so don't get revised as often. I expect sales have suffered because they're aimed at travellers for whom, like me, travelling sustainably is important rather than at mainstream travellers who like their days planned out for them.

[pause]

Speaker Four: The *Into Guides* were started by a graphic designer, which shows in the extraordinary pictures they're famous – and widely praised in the press for – and these are accompanied by huge amounts of historical detail. That's not to say they don't contain some useful stuff too – there's a certain amount at the end. But I just feel there isn't quite enough organisational stuff to help you plan a schedule each day. Overall though, I'd say despite the fact that it reads a bit like an encyclopaedia at times, there's nothing like it for really getting an in-depth understanding of a country before ever setting foot there.

[pause]

Speaker Five: I bought the *Footsteps Guides* because it includes several sections written by some of the big names in travel writing. And I wasn't disappointed. I prefer guides that really bring a variety of perspectives to a place and its culture. The standard sections suffer by comparison – a little more description and emotion here would be welcome – the text here can be pretty matter-of-fact. Overall though, there are still far more pluses than minuses. It's got accommodation and things to do and it's pretty good on transportation, which may help with planning. I expect some will find the books a bit bulky – although I personally don't mind it.

[pause]

Now you'll hear Part Four again.

tone

[The recording is repeated.]

[pause]

That's the end of Part Four.

There'll now be a pause of five minutes for you to copy your answers onto the separate answer sheet. Be sure to follow the numbering of all the questions. I'll remind you when there's one minute left, so that you're sure to finish in time.

[Teacher, pause the recording here for five minutes. Remind students when they have one minute left.]

That's the end of the test. Please stop now. Your supervisor will now collect all the question papers and answer sheets.

Test 4 Key

Reading and Use of English (1 hour 30 minutes)

Part 1

1 A   2 D   3 B   4 C   5 D   6 A   7 A   8 D

Part 2

9 as   10 not   11 like   12 to   13 off / from   14 before   15 there   16 for

Part 3

17 mindlessly / absentmindedly   18 involuntary   19 accompanies   20 viewers
21 pleasure   22 inappropriately   23 unplanned   24 thoughts

Part 4

25 the FIRST time | she had / she'd (ever)
26 was MEANT to | turn / show
27 CAME as | no surprise
28 took (absolutely) no | NOTICE of; did not / didn't take (any) | NOTICE of
29 has / 's been a | DROP in
30 had / 'd BETTER | put

Part 5

31 D   32 B   33 C   34 D   35 A   36 B

Part 6

37 B   38 A   39 D   40 D

Part 7

41 E   42 G   43 A   44 F   45 D   46 C

Part 8

47 A   48 D   49 A   50 D   51 C   52 A   53 B   54 C   55 D   56 B

Writing (1 hour 30 minutes)

Candidate responses are marked using the assessment scale on pages 108–109.

Listening (approximately 40 minutes)

Part 1

1 B   2 A   3 B   4 A   5 C   6 B

Part 2

7 (some) (magazine) editors   8 wide-angle   9 lost cities   10 blue filters   11 test beds
12 (helicopter) pilot / pilot (in a helicopter)   13 (repeated) circles   14 hero image

Part 3

15 D   16 A   17 B   18 C   19 B   20 A

Part 4

21 G   22 A   23 D   24 E   25 C   26 E   27 G   28 B   29 H   30 C

Transcript

This is the Cambridge English Advanced Listening Test. Test Four.

I'm going to give you the instructions for this test.

I'll introduce each part of the test and give you time to look at the questions.

At the start of each piece you'll hear this sound:

tone

You'll hear each piece twice.

Remember, while you're listening, write your answers on the question paper. You'll have five minutes at the end of the test to copy your answers onto the separate answer sheet.

There'll now be a pause. Please ask any questions now, because you must not speak during the test.

[pause]

Now open your question paper and look at Part One.

[pause]

PART 1

You'll hear three different extracts. For questions 1–6, choose the answer (A, B, or C) which fits best according to what you hear. There are two questions for each extract.

Extract One

You hear two friends talking about their children's reading habits.

Now look at questions one and two.

[pause]

tone

Woman:	Your daughter likes reading, doesn't she?
Man:	Yeah. She reads all sorts of books, often about things outside her personal experience – in fact, anything from historical legends to science-fiction stories, provided the characters are strong. We keep an eye on her choices, but there's never been a problem and encouraging her to go for what she wants keeps her enthusiasm going. Some of her books are beautifully illustrated, too – but, good as the pictures are, she's got such a strong imagination that she says they can actually contradict the mental images she creates herself.
Woman:	I only wish my own kids were the same! They're used to seeing me with my nose in a book and I thought they'd copy my example. Perhaps they just see reading as boring, something teachers ask them to do. I guess there's so much competition now for their attention, too, and they spend so much time online.
Man:	Well, there's always room for a good book, if only kids realised the fun of escaping into the world of fiction. Admittedly, literature classes can be a drag, when you're always analysing everything – no wonder that puts some kids off. I admit my own mum and dad weren't great readers, but they did encourage me from an early age – they were always buying me books.

[pause]

tone

[The recording is repeated.]

[pause]

Extract Two   *You hear part of an interview with a man who worked as a team leader with students doing voluntary work in the rainforest.*

Now look at questions three and four.

[pause]

tone

Woman:	And you were a team leader on a volunteer project?
Man:	Yes. I'd been looking for ways to get experience in international development as well as leadership, so when I heard about the opportunity to set up a sustainable method of processing coffee beans in the rainforest, I jumped at the chance to lead a team of multinational volunteers on a three-month project! They had no previous work experience, so it was incredibly fulfilling to witness their evolution. As they came out of their shells, they formed friendships and gained valuable life skills in the process. It may have been their first time away from home, but that didn't stop them giving pretty much everything a go.
Woman:	Right.

| Man: | Before, I lacked experience of leading a team, which is essential in the workplace nowadays. Like, I learned to take on responsibilities for the rota, whilst acting as mentor and ensuring that the project's goals were achieved. But all that paled in comparison to what I actually walked away with. The sheer intensity you experience when operating in a tight-knit group such as this isn't just an integral part of being a successful leader, it's personally transformational in nature. Now I feel ready for whatever the world has to throw at me. |

[pause]

tone

[The recording is repeated.]

[pause]

Extract Three *You hear two students talking about fast food.*

Now look at questions five and six.

[pause]

tone

Woman:	Hey, is that a fast-food bag you've got there?
Man:	It is ... and it's quite rare for me! My housemates rely heavily on fast food though – they're watching their budgets and reckon it's a cheap deal. But when you look at the minuscule portions, it's hardly economical compared to making your own meals from scratch. They don't like to admit that's beyond them, I reckon – so they can't resist stopping by the burger bar. Lots of fast food companies are targeting kids and students, too, in their advertising, though I think my housemates would just buy the stuff anyhow.
Woman:	I know what you mean. I personally eat a lot less of it now.
Man:	That's good.
Woman:	Well, I must admit when I'm really pressed for time, it occasionally comes in handy and I guess that applies to most people. No matter how tasty they try and make it look though, I always find it really unsatisfying and end up hungry an hour later! Fast-food companies are making an effort to include more fruit and veg on the menu now though, which is a real step forward. I wonder if they'd be more filling. I do think many people eat fast food out of habit, and when companies have to display the calorie content of everything, customers will think twice.

[pause]

tone

[The recording is repeated.]

[pause]

That's the end of Part One.

Now turn to Part Two.

[pause]

PART 2   *You'll hear hear an architectural photographer called Jack Gollins talking about his work immediately after receiving a professional award.*

For questions 7–14, complete the sentences with a word or short phrase.

You now have 45 seconds to look at Part Two.

[pause]

tone

Jack: My name, as you've probably gathered, is Jack Gollins, and I'd like to express my thanks for this wonderful award.

Frankly, I'm a bit of a workaholic, busy trying to satisfy my architect clients, and come up with a photograph that will put them on the map, as well as trying to satisfy my own artistic ambitions. So to be honest, it was only when I was talking to some magazine editors recently who were consulted over my nomination, that I realised what I've actually achieved so far in my field. I was genuinely taken aback by the number of projects I've done.

So, how do I actually go about shooting a building? Well, I have self-imposed rules – and some of them are quirky and particular to me. I tend to use a wide-angle lens, rather than a fish-eye lens that some photographers prefer. I show more context than many of my colleagues too, and my compositional rules break all the normal aesthetics.

I'm often asked if there are particular places, in Australia or overseas, that have had a big impact on me. The short answer is yes. I've spent quite a few years in countries like Cambodia photographing what are called lost cities. These were generally built by the leaders of the time, and I've been very influenced by the quality of the buildings there. There are practical issues working in such places – maybe if the building's half in ruins I'll work at night and only light the existing half, and leave the other half to the imagination. And in India, I've had to work with strong blue filters to separate the stone from the vivid sky. But I avoid fancy gimmicks out of a respect for historic buildings – they're intrinsically remarkable buildings which don't need any special effects. I use such trips as test beds for practising particular photographic techniques. A lot of them, like lighting buildings at night, were first tried out on my own projects – and then brought to bear on clients' modern buildings.

I guess I'm well-known now for my elevated shots. You can get in so close in a helicopter, and a few years back myself and the pilot I always use – he's awesome at the controls – worked out techniques for making the most of this. We can get amazing shots, by performing rapid, repeated circles, and be finished before local people and tourists start complaining! I've recently shot extraordinarily beautiful night-time pictures this way – which couldn't have been done ten years ago.

Now, potentially, an iconic building can bring in lots of money for everyone associated with it – so the pressure's on from clients for me to produce award-winning photos. But I'm a very harsh critic of my own work, and will keep going back to a project until I basically think I've achieved what's known as the hero image – the definitive shot of a building which brings in the money. And it can take a lot of visits to get it right, believe me. That's one of the reasons I'm so delighted to receive this award in recognition of my work – thank you so much.

[pause]

Now you'll hear Part Two again.

tone

[The recording is repeated.]

[pause]

That's the end of Part Two.

Now turn to Part Three.

[pause]

PART 3   *You'll hear part of an interview in which a science writer called Andy Hicks and a psychologist called Dr Karen Ferrigan are talking about how technology affects our brains. For questions 15–20, choose the answer (A, B, C or D) which fits best according to what you hear.*

You now have 70 seconds to look at Part Three.

[pause]

tone

Interviewer: Hello everyone. Today I'm talking to science writer Andy Hicks and psychologist Dr Karen Ferrigan about how technology affects our brains.

Andy: Hi.

Karen: Hello.

Interviewer: Andy, your latest book claims we shouldn't be texting, emailing, cooking and watching television all at the same time because our primitive hunter-gatherer brains are poorly suited to such high-tech multitasking.

Andy: That's one way to put it, but there's more to it. I'd argue that we think we're doing all these things simultaneously – all of us do – but in practice, the brain doesn't work that way. In terms of paying attention, what we're doing is rapidly shifting focus from one thing to the next and the next then back around to the first. All of that comes at a cost. It depletes the resources that we need for functioning effectively. Basically, it's an illusion.

Interviewer: You've written about the effect of having unread emails. Can you tell us about how that affects intelligence?

Andy: Well, there was one study that showed that the distraction of knowing you've had an email that you haven't read, while it doesn't lower your overall level of intelligence permanently, it does effectively lower it at that moment because your mind is now divided, there's a little voice inside your head asking, 'Who's that from? Is it good news? Is it something that needs sorting out right now?' All these thoughts are crowding your head, taking up the place of thoughts you would rather be directing at the task at hand.

Interviewer:	So what can we deduce from this?
Andy:	We see in studies done in various workplaces that people who are allowed to multitask get less done than people who work more methodically. But the interesting thing that comes out from the studies is that the multitaskers believe that they've been more productive. And you could say, well, why is it these people are so deluded? I'd say, just because you think something's so, doesn't make it so. One of the things we do know is that the brain is really good at tricking itself. I've seen this myself. I happen to think I tell brilliant jokes, but people around me say it isn't the case.
Interviewer:	Karen, would you agree then that our memories aren't designed for the demands of technology, including things like remembering passwords?
Karen:	Well, in terms of short-term memory, what you can hold in your consciousness is limited to three or four things. Your long-term memory, the memory you have for facts and figures, the stories that you've told about different things you've done, that's apparently unlimited. But the challenge with passwords is that they tend to be arbitrary. Different websites impose different restrictions – in some passwords you have to have special characters whereas others don't allow them, some have to have at least one number and so on. You can see the problem with trying to sort it all out. But I think we're digressing here.
Interviewer:	So, let's move on. And would you say our brains are changing over time?
Karen:	Of course we – and our brains – are evolving all the time, but so slowly that we can't easily measure it. It can take a great deal of time for us to respond to developments in our circumstances. Our brains could keep pace with the world of 20,000 or more years ago. There wasn't a whole lot of information coming in back then, nor much technological change. There were hundreds of thousands of years between, say, harnessing fire and developing agriculture. Now, though, your cellphone constantly updates its software and you've got to learn completely new things all the time. The result seems to be we all feel busier than we used to, less effective at work, and find it more difficult to make decisions.
Interviewer:	But there are advantages that come with this information age, aren't there?
Andy:	Absolutely. With the greatest respect to Karen, one of the best things actually is this unprecedented access to reliable information. Think back 20, 30 years. Say you wanted to know what the Krebs cycle was from biology; you'd either have to find somebody who knew, or go to a library and look it up. This can now be done instantly. Almost anything you'd want to know is easily available.
Karen:	The problem is that in there with all that information is so much misinformation. And it's got very difficult to know which is which. Back then, you could pick up a particular magazine and everything about it screamed 'this is an unreliable source'. Now bad websites look just as good as good websites. The most important thing we can teach is information literacy: how to tell the difference.

Interviewer: So, of all the interviews that we've had ...

[pause]

Now you'll hear Part Three again.

tone

[The recording is repeated.]

[pause]

That's the end of Part Three.

Now turn to Part Four.

[pause]

PART 4   *Part Four consists of two tasks.*

You'll hear five short extracts in which people are talking about their experiences of doing volunteer work.

Look at Task One. For questions 21–25, choose from the list (A–H) the reason each speaker gives for doing volunteer work.

Now look at Task Two. For questions 26–30, choose from the list (A–H) the change each speaker identifies in themselves as a result of doing volunteer work.

While you listen, you must complete both tasks.

You now have 45 seconds to look at Part Four.

[pause]

tone

Speaker One: My mate volunteered at an animal rescue centre last year and said it was brilliant. I didn't know much about animals, but I was prepared to give it a go, 'cos I was at a loose end over the summer with nothing else lined up, I reckoned this'd fit the bill. Actually, you didn't need to be an animal expert, you just had to be willing to work hard, cleaning cages and dragging bags of feed around and so on. I developed muscles I never knew I had, and though the first week was exhausting, by the end I'd toughened up. The hours were long but they flew by, 'cos it was never boring.

[pause]

Speaker Two: I volunteered for a local Woodland project, leading guided walks in the woods nearby. I was surprised at the variety of fellow volunteers – I've made friends with people from eighteen to eighty! I not only got to know them, but, daft as it sounds, myself as well. I've got six brothers and sisters and, much as I love them, it's hard sometimes to feel you're an individual, so doing this – away from them – has been a revelation. Leading walking groups and explaining issues about the woodland environment has been useful, too – the thought of speaking in public used to keep me awake at night, but I signed up hoping this'd be a way of conquering that feeling.

[pause]

Speaker Three: I joined a local charity as a media volunteer, doing proof-reading and press releases. It required an eye for detail and the ability to focus, which is where my talents lie anyway. I'd no idea where these skills could take me career-wise and hoped that volunteering would give me some ideas. I can now see myself as a self-employed PR person. I'd enjoy being my own boss – the managers at the charity could be quite temperamental. I gradually realised the way to handle such individuals was not to get upset when they let off steam, but to listen quietly before saying my bit. It meant things took longer to get through, but the strategy worked.

[pause]

Speaker Four: Last weekend, I volunteered on a river clean-up and persuaded my mates to join too – and they didn't let me down. There were several volunteer activities I could've done, but here I felt I'd make a tangible difference, which was what I was after – I'm someone who needs concrete results. It did me good being in a team, too. It meant negotiating who did what, which brought home the fact that not everyone was comfortable doing challenging physical stuff, like clearing the riverbed. I'd just presumed everyone'd be up for that! But several people opted to do things I'd have found boring, like removing rubbish from the riverbank – but, fair enough – that affects local wildlife.

[pause]

Speaker Five: When my brother mentioned a volunteer scheme for helping elderly people maintain their gardens, I jumped at it. I was already pretty knowledgeable about plants, having studied botany as a university option, but I confess I'd had no experience of actually handling a spade or cutting back trees and stuff – and here was my chance. If you'd told me last month that I'd happily spend hours focusing on weeding and digging, I wouldn't have believed you. But it's actually been riveting – time really flies by as I'm totally engrossed in the task in hand, something I'd have found impossible before. And it's incredibly satisfying to stand back afterwards and see things looking so much better thanks to my efforts!

[pause]

Now you'll hear Part Four again.

tone

[The recording is repeated.]

[pause]

That's the end of Part Four.

There'll now be a pause of five minutes for you to copy your answers onto the separate answer sheet. Be sure to follow the numbering of all the questions. I'll remind you when there's one minute left, so that you're sure to finish in time.

[Teacher, pause the recording here for five minutes. Remind students that they have one minute left.]

That's the end of the test. Please stop now. Your supervisor will now collect all the question papers and answer sheets.

CAMBRIDGE ENGLISH
Language Assessment
Part of the University of Cambridge

Do not write in this box

SAMPLE

Candidate Name
If not already printed, write name in CAPITALS and complete the Candidate No. grid (in pencil).

Candidate Signature

Examination Title

Centre

Supervisor:
If the candidate is ABSENT or has WITHDRAWN shade here

Centre No.

Candidate No.

Examination Details

Candidate Answer Sheet 1

Instructions

Use a PENCIL (B or HB). Rub out any answer you wish to change using an eraser.

Part 1: Mark ONE letter for each question.

For example, if you think **B** is the right answer to the question, mark your answer sheet like this:

Parts 2, 3 and **4:** Write your answer clearly in CAPITAL LETTERS.

For Parts 2 and 3 write one letter in each box. For example:

| 0 | E X A M P L E |

Part 1

1	A	B	C	D
2	A	B	C	D
3	A	B	C	D
4	A	B	C	D
5	A	B	C	D
6	A	B	C	D
7	A	B	C	D
8	A	B	C	D

Part 2

Do not write below here

9		9	1 0 u
10		10	1 0 u
11		11	1 0 u
12		12	1 0 u
13		13	1 0 u
14		14	1 0 u
15		15	1 0 u
16		16	1 0 u

Continues over ➡

CAE CPE R1

DP801

© UCLES 2018 Photocopiable

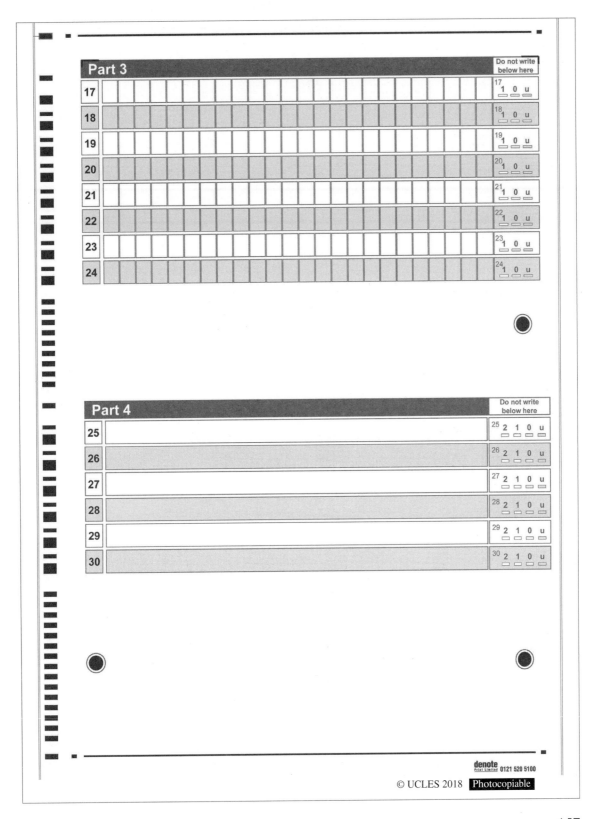

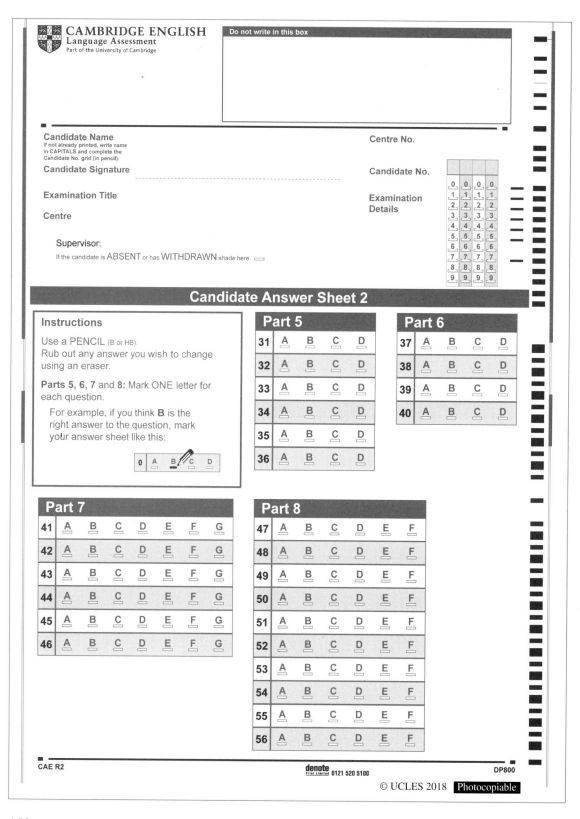

CAMBRIDGE ENGLISH
Language Assessment
Part of the University of Cambridge

Do not write in this box

SAMPLE

Candidate Name
If not already printed, write name
in CAPITALS and complete the
Candidate No. grid (in pencil).

Candidate Signature

Examination Title

Centre

Supervisor:
If the candidate is ABSENT or has WITHDRAWN shade here

Centre No.

Candidate No.

Examination Details

Candidate Answer Sheet

Instructions

Use a PENCIL (B or HB).
Rub out any answer you wish to change using an eraser.

Parts 1, 3 and **4:**
Mark ONE letter for each question.

For example, if you think **B** is the right answer to the question, mark your answer sheet like this:

Part 2:
Write your answer clearly in CAPITAL LETTERS.

Write one letter or number in each box.
If the answer has more than one word, leave one box empty between words.

For example:

Turn this sheet over to start.

CAE L

DP803

© UCLES 2018 Photocopiable

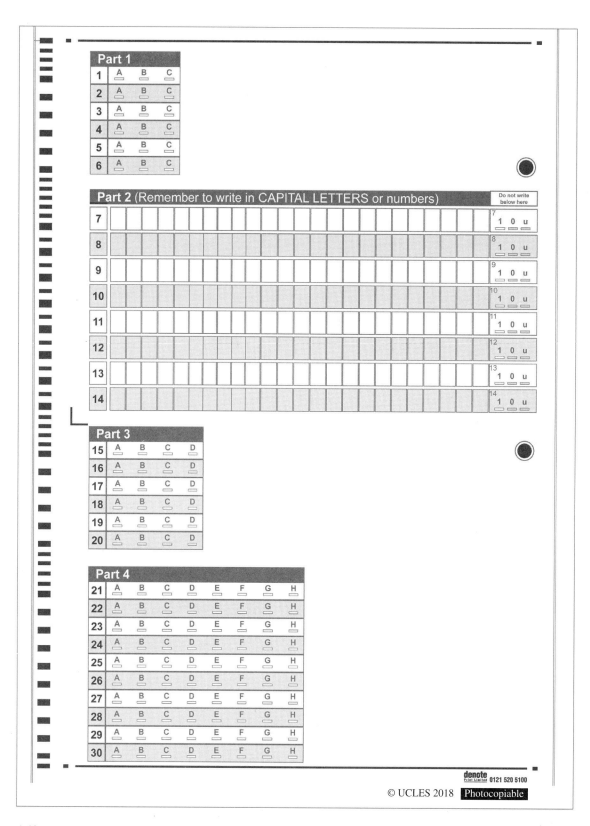

Acknowledgements

The authors and publishers acknowledge the following sources of copyright material and are grateful for the permissions granted. While every effort has been made, it has not always been possible to identify the sources of all the material used, or to trace all copyright holders. If any omissions are brought to our notice, we will be happy to include the appropriate acknowledgements on reprinting and in the next update to the digital edition, as applicable.

Key: TL = Top Left, CR = Centre Right, BL = Below Left.

Text Acknowledgements

Guardian News and Media Limited for the text on p. 16 adapted from 'Is London such a terrible place to live?' by Sam Jordison and Liz Hoggard, *The Guardian*, 23.08.2014. Copyright © 2014 Guardian News and Media Limited. Reproduced with permission; Syon Geographical Ltd. for the text on p. 18 adapted from 'Beavers create nitrogen sinks' by Laura Cole, Geographical website, 23.10.2015. Copyright © 2015 Syon Geographical Ltd. Reproduced with permission; James Willstrop for the text on p. 21 adapted from 'How should squash react as sport climbing and skateboarding are prioritised for the 2020 Olympics?' by James Willstrop, 30.09.2015. Copyright © 2015 James Willstrop. Reproduced with kind permission; Associated Newspapers Ltd for the text on p. 30 adapted from 'Learn to read the slow way' by Louise Heighes, *Metro*, 10.11.2010. Copyright © 2010 Associated Newspapers Ltd. Reproduced with permission; Guardian News and Media Limited for the text on p. 36 adapted from 'Charles Spence: the food scientist changing the way we eat?' by Amy Fleming, The Guardian, 24.09.2014. Copyright © 2014 Guardian News and Media Limited. Reproduced with permission; Independent Digital News & Media Ltd for the text on p. 40 adapted from 'Where the wild things are: Animal attraction in Costa Rica' by Mike Unwin, *The Independent*, 21.09.2012. Copyright © 2012 Independent Digital News & Media Ltd. Reproduced with permission; The Financial Times Ltd for the text on p. 43 adapted from 'How to identify a real Rembrandt?' by Bendor Grosvenor, *The Financial Times*, 10.10.2014. Copyright © 2014 The Financial Times Ltd. Reproduced with Permission; The Conversation Media Group Ltd. for the text on p. 58 adapted from 'The examined life: why philosophy needs to engage with the world, but hasn't' by Matthew Beard, The Conversation website, 08.06.2015. Copyright © 2015 The Conversation Media Group Ltd. Reproduced with permission; Guardian News and Media Limited for the text on p. 62 adapted from 'How I deal with the unbearable hypocrisy of being an environmentalist' by Madeleine Somerville, *The Guardian*, 05.04.2016. Copyright © 2016 Guardian News and Media Limited. Reproduced with permission; Guardian News and Media Limited for the text on p. 65 adapted from 'A girl growing up on film' by Anna Moore, The Guardian, 09.04.2016. Copyright © 2016 Guardian News and Media Limited. Reproduced with permission; Times Newspapers Limited for the text on p. 80 adapted from 'So why the long face?' by Tom Whipple, *The Times*, 31.08.2010. Copyright © 2010 Times Newspapers Limited. Reproduced with permission; Guardian News and Media Limited for the text on p. 84 adapted from 'Rain is sizzling bacon, cars are lions roaring: the art of sound in movies' by Jordan Kisner, *The Guardian*, 22.07.2015. Copyright © 2015 Guardian News and Media Limited. Reproduced with permission; Guardian News and Media Limited for the text on p. 87 adapted from 'The myth of the know-it-all scientist' by Dean Burnett, *The Guardian*, 01.03.2016. Copyright © 2016 Guardian News and Media Limited. Reproduced with permission.

Photo Acknowledgements

All the photographs are sourced from Getty Images.

p. C1 (TL): Dan Brownsword/Cultura; p. C1 (CR): Sharie Kennedy/Corbis; p. C1 (BL): Dylan Ellis/Photodisc; p. C2 (TL): Tom Merton/Caiaimage; p. C2 (CR): praetorianphoto/E+; p. C2 (BL): G. Baden/Corbis; p. C4 (TL): Prasit photo/Moment; p. C4 (CR), p. C5 (BL), p. C10 (BL): Hero Images; p. C4 (BL): Stuart Ashley; p. C5 (TL): Dan Dalton/Caiaimage; p. C5 (CR): Westend61; p. C7 (TL): f4foto/Alamy; p. C7 (CR): Hill Street Studios/Blend Images; p. C7 (BL): Heiner Heine/imageBROKER/Alamy; p. C8 (TL): allesalltag/Alamy; p. C8 (CR): Flying Colours Ltd/Photodisc; p. C8 (BL): OMG/The Image Bank; p. C10 (TL): rubberball; p. C10 (CR): Mint Images RF; p. C11 (TL): Aliyev Alexei Sergeevich/Cultura; p. C11 (CR): Caiaimage/Chris Ryan/OJO+; p. C11 (BL): Dave and Les Jacobs/Blend Images.

Visual materials for the Speaking test

- Why might the people be reading together?
- What might they do next?

1A

1B

1C

- Why might the people be getting advice?
- How useful might the advice be?

1D

1E

1F

1G

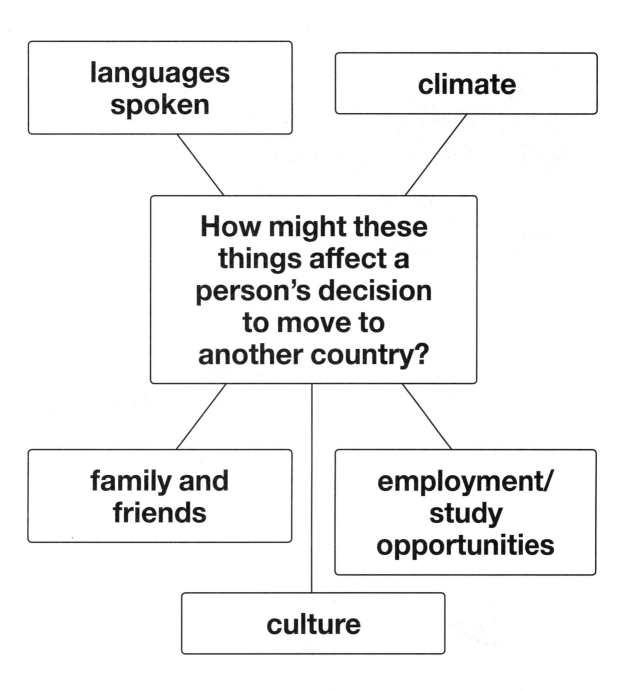

Visual materials for the Speaking test

- Why is water important to the people?
- How might they be feeling?

2A

2B

2C

- Why might the people be eating outside?
- How memorable might the experience be?

2D

2E

2F

2G

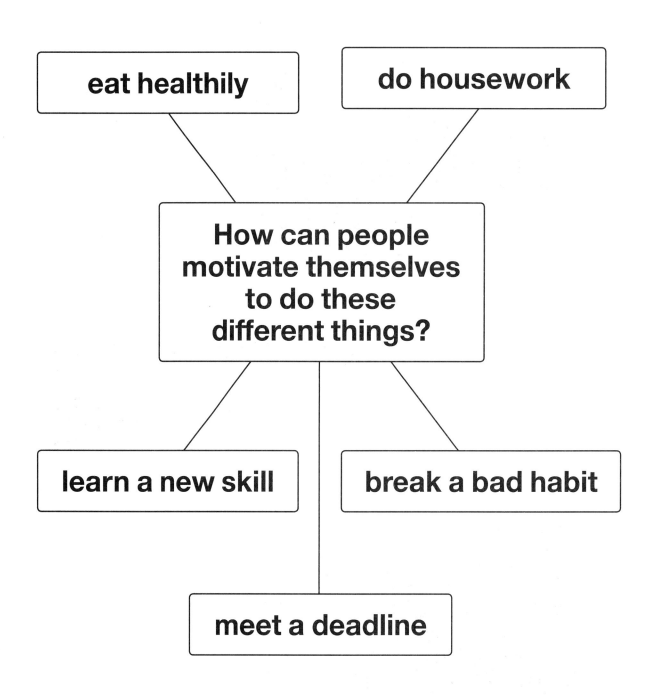

- Who could they be preparing the meal for?
- How might they be feeling

3A

3B

3C

- Why might these people be making a complaint?
- How could their complaint be dealt with?

3D

3E

3F

3G

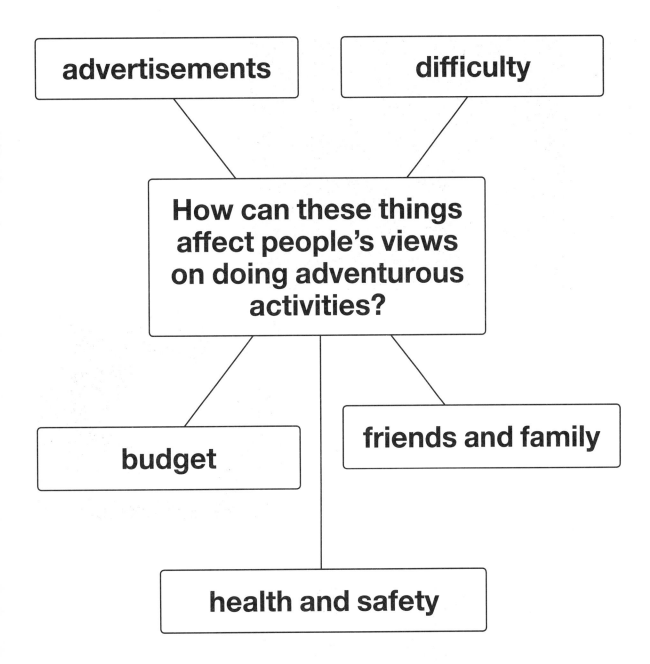

advertisements

difficulty

How can these things affect people's views on doing adventurous activities?

budget

friends and family

health and safety

- What skills are needed to solve the problems?
- What difficulties may the people face?

4A

4B

4C

- Why might the people have decided to take photos in these situations?
- How carefully did they need to prepare?

4D

4E

4F

4G

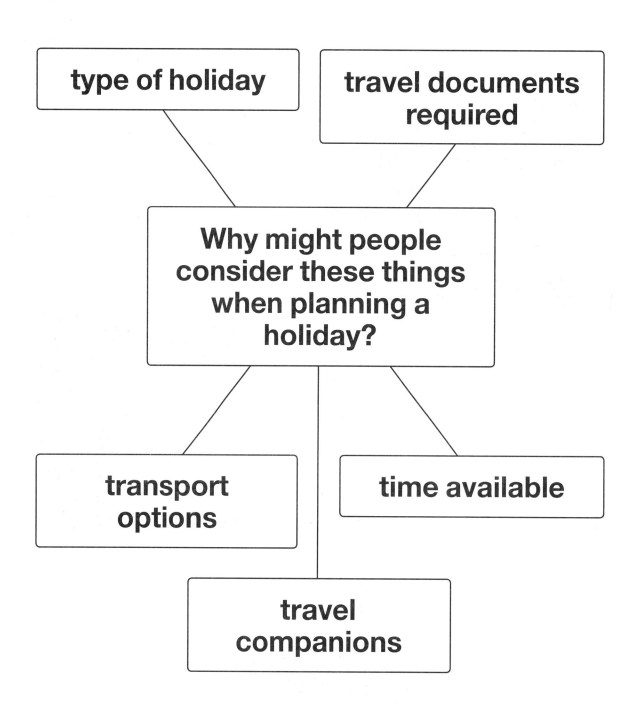

type of holiday

travel documents required

Why might people consider these things when planning a holiday?

transport options

time available

travel companions

Cambridge English

OFFICIAL EXAM PREPARATION MATERIALS

CAMBRIDGE.ORG/EXAMS

What do we do?

Together, Cambridge University Press and Cambridge English Language Assessment bring you official preparation materials for Cambridge English exams and IELTS.

What does *official* mean?

Our authors are experts in the exams they write for. In addition, all of our exam preparation is officially validated by the teams who produce the real exams.

Why else are our materials special?

Vocabulary is always 'on-level' as defined by the English Profile resource. Our materials are based on research from the Cambridge Learner Corpus to help students avoid common mistakes that exam candidates make.

Authentic examination papers: what do we mean?

INVOLVING WRITING TEAMS AROUND THE WORLD

PRETESTING

VALIDATION

PRACTICE PAPERS

← SELECTION →

LIVE EXAMS

Testbank

NOW ALSO AVAILABLE ONLINE IN Testbank

Practice makes perfect!

Testbank

AUTHENTIC PRACTICE TESTS

FLEXIBLE APPROACH

IMPROVE CONFIDENCE

PERFECT PRACTICE

DETAILED GRADEBOOK

INSTANT MARKING

PROGRESS CHECKER

NOW ONLINE

TEST MODE

PRACTICE MODE

SPEAKING PRACTICE

Experience 'exam' conditions

Enhance learning and practice

Timed video simulation

Go digital! Go Testbank.org.uk

Discover more
Official Preparation Materials

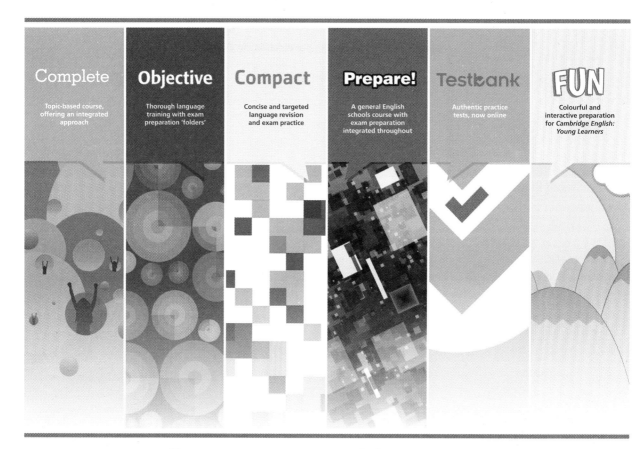

Complete — Topic-based course, offering an integrated approach

Objective — Thorough language training with exam preparation 'folders'

Compact — Concise and targeted language revision and exam practice

Prepare! — A general English schools course with exam preparation integrated throughout

Testbank — Authentic practice tests, now online

FUN — Colourful and interactive preparation for *Cambridge English: Young Learners*

Courses, self-study, learner support

CAMBRIDGE.ORG/EXAMS

CW00687781

Miners' March, Camborne, 7 March 1998

THE WHEAL OF HOPE
South Crofty and Cornish Tin Mining

Poems by James Crowden

Photographs by George Wright

AGRE

In memory of all Cornish miners past and present

First published in 2000
by AGRE BOOKS
Groom's Cottage, Nettlecombe,
Bridport, Dorset, DT6 3SS

www.agrebooks.co.uk

All rights reserved. No part of this book may be reproduced in any form
or by any means without permission in writing from the publisher,
except by a reviewer who may quote brief passages in a review.

Copyright © 2000 text James Crowden
Copyright © 2000 photographs George Wright

The authors have asserted their moral rights

Typeset and printed in the British Isles
by R. Booth Ltd, Penryn, Cornwall

ISBN 0 9538000 2 4

A CIP catalogue record for this book
is available from the British Library

Cover photograph shows Mervyn Randlesome at 410 sub level.

Contents

Acknowledgments....................7

Introduction 8

Below Carn Brea....................11

The Dry....................12

The Tally....................14

The Surface....................17

The Cage 18

The Shaft....................21

At 400 Fathoms 22

A Long Walk To The Face 24

The Tunnel....................26

The Miner....................29

The Sub Level 30

Geography....................33

The Sharp End....................35

Drilling 36

The Reckoning 39

Geological Survey....................40

Language....................43

Croust, Morzel And Crib....................44

The Gospel 47

The Power Of The Past....................48

Naming The Mine....................51

The Roll Call....................52

Old Engine Houses 54

Ancestors 56

Faces Old & New....................59

Old Workings 60

Dick Trevithick 62

Arsenic And Strong Women....................64

A Rough Apprenticeship....................66

Uncertainty - The Final Act 69

Postscript 71

Notes 72

The Uses Of Tin....................91

The Workforce 93

Further Reading 95

About Agre....................95

About The Printing 95

About The Authors 96

Croust

Acknowledgements

WHEN I first heard in August 1997 that South Crofty was closing, I wrote to David Giddings, the managing director, to ask if George Wright and I could go underground. I had been down South Crofty in 1975, a trip which left me with vivid impressions that I wanted to capture in words. Some of George's pictures appeared in the national press, notably the *Sunday Express*, *The Observer* and *The Financial Times*. I also managed to initiate a Radio 4 *Kaleidoscope* documentary about Cornwall which took the plight of the mine as its central theme. Since then I have been hard at work researching tin mining in general and South Crofty in particular.

George and I would like to thank David Giddings for letting us proceed, Steve Gatley the mine manager and Mark Owen the chief geologist for allowing us down, Chris Rogers and John Usuro for accompanying us and answering endless questions. Special thanks also to Allen Buckley the mine historian and former miner whose own book on the history of South Crofty is a fascinating delve into the records; to Jennie Hinton for keeping us up to date with what was happening; to miners Mervyn Randlesome and Micky Roberts for their time and witty comments; and to Paul Bray the last mine captain who helped make a second Radio 4 programme for *Open Country*.

Thanks also to George himself who, apart from being excellent company, managed to take some outstanding photographs in adverse conditions. For helping to finance the photography, I am very grateful to Kerrier District Council and its Amenities Committee, to His Royal Highness the Prince of Wales, Duke of Cornwall, to the Kobal Foundation and to a charity in Devon that wished to remain anonymous. Also, Jenefer Lowe, Cornwall County Council's Arts Officer; Mark Richardson of the Camborne, Pool & Redruth Action Team; I am very grateful to Morag MacRae, the Poetry Society and its Poetry Places initiative, the Arts Council and the National Lottery Arts for All scheme which sponsored a Poetry Residency at Wheal Jane in May 2000. This allowed me space and time to write up the project in situ, which was vital.

Jonathan and Sara Hudston of Agre Books for their excellent editing and persistent advice; Stuart Brill of Senate Design for the cover; South West Arts for help with the publishing and Booth's of Penryn for reprographics, printing and binding. Thanks also to Bernie Ballard of Carnon Enterprises at Wheal Jane for all his help in many ways and for being prepared to assist with the publication - an interesting mixture of poetry and heavy-duty engineering.

My thanks also to my father Guy Crowden who has produced all sorts of interesting information. To Mike Cudmore for the loan of mining books. To Sue and John Wilson of Zennor for bed & breakfast over the years and my partner Sue Bell who has been very patient with the ups and downs not only of writing but of covering a mine story at a distance.

My main thanks again are to the miners, without whom there would be no mine, no story, and no book.

James Crowden

Introduction

CORNISH tin mining was one of the wonders of the industrial world and it has stamped its mark indelibly on the Cornish people. For nearly 4,000 years tin has been mined in Cornwall and traded the length and breadth of Europe. Without Cornish tin added to copper, there would have been no Bronze Age and history would be very different. Stable and non-toxic, tin is also an essential ingredient in other alloys such as pewter and brass. Could we survive without tin cans, tinplate and electronic solder for microcircuits? If tin was valued as highly as silver or gold, Cornwall would be another Eldorado. In the 19th century large fortunes were made and lost - in the 20th century many mines struggled to survive.

The recent crisis stems from October 1985 when the International Tin Council ceased trading. Overnight the price fell from about £10,000 a tonne to below £2,900. Cornwall could barely compete. One by one other mines like Wheal Jane and Geevor shut, but South Crofty managed to keep going with a substantial government grant. In 1994 there was a successful share issue, but in August 1997 it was announced that tin mining would have to cease. South Crofty's plight became national news. There was a prolonged campaign for a rescue package from the DTI, but it all came to nothing. On 6 March 1998, South Crofty shut. It was the end of an era. The deep pumps were turned off, the mine gates closed and redundancies worked out. There were miners' marches and beer tents, a sea of faces and helmets, Cornish flags and banners, brass bands and pasties. Some miners went to Falmouth docks, some went fishing, others went to Brazil. For a while the Welshman Wilf Hughes looked a hopeful buyer; he signed a contract but never completed. As the mine steadily filled with water, scrapmen appeared like vultures, machinery was salvaged and museum curators rubbed their hands in anticipation. Steel wire cables were coiled up and greased, wind whistled through the headframe and old dynamite wagons suddenly appeared at roundabouts sprouting daffodils.

One thing Cornish tin does not lack is words. For every ton of ore raised to surface, reams have been written. What concerned me most about mining was not the politics or the global finances which forced the closure, but the feelings and sensations of working underground, which I did not want to go unrecorded. It is a remarkable thing to be half a mile beneath the surface and talk to men whose lives have been fashioned in the half-darkness. Conditions were hard, sweat flowed, the humour was wicked. If these few words and photographs go some way towards highlighting what it was like in Cornwall's last working tin mine, then the project will have been worthwhile.

Mining is still an unpredictable business. South Crofty has already closed twice in its long history, once in the 1790s, and again in 1895. Even now, though the main pumps are flooded and the 'house of water' is filling well, there are two interested parties. The SW Regional Development Agency wants the land to set up a high-tech business park, but a local firm called Baseresult has already exchanged contracts. It's aiming to re-start mining within two years and create 200 jobs. I hope this book will bridge the gap between the closure of South Crofty and whatever the future holds.

James Crowden, October 2000

Garry Dunn, shift boss

Below Carn Brea

Hard rock breeds hard men
Who slip between the earth's cracks for a living,
The dark chasm which closes round you,
Tight like a fist, draws you down
Into the mine's gullet, the belly of the beast,
Hewn out of granite, the ledger of tin,
The ingot of tradition, a labyrinth of strong voices
That still chisel the dark, the rich seam,
A stream that runs through each generation,
A lode that anchors a man's life,

And leads him by the hand
Down the slender ladder of the night
Deeper and deeper into the dark maze,
Honeycombed with shaft and adit,
The ancient sorcery of stope and rise,
Winze, stull, level and gunnis,
Beckoning him on relentlessly
Into uncharted waters
Like a tide that has just turned,
The Wheal of Hope still tugging at your sleeve.

The Dry

In a thin locker, in the locker room,
You place your belongings,
Your last will and testament
Stamped and sealed,
Strip down to your smalls
And glide into blue overalls
Which miraculously have enough buttons.

No turning back.
The initiation of miner's lamps
Boots, gloves, helmets,
Emergency breathing apparatus
And thick set batteries
Which are strapped onto your belt,
Till the belt sags, convincingly.

Time travellers, you test the lamp,
Admire each other's Cyclops eye.
Glowing in the corridor,
Illuminating the earth's secrets,
The unconscious mind,
This voyage into the underworld -
Jung would have approved.

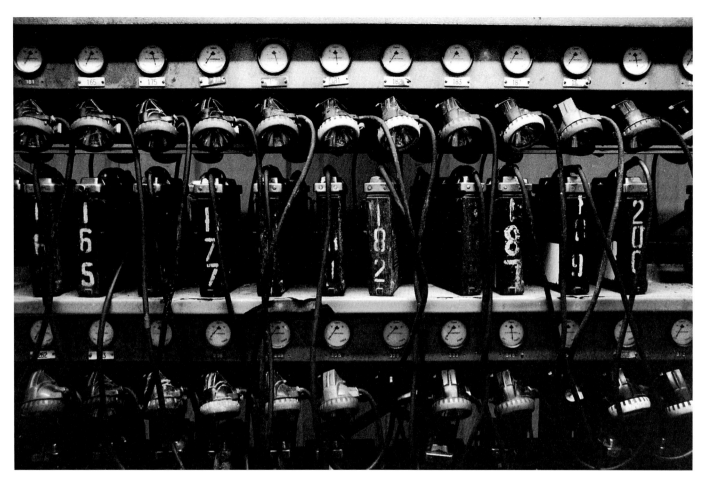

Recharging batteries

The Tally

It is hot down there, they say.
Cornwall's only deep sauna.
You might lose some weight
But that would be no bad thing,

Very strenuous in places,
Better than an exercise bike or a workout machine.
Not quite the place for a dicky heart
Or a zimmer frame.

Being diplomatic and practical
They get you to sign a piece of paper
About Radon
And other extra-terrestrial beings,

Then, off a vast board
Hand you a tally
Which certifies that you were still alive
And kicking at the surface.

Identity whittled down
To a small copper disc,
A dog tag, smooth, round and numbered
That checks you in and out of the mine

A token for the underworld,
A gift for the man in the lander's hut.
Who takes it nonchalantly,
Like a doorman at the Ritz.

The lander's hut

The Surface

Out of the DRY into the WET.
The world is narrowed down to a short walk
Along a narrow plank. New Cooks Kitchen.
The stubborn headgear, a reassuring skyline.

Patiently you wait your turn
And reflect upon
The finer points of Cornish History.
Wrecking, smuggling, piracy and pilchards.

At last the giant wheel turns against the sky,
Cornish Roulette, gambling with the earth's core
The only visible sign of movement
Amidst the shanty town of sheds

That is your last glimpse of the world above
With its rain and seagulls,
Fish and chip shops, wet tarmac
DIY and building supplies, re-cycling...

A desolate, scarred, pitted landscape
Riddled with old workings and rare flowers -
Like underground streams, rich stories
Still run through each kitchen sink

An intimate part of the family jigsaw,
The Celtic Parliament of old engine houses,
Standing out, derelict and stubborn,
Sore thumbs above the yellow gorse.

The Cage

Huddled on narrow benches
A clutch of miners wait for the next lift,
By the winding house,
Wrapped in silence, scan the papers,
Exchange looks, Page Three and the odd word.
Tucked under their arm, and folded neatly,
The female form, curvaceous like a mermaid

Slipped into the pocket, to be perused at length
When time permits, creature comforts
Admired, absorbed, the essential talisman
Taken back to mother earth,
By Cornwall's most rugged commuters,
Squeezed into the cage
Like sheep going to market.

They budge up and jostle,
Like a rugby scrum or a line-out,
The male thing, bonded
A kind of equality,
Each man with his own thoughts,
As if eternity was just round the corner
And the cable going under the ocean.

John West, south winder

The Shaft

The lander gives you a strange look,
Charon the ferryman, with his silver sideburns,
Says nothing. He's seen it all before.
A slight nod and the gate clangs to.
Wet drips down your jacket,

The cage lurches
And the darkness grabs you
By the scruff of the neck
And propels you down shaft.
Faster and faster, old levels flit by.

Vertical, the strange sense of falling,
For minutes on end, as if in flight,
Swallowed at one gulp
Down the earth's throat,
Glimpses of floors you never knew existed,

And better than Harrods,
Ladies Lingerie, Children's shoes,
Men's ties and cravats, hardware, software.
All of us destined for the bottom draw,
The Bargain Basement at 400 fathoms.

At 400 Fathoms

The amphitheatre, a vast vault
A granite cathedral, unexpected
Like Paddington Station opens up
And we step into it with awe and disbelief,
Like Jonah into the belly of the whale.
Filled with old pumps and strops,

Bolts, winches and compressors,
Oxy-acetylene bottles,
Steel rods, baulks of timber,
Remains of ladders piled up and thrown to one side,
The paraphernalia of getting on with it,
As if a tidal wave has just swept through.

We pause a minute, look around,
Breathe good air, say a prayer
And then enter the solid rock
Following the geologist, who, like a ferret,
Legs it down the nearest tunnel,
Checking samples and pegs.

Navigation underground
A skilled art in three dimensions
A badger warren that imprints itself
On the mental processes
As something rather extraordinary
And better left to those that know.

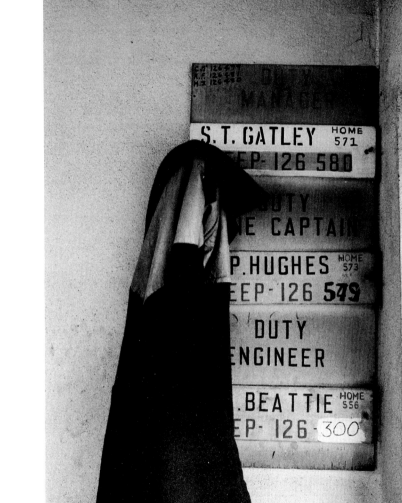

A Long Walk To The Face

Trudging between rails and pools of water
A small stubby engine slides by
Powered by a small stubby miner
Who looks as though he can -
And will - sink as many
Beers as possible on Saturday night.

Narrow gauge tramming,
Perfectly suited
For this kind of thing, trucks trundle by
Weighed down by great lumps of ore
Which have to be smashed with sledge hammers
Or blown to bits on the grizzly bars.

Snow White is nowhere to be seen
But above ground
She still has to calculate
Their overtime and production bonuses
Peers into her crystal ball -
The mine's future a phone call away.

Brian Jenkin

The Tunnel

The tunnels are wide and generous,
It's half a mile at least
And then down the decline
Following thin veins of probability,
The air warm and moving.
Like fireflies, lights ahead bob and duck
The murmur of voices, as if only Cornish

Should really be spoken down here.
As if somehow the rocks respond better
To their own language, a bond between them,
A pact forged in the days
When Fogous were breeding fast.
And the magical wealth
Travelled the length and breadth of Europe

And the terrors of the dark
Were overcome with tallow, superstition
And chapel singing,
As if their daily voyage
Into the bowels of the earth
Has a hidden necessity
Which still touches us all deep down.

Danny Penhaligon

Paul Merton

The Miner

Every miner is infinitely connected with the earth.
All his friends and relations are tucked up here,
The wife's grandfather,
His second cousin twice removed
Who's now in Bolivia
But was in Peru, or was it Saudi Arabia?

The cosmic universe tattooed on their Christmas card list,
Indonesia, Australia, Angola and Canada,
Greece and Bulgaria. Each miner a satellite
Thrown into the darkness of other countries,
With a bit of explosive, firm muscles,
Cornish grit, computerised.

Everything here is compressed,
Even the air which drives all the machinery.
Fingers, toes, eyes and ears
These are at a premium.
Rocks can fall suddenly, squashing a man
Like a poached egg, but accidents are rare.

The Sub Level

In the dark we climb sixty
Seemingly endless feet,
Safe in its own way, the sub level,
A small hole above our heads.
One rung is missing, but that's nothing.
Bits of rock float down -
The helmet is useful, it keeps the brain intact.

At the top of the ladder,
A small gallery and a narrow plank.
Faces are caught briefly
In each other's headlamps
Like Old Masters,
Or Joseph Wright of Derby,
Then return to their job.

Each drill, a vibrating arm that reverberates,
And holds a man in its gyrating grasp,
The face of granite, sleek and flecked,
Solidity compressed,
The dust and water fuelling a stream,
A haze within which they live,
A cliff edge in a storm.

Peter May

Kelvin Gay

Geography

It's like the Amazon Basin,
Cornwall's rainforest, half a mile underground,
And at the ends, sweltering, airless,
98 percent humidity. Triste Tropique,
For those that are adventurous,

The anthropology of tin,
A lost tribe on the edge of extinction.
Remote and distinct.
Herodotus no doubt knew of their existence
As did Ptolemy and Caesar.

From 400 fathoms you walk down
The decline to 420,
And then down to 445.
Another numerical world replicated,
Each fathom another step of improbability,

Each notch a man's height, near enough
And below that 470 and the sump
From which mad water is pumped
Gurgling to adit. The cost,
Only a million pounds a year.

Clarence Matthews

The Sharp End

At last the face itself, the ultimate frontier,
Chiselled away, blasted,
Explored, plotted, eased out
This is the front line,
Preparing the way for production stopes,
The rock eased out,
Like enormous slabs of Christmas cake.

It is here, in countless other dead ends
And cul-de-sacs, the miners work.
It is here they ponder their fate
An endangered species,
Habitat slewed by world prices,
Sliced into by dollar exchanges and interest rates.
Piracy on the high seas of investment.

Three maybe four thousand years
Gone in a twinkling,
A steady head for heights,
An inner confidence
Keeps them alive in the small places
In the backwaters, where a cry for help
Would not be heard on the surface.

Drilling

Longhole drillers say little
They are paid by the metre
The air pumped down to them like divers,
The angle of each hole
A pattern of stars that shear off
Into the dark galaxy of the nether regions.

Others, mining a raise, clamber up chains
Like powder monkeys,
Balancing bits in their teeth
The slippery slope, defying gravity
The uphill grind,
As if pushing the very rock on their shoulders.

Each miner is known by his face
His ability to make and take jokes
The constant ribbing, years of crack
Rubbed off on one another,
The internal push and shove
Of mine politics,

Tunnelling into wage packets.
As they open another box of explosive.
Pump in the ANFO, a fist full of detonators.
The force of each explosion,
Addictive and sudden, like a loose billiard ball,
The shock wave ricocheting round the mine.

Rock-bolting and meshing at a draw-point

Dave 'Vokem' Buzza

The Reckoning

Everything here is numbers, tons, cubic metres
Mother earth cut down to size.
It's a big thing to get your head round
The millions of tons of rock and ore,
Manhandled to surface,

Lifted out of the earth's belly,
The dark chasm left behind, a hernia,
A gaping rift within which men's lives
Are suspended like gossamer.
The spider's web of det cord,

Hanging in mid-air,
Each hole rammed home,
Linked, primed, a shot in the dark,
Demolition charges gnawing at the rock,
Burrowing into the earth's overalls.

Each lode a family affair, tribal activity.
An old friend tapped into at odd intervals.
No 4 West / East No 8 / Pryces / Tincroft
Dolcoath South / Dolcoath North,
North Pool / Roskear B / Roskear A.

Surveyed and logged, each week's progress,
Followed faithfully like a local rugby team.
The score measured
In hundreds of tons of ore
And cubic metres of dirty washing.

Geological Survey

Plumbing the depths,
Like tickling trout with diamond drills,
Geology at its most inventive
Surveyed, plotted, sampled
The tin hunted, tracked down
Eased out of the rock's grasp.

No ordinary maps these
The metamorphosis on a slant,
Above and below ground,
Minerals catapulted to the surface
Breathing for the first time
In millions of years.

At every level, a world shifted, replicated,
Linked at impossible angles,
Theodolites in the dark,
Plotting the heavy vein,
Cassiterite caught gleaming in the headlights,
A gift from the Gods.

John Usoro, geologist

Micky Roberts

Language

Deep underground a man's spirit expands
Like his chest and absorbs the sweat,
Salty water pouring through the ceiling,
Like a warm shower.

For years on end miners work together,
In pairs take a solemn vow,
A married couple that no words can explain.
The machinery so loud only gestures will do.

Hand signals and the odd glance over the shoulder.
Language without language
Intuition honed down to a fine edge
Upon which their lives depend.

And in the silence that follows each blast,
You can sometimes hear the earth talking,
Spellbound, as sheaves of granite move and buckle
Like a giant turning over in his sleep

Settling back into the crevasse,
Each crack a coded warning,
A signal to the outside world
Great forces are still at work.

Croust, Morzel And Crib

A time to sit and rest, rub sore limbs.
Stoke the furnace of a man's belly.
In the darkness, talk softly,
As if on night patrol,
The feeling of being watched,
Mine spirits hoisted from the past,
Superstition swallowed, digested in the shadows.

Quiet and private, Cornwall's unlikely heroes
Lever open sandwiches, twist the tops of Thermoses
Discuss each other's wives, cars, rugby,
The lottery of life
What they will do at the weekend
When eventually they re-emerge
Like moles, blinking in the sunlight,

To wonder at the beauty of grass and heather,
The sight of women and children,
Walking on the surface,
Talking to the sea in whispers
To wonder which world is real
Which one they really belong to
Which is it truly holds them in its grasp.

Croust at 420

Jimmy Pellow

The Gospel

To understand the true meaning,
The message, the Word
The Phoenician Epistle to the Cornish
The one they lost at sea
Off Finisterre in a storm,
You have to have grown up with shafts,

Calciners, buddles and flues
The Gospel of tin and copper,
The Creed of lead, silver, arsenic and wolfram
Had them growing out of your ears
Thick with gorse, a diet of tallow
Hidden in the valleys of tall chimneys.

St Piran would have been impressed
By the Old Testament of engine houses,
Pillars of the community
Nonconformist beam engines
Which, like the Cornish themselves,
Relied on the eccentric

And the honest power of steam
The sermon of engineering pioneering the scalp,
Pumping the baptismal water
From unseen depths.
Confirmation of the lode.
Communion with unseen forces.

The Power Of The Past

Scattered to the four winds,
Lie the bones of countless mines,
The ghosts of Jurassic dinosaurs,
That chewed on the night, ate fire, spat steam,
And devoured whole parishes
Everyday regurgitating their strongest men
Brought back from the brink,

Each shift catapulted into sunlight and fresh air
Like yellow canaries caged
And singing in chapel, miners' lives
Lay perched on the accountant's books.
Blessed are the poor and the meek
Those that don't grumble too much.
Slight unease when the candle goes out.

One slip is all it takes, the weight of tools
Pulling you back down the eternity of ladders,
Disappearing rungs, hundreds of feet,
Black silence swallows you up in an instant.
Muffled explosions, thick curtain of dust.
Like a rood screen between past and present
The widow's chant still hangs in mid-air.

Workings old and new

Core samples from diamond drilling

Naming The Mine

Each name a focus, a count house,
A powerful lens through which
Whole communities lived and died
A potent force to be reckoned with.

Each name a rich mythology
Hope that fed a thousand children
Put bread upon the table.
Clothes upon the wife, latch upon the door.

Each name a rough passage
A voyage into deep pockets.
A deal struck with the earth
The rich lode smelted down.

Each name a hard grindstone
Pitted against men's wits,
A ship's crew bound together,
Old before their time, the mast of tin.

Each name an inventory of untimely disasters
Flash floods and fires,
Explosions and rock falls
Sending up small flurries of gravestones.

Each name rolled off the tongue
Biting the bullet,
Another closure like a volcanic island
That sinks back beneath the waves.

The Roll Call

Wheal Spinster, Poldice and Wheal Jewel,
Poldory and Cupboard, Ale and Cakes
Ting Tang and Wheal Squire,

  Merry between, Cloam Dish
  Little Dagger, Down dribble

Wheal Pink, Wheal Comfort
Unity and Consolidated
Penstruthal, Wheal Music, Trethillan

  Pitpaddy and Pitspry
  Goodmorrow neighbour

Wheal Busy, North Downs and Carn Brea,
Tehidy, Wheal Cupid and Tolgus
Hallen Beagle, East Pool and Dolcoath

  Piskey Meadow and Jew's House,
  Stennack Filly, Bold Adventure

Roskear and Wheal Bassett
Condurrow and Wheal Curtis
Fortescue, Grenville and South Frances,

  Come by Chance, Lower Gun Deep
  St Gracious and North Goodluck

Best-to-agree and Poor man's work
Biscuppa Skence and Killifreth
Botallack, Levant and Tincroft.

  Mount Wellington, Pendarves,
  Geevor, Wheal Jane, South Crofty.

Emergency breathing apparatus

Old Engine Houses

The God of granite worshipped here like none other
Cornish cathedrals, sacrificial altar,
The shaft of water hauled to the surface,
Life blood of the mine, communion
Powered by a thousand chimneys
That once belched smoke and sulphur
Like a fleet of battleships at full power.

Night and day they devoured Welsh coal.
The beam's incessant nodding,
Slender rods and valves that defied gravity,
Kept the mine from drowning, powered the stamps,
Now lie trapped, unable to move,
Like Knights on a vast chessboard,
Each with their own lance impaled in rock.

Rich veins that could be worked no further.
Stalemate, capped with jackdaws,
Chequered memorials open to the sky's echo
Empty fortresses through which the wind now blows.
Shrines still worshipped with wild flowers
As if at some ancient Celtic wishing well,
Where miracles once took place.

Fortescue

Ancestors

Each ancestor that ever got
Within spitting distance of a mine,
Is logged, plotted and talked about
In terms of reverence and fathoms
To be steered around
Like a rock off Land's End
In times of uncertainty and tempest

When boulders and beds of shingle
Dance on the sea floor like thunder overhead,
The narrow salty ceiling of rock
Shifting with the ocean's tide,
More than one lode on your mind
As giant waves enter the cliff adit,
Half drowned men re-emerge like sea urchins.

Underwater these mines became famous wrecks.
White finger and broken bones the least of it,
Arthritic limbs and wheezing lungs
Bellows that crave an honest breath,
Windows jammed open on stormy nights,
Fresh air, a powerful resource, telling stories,
Slender threads that gently float to surface.

Paul Hoskin

Fitters' croust at 445

Faces Old & New

Faces that have eaten a thousand pasties
Glimmer in the darkness,
Outstare you from countless photographs.
Each head locked on with cap and candle.

Faces that have worked underground
Notch up their own history
Of scars, sharp rocks and narrow escapes,
Gunpowder tattooed beneath the skin.

Faces that believe in minerals and each other,
The pulpit of endeavour.
Brought to bear in times of need.
Faith that cannot easily be broken.

Faces that once looked clean
Appear sullen and introspective
Parade their good looks for posterity
And books that have not yet been printed.

Old Workings

Sunk into generations of bed rock,
The deep necessity of rope and explosive.
Glimmer of candle against the ore.
Following a vein, marvelling at its twists and turns
The whole county stunned by cat's-head mallets
Needled by borers and shafts,
Acupuncture on a vast scale.

Still unhealed, scabs of waste tips
Pockmarked by shovels and picks,
Man traps lurk behind brambles
The pits of waterwheels and foundries
Smelting houses, stout walls made of copper slag,
And by the sea, neat, empty harbours
Where schooners once docked plump with Welsh coal.

Sucked into black holes, long capped
Their inheritance, dark ancestral waters,
A thousand miles of flooded passage,
Opening up for the millennium
In driveways and people's gardens,
Identity and independence
On the tip of the tongue, old language re-emerging.

Dick Trevithick

Wildman of engineering, patron saint of locomotion,
He amazed the local women on Christmas Eve
With his strength and power,
The iron horse wheeled out
Bit rattling between the teeth.
First triumphant ride up Camborne Hill.

Alas, came to grief four days later,
A rut on the turnpike, left unattended,
Keeled over into history, nonchalantly,
Unlike the roast goose and ale in the nearest hostelry.
Water boiled away, iron red hot.
Engine burnt to a frazzle.

By Cornish rights,
Dick's face should appear
On the back of every five pound note.
Treasury of the Nation,
Each round of drinks and flutter on the horses,
Groceries and petrol stations.

He'd follow your every move,
The power of locomotion lurking in your pocket.
'Catch me if you can'.
And Dick himself?
He went to South America
In search of silver, crocodiles and Simon Bolivar.

Arsenic And Strong Women

Whole families struggled above ground
Under the 'Grass Captain'
Whose slow revolutions powered the stamps
And dressing floors, the relentless tyranny
Of buddles, frames and launders,
Tended by bal maidens
Whose good looks, favours and prayers,
Sunk many a shaft in a man's heart

And brought him safely to the surface,
Cooked his meals and mended his clothes,
Buried him when the time came.
Dressed like nuns in their long skirts and white aprons
They washed and crushed the ore
Their devotions, neat like the head-dresses,
Textured the mineral, spalling and barrowing.
Till the ore could be smelted and sent away

Like the children up the arsenic flues
Who scraped at the white serpent
That went into paint and battered wives'
Husband's dinners, worldwide,
Wall papers and insecticides,
Colorado beetles and Boll weevils
Sheep dips between the wars,
Cures for syphilis, glass, lead shot, mustard gas...

The Red River

A Rough Apprenticeship

Forged in the teeth of necessity,
The long walk from each village
The smell of hose and pony
Circling all day like the barefoot boys
Walking in the slime to stir it up,

Before being sent below decks
Where whole forests of timber
Were stacked and re-assembled
Fresh from the Baltic, the grain's muscle
Employed in chutes, stulls and shafts

Holding the earth and accidents at bay.
A nod is often all you get at the face,
Time is too precious,
And breath a rare commodity,
In the heat of the moment.

They size you up, prod you in the belly
Pull the wool if they can,
Slip in the odd jest,
A voyage into solid rock.
Passed on from father to son.

Fitters' bay at 445

Ken Tucker at the ore bins

Uncertainty - The Final Act

Promises from distant places are weighed up,
Measured out with a pinch of salt.
But no signature floats to the surface
No arm is quite long enough. The telephone is silent.

After the last blast, exhausted men reach the surface,
Hand in their lamps, tallies to the board,
Shower their bodies with hot water, soap and steam.
The final act, performed with a towel,

And if you are lucky a comb.
Ice cream, surf and car parks are no substitute
As locker doors slam shut.
The economy smelted down to myth and sentiment.

Pumps are turned off and the dark night of water
Starts to crawl back up the shaft,
Feeding on its own silence.
The dark maze, the labyrinth abandoned

And cast adrift within sight of shore,
The last mine slowly sinking beneath the waves,
Like a schooner in distress, whose last flares
Have gone up into a troubled sky.

South Crofty, Christmas 1997

Postscript

The boardroom clock disappears -
Exit time.

       Pipe and ladder are snapped in two -
       Await the scrapman's chalk.

In silence, belts are tightened -
The house of water slowly fills

       Headframe glistening -
       Full moon above the shaft

Wheels turn idly in the wind -
The cry of tin eclipsed

       Their sorcery outdone -
       Miners disperse

Four corners of the world -
What else are Cornish boys to do?

Notes

The occasional decorations in the notes are old Cornish smelting marks. I've also inserted a few italicised quotations from past writers to try to bring extra light and shade to certain points; such as this on Cornwall:

'This County... is for the most part mountainous... The sea-coast is beautify'd with very many Towns which are able to man out a considerable fleet. The inner parts abound with rich mines. For tinn, to the vast advantage of the inhabitants, is digg'd up in great plenty...' William Camden, 1586 (translated from Latin into English 1695)

Below Carn Brea: Anyone who has been to the top of Carn Brea and looked down at South Crofty and the area surrounding Camborne and Redruth will not have failed to notice the residual strength of the industrial landscape, a landscape that a hundred years ago must have seemed more like the devil's kitchen with smoke and fires burning to power the vast beam engines that kept the pumps working day and night deep underground. For miles in every direction the earth is riddled and pockmarked, each derelict engine house and chimney stack surrounded by countless shafts, now fenced off with rusty barbed wire. Bare waste heaps abound, still rich in arsenic and other minerals, a haven for rare plant species, lizards and dragonflies. Cornwall owes much of its unique and remarkable character to mining.

Miners' language reverberates with technical terms evolved over centuries, some peculiar to particular mines or areas of Cornwall, others more general. Most common is wheal, the Cornish word for work, and by late medieval times also used to refer to stream work or mine work. It was deployed as a prefix for individual mine names such as Wheal Jane, Wheal Jewel, and Wheal Vor. This usage travelled over the border into West Devon, where I grew up. Around Tavistock you can still find Wheal Crebor, Wheal Friendship, Wheal Betsy, Wheal Russel, Wheal Maria, Wheal Josiah, Wheal Fanny and many more. However, the miner's name for a mine was more commonly bal, hence also the term bal maidens for the women who worked at the surface breaking the ore. Bal started off as a Cornish word for a group of tin bounds, hence names like Baldhu and Bal West.

Some other terms: an adit is a horizontal tunnel driven into a hillside and used for drainage. Mine water pumped to adit level was left to discharge into the nearest river, or in the case of the mines around Pendeen, straight out to sea via the cliff face. There are stories of mines flooding during storms when waves pounded the cliffs and entered the adits. Some of the adits in use today were dug 300 years ago and are still checked to make sure they are safe. Adits could also serve as emergency exits and they helped to ventilate mines. Levels are key parts of the mine, reached by shafts going vertically down from the surface. In old mines, levels were systematically driven at eight, ten or twelve fathom intervals. In some of the more modern mines, the distance between levels was twenty fathoms (ie 120ft), though in South Crofty, they went twenty-five fathoms down to the 445 level, then down the same again to 470. The main levels are horizontal but at places where they intersect the lode, workings are made up to the previous level and called raises. Workings that go down to the next level to meet the raises coming up are called winzes. Intermediary seams of ore are worked out either by underhand or overhand stoping. Different mines favoured different methods of extracting ore. The result of one kind of open-caste excavation was known as a gunnis (cf the village of Gunnislake in the Tamar Valley). A gunnis would usually be narrow, like a big open grave, hence probably its alternative name of coffin. Underground, the word gunnis could also be used to refer to an old stope from which ore had been extracted. Gunnises can be very deep; to look

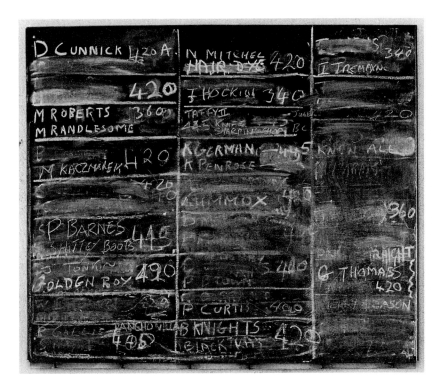

over the edge of a 300 foot gunnis and realise there is also 300 foot above, is quite a sobering experience. One slip and you'd plunge into eternity.

Below Carn Brea is also a tribute to the generations of miners who have worked that ground - a tribute in fact to all Cornish miners, particularly as the word tribute also has mining connections - it refers to the old system by which groups of miners bid for a stretch of ore. Once every two or three months on the steps of the count house, group leaders (called takers) would compete for the rights to different pitches. Eventually the mine captain would take a pebble and throw it up into the air. If no one put in a higher bid before the pebble hit the ground the last bidder got the pitch at the price he'd stated. So group fortunes depended on their leaders' skill at estimating likely yields and bidding accordingly (and then trusting to luck).

The Mineral Lords, who owned the mineral rights, would take a cut of perhaps one-twelfth of white tin at smelting, or one-ninth of stone at grass. The fractions varied from mine to mine depending on the mining difficulties and the cost of keeping the mine dry. This was more democratic than the coal mines on fixed wages.

The Cornish system of tribute interested 19th century economists such as John Stuart Mill as an even-handed method of allocating profit between workers and owners. However, miners on tribute did have to pay for their explosives and tools, and they sometimes had to borrow money at extortionate rates of interest to be paid back when they struck lucky. Some say this system encouraged undue recklessness but it was better than farm work from which there was no release.

'A tinner has nothing to lose.' Old Cornish proverb

The Dry: The Dry was the changing rooms but also far more than that. It was, for working miners, the day-to-day nerve centre of the mine where the main tally board was kept and where the shift bosses and mine captains had their offices. Here you charged batteries, tested headlamps, adjusted belts and helmets. Here also the sets of emergency breathing apparatus were kept, small flasks containing charcoal, strapped onto your belt like small water bottles. An attached mouthpiece allowed you to breathe in oxygen for half an hour. Mercifully, gases like firedamp or methane, often associated with coal mines, were very rare in Cornish mines. Such gases could ignite disaster. The worst Welsh explosion was in 1913 at the Universal Colliery at Senghenydd when 439 men and boys died. In 1901 at the same colliery eighty-two men had died. By contrast the worst Cornish disaster was at the lead mine East Wheal Rose in 1846 when thirty-nine miners were drowned in a flash flood that filled the mine from the surface.

There is more to the expression 'home and dry' than first meets the eye. Only when you re-entered the warmth of the Dry did you feel really safe. Here were the lockers and showers, here you changed and handed in your dirty overalls for washing. The water was hot, the soap liberal, the towels small. Miners liked the distance from the head of the shaft to the Dry to be kept as short as possible. Coming up from the depths wet and warm on a summer's day was one thing, coming out into wet and windy weather was quite another...

In 1997 the man in charge of the Dry was Lewis Pascoe, who - when he wasn't sorting out washing machines - would be issuing explosives and detonators from a small hut. He had spent many years working underground. The mine captain then was Paul Bray, the shaft and surface foreman Martin Wolstenholme, the safety officer Peter Hughes, the mill manager Mike Hallewell, and the union leader Mark Kaczmarek, who was often in the news. When I met Mark briefly in the Dry he was showing people the injury on the back of his neck sustained a few weeks earlier during a small rock fall. Twelve stitches and lucky to survive. The Dry was where impromptu meetings were held about the future of the mine.

The Tally: Tallies were small discs like dog tags, made of brass, copper or plastic. They bore your name and number and came in pairs. One you left on the board, the other you gave to the man at the head of the shaft. Known as the lander, he operated the cage gate, checked you in and checked you out. It was up to each pair of miners to tell him where they were going to be working. At the top of the shaft there was a small shed like a bus shelter where men could sit and wait. Tallies were left there. Some were very worn, like talismans - the mythological small coin placed in a man's hand so he could pay the boatman Charon to get across the underworld river of the Styx. The Charon of New Cook's Kitchen wore a donkey jacket and had large white sideburns...

The Surface: Your last sight of the world as you knew it. A quick glimpse up at Carn Brea and the monument. A hill which meant so much to John Harris, the mining poet of the 1850s: 'O wondrous mountain, 'neath thy ribs of rock / Lie beds of precious metal...' (Carn Brea). South Crofty is at Pool between Camborne and Redruth. The rivalry of these two towns is legendary and even old ladies have been known to get really worked up at the annual rugby match held on Boxing Day, where language you would not expect to hear emerges from behind the daintiest of teapots. I've heard one old lady saying she hoped Redruth would 'beat the shit out of Camborne this year.' The rivalry used to be mostly economic. Each town had its own port - Camborne had Hayle, Redruth had Portreath and then Devoran. Even underground the miners used to know which parish they were working in and where the boundaries lay, and make odd jokes about passports and asking permission to cross the border. Both communities thrived in the past but sadly they are now economically depressed and in need of realistic development plans. Driving through they can seem more like Yorkshire or Durham mining towns, but I like them both because they have a character and a history that is closer to the real Cornwall than the tourist Cornwall. There are rows of small affordable houses, and some derelict properties could easily be reinstated as good starter homes for young people. It's a face of Cornwall that visitors rarely see as they speed past on the A30 desperate to get to St Ives, Penzance, Land's End and ice creams.

The Cage: The wheel turns, the cage comes up and with it several miners coming off shift. Your turn next. Squeezed into the cage you have to jostle up tight. Eight to a cage and one cage on top of another. There's no first or second class. When the gate clangs to that's it. The bells ring and you are hovering over a shaft that's 400 fathoms deep - that's 2,400ft or nearly half a mile. Dropping at 21mph the journey takes less than two minutes... Operating the winding gear was a skilled business. The brake men had to stop the cages at each level, and not let them move again until the correct signals were received. A whole Morse code of bells and messages could be sent up and down. The steel wire ropes holding the cages cost about £26,000. They were inspected and renewed every so often; snapping could be fatal.

The biggest shaft disaster was at Levant in October 1919, when the man engine collapsed and thirty-one men were killed. The man engine was a series of interconnected rods driven up and down by an engine at the surface. Attached to the rods - which moved twelve feet up and down, again and again and again - were small metal plates, just big enough for a man to stand on. Miners stepped on and off these plates onto platforms placed twelve feet apart on each side of the shaft. Gradually, they got to where they wanted to go. For its time, the system was ingenious. It allowed one shift to go down as another went up, much better than climbing 1,000ft of ladders, though you had to beware in the darkness of losing an arm or a leg. What happened in Levant was that one of the caps broke, which helped to fasten the rod at the top of the shaft to the main beam of the engine. The whole apparatus shot down past the safety catches, then a rod broke at 60 fathoms, sending the miners to the bottom. Coming as it did less than a year after the end of the First World War, this tragedy must have shaken the whole community. In St Just in 1972 I met a man in a pub who claimed to be the last-living survivor of the disaster and he had a silver watch to prove it. He broke several bones on the way down. Thankfully such accidents are rare in Cornwall's mining history. South Crofty was, I think, a particularly safe mine.

The Shaft: There's a world of difference between the fancy lifts in Harrods and the one at South Crofty, and I know which I prefer. At least at South Crofty there were no poodles and high heels. As you glimpsed men working it was like a film, slowed to three frames a second. Odd lights, water dripping, old levels - whole worlds flipped past, and it was a sobering thought that the upper reaches were carved out by men long dead and buried. The cage was wet and when the sky was raining you got it down the neck, even when you were deep down in the earth. In a mine water gets everywhere.

'they were digging in the Tinn mines, there was at least 20 mines all in sight which employs a great many people at work, almost night and day, but constantly all and every day includeing the Lords day which they are forced to, to prevent their mines being overflowed with water...' Celia Fiennes, 1698

At 400 Fathoms: At the bottom of the shaft I was amazed at the vast cavern I walked into. It was blasted out in the 1980s to form a massive underground pumping station though due to financial problems the scheme was never completed. The vast space left was full of all sorts of paraphernalia, a kind of junkyard where equipment and materials waited either to go deeper into the mine or be hoisted up to the surface. Men appeared then disappeared. The only noise apart from the distant hiss of the odd ventilation leak in the compressed air lines was the occasional exchange of bells with the surface winder. Choirs occasionally sang down there, and there was a Wagnerian feel to it all, as if the forces of the underworld would gather here when men had gone to the surface.

'They have a pallor, but they are very wiry men, capable of enduring a great deal of fatigue and possessed of great muscular power.' Western Morning News, 1865

A Long Walk To The Face: In the old days miners had a long walk to work, sometimes six miles each way. In the summer it must sometimes have been a rather wonderful contrast to the mine, but in bad weather or the dark of winter, just a hard trudge. On arrival they would have to climb down long ladders, carrying their gear and food. Then there was the long walk to the face. They must have been superbly fit, but even so the work could make them old before they were forty. Lungs often suffered with pneumonia, bronchitis and silicosis, and there were other problems. One man I spoke to recently, Ken Williams, told me that his grandfather died in the 1890s of hookworm, brought back to Dolcoath from Mexico by a fellow worker. In 1912 a Royal Commission examined the problem of hookworm throughout Cornwall. In South Crofty eleven percent were affected, in nearby Dolcoath the rate was a shocking sixty-nine percent. Such unpleasant phenomena could occur when miners returned from South and Central America as well as Africa. (Many emigrated out of financial necessity and never came back. A quarter of the county's working population left during the last half of the 19th century. Between 1871-78 a third of the mining population went).

I found the walk to the face a bit of a trudge but not unpleasant - there was none of the stooping you get in a coal mine. The rock was granite and the tunnels were wide. It was like an underground city. At every level there were fitters' workshops with lathes and welding gear to keep ageing equipment going. At every level ran small narrow-gauge railways and battery-powered locomotives. You could see and hear them a fair way off, but familiarity has always bred contempt and people lost toes, and feet, and bits of their hands, through not being careful enough. All the tramming machinery was robust and powerful like the miners themselves.

Every ounce of ore was hauled and tipped onto grizzly bars, a form of grid. Bits that didn't go through had to be broken up with a sledgehammer or even, in extreme circumstances, with explosive. Tasks like this were sometimes used as a punishment for miners who had behaved badly or broken rules in the past. Another sanction available to the mine captain was to send you for a few weeks to the more unpleasant and wet parts of the mine, for a job like excavating a sump at the lowest (and hottest) level. Good training for the Eden project... Ore used to reach the surface by going along an elaborate system of conveyor belts and crushers before being hoisted up in the main shaft.

The Tunnel: Quite often you walked for a mile at least, as the levels extended for about two and a quarter miles from east to west, over an area about half a mile wide. There were hundreds of miles of tunnels at numerous different levels. Many never yielded ore, but provided access. Only at the lode itself was ore prised out. And the two per cent average of tin in the lode had to pay for all the other non-productive work. Quite a thought. Navigation underground was a skilled art, even when you had logged various landmarks. Odd bits of graffiti, abandoned trucks, small lights, even the smell of pipe tobacco, were all useful to steer by, but it felt like being at sea, always looking for longitude and latitude in oceans of rock.

In the old days miners used to work by candle light (and in the last war, in the ore sheds, they chose to again to avoid attracting German bombers). Underground, men would fix candles to their hardened felt helmets with a special clay from St Agnes, and place them on a nearby rock. The length of miners' shifts used to be measured by the number of candles they got through, but as candles burned at different speeds, time-keeping was not always precise. In some mines ten candles a day were issued per man, in South Crofty it was six, but even then it's said that some workers would manage to save one a day to take home to their families. Candles were expensive (as were explosives), they served as a currency and could be traded above ground for tobacco and food.

In the past men would sing hymns as they went down the shafts in their cages and they would sing as they walked underground, if they had the breath for it. The tunnels must have echoed magnificently as dozens of voices reverberated throughout the mine. Choirs were just as important here as in Wales.

Connecting the various levels below 400 in South Crofty was the decline, a steep path down which a conveyor belt ran. When this was working it took ore up to the bottom of the ore shaft. Men could ride on it but visitors were advised not to. The path's gradient was steep at about 25 percent - the climb up was always more exhausting than the walk down. The decline went down to the 470 level. Below that was the sump where the pumps were. It was hot down there and very wet.

'The late storms have brought several vessels ashore and some dead wrecks, and in the former case great barbaritys have been committed. My situation in life hath obliged me sometimes to be a spectator of things which shock humanity. The people who make it their business to attend these wrecks are generally tynners, and, as soon as they observe a ship on the coast, they first arm themselves with sharp axes and hatchetts, and leave their tynn works to follow those ships. Sometimes the ship is not wrack'd but whether 'tis or not the mines suffer greatly, not only by loss of their labour, which may be at about £100 per diem if they are 2,000 in quest of the ship, but where the water is quick the mine is entirely drowned. They seldom go in a less number than 2,000...They'll cut a large trading vessell to pieces in one tide, and cut down everybody that offers to oppose them. Two or three years ago a Dutchman was stranded near Helston, every man saved, and the ship whole, burthen 250 tons, laden with claret. In twenty-four hours time the tinners cleared all.' George Borlase, February 1753

The Miner: Mining is one of the last real macho industries left, alongside coal-mining, steel-working, ship-building, sheep-shearing and deep sea fishing. But it's not just brute strength. Much has been written about the stoical nature of Cornish miners, their bravery and craft. For centuries observers have praised their intelligence, their wonderful art, the way, for example, in which they smelted ore. 'Nothing can be more ingenious', noted William Camden in 1586. But many miners in the past were only ever part-time, being also farmers or fishermen. So writers, lauding Cornish miners, were really acclaiming Cornish men, though it should be said that self-consciously respectable observers were dismayed by some of their occupations - chiefly wrecking. 'They'll cut a large trading vessel to pieces in one tide,' wrote George Borlase in the 1750s (it would be unfair to accuse Borlase of hypocrisy, but he wasn't disinterested; he was only able to live at Castle Horneck near Penzance thanks to income derived from mines in the St Just area).

Modern miners have remained very flexible, they are well-read and well-travelled. Many have gone abroad and they have friends and families in remote spots around the globe. Wherever minerals are being extracted from the ground, there is a potential job for Cornish men. Not surprisingly, their views on the world are well worth listening to.

Miners in South Crofty included development miners, production miners, trammers and fitters, all with different rates of pay. Towards the end of the mine's life most received a low basic wage, about £3.86 an hour, with production bonuses on top (so in a sense the old profit-sharing tribute method still lived!). Some miners earned £30,000 a year when the price of tin peaked at around £10,000 a tonne in the 1980s, but by the mid-1990s their income had halved. A big part of the problem was the world price of tin, worked out in US dollars. Large amounts of cheap alluvial river tin dredged from Malaya, Indonesia, Brazil and China kept the price down to just under £3,600 a tonne. South Crofty's tin ore was processed at Wheal Jane, twelve miles away, where it was crushed, frothed, scavenged, floated, shaken (not stirred), and then sent to Falmouth docks to go halfway round the world to Thailand. There it was smelted and only then would they really know the grade and value of the ore. With the percentage of actual tin fluctuating between 1.5 and 2 percent small variations could make all the difference between profit and loss.

'Miners are never very florid or robust, but to see the men... arriving at the surface after eight hours work is a most sickening sight. Thin, haggard, with arms apparently very much lengthened and hanging almost uselessly by their side, they seem like men worn out rather than tired.' Richard Q. Couch, Royal Cornwall Polytechnic Society, 1858

The Sub Level: When levels had been driven and raises mined, there was a need for sub levels. These were smaller and designed to be connected, so men could go long-hole drilling to blast the stopes. Sub levels were reached by climbing up or down sixty foot wooden ladders with iron rungs. So, for example, between the 400 and 420 levels there was a 410 sub level, running with a particular lode. If you said you were working at 410 on Roskear B, people would know exactly where to find you. Air quality was always good, except in the sub levels when pushing forward without a connection from below. When air could not circulate, it had to be passed to the miners down a thin pipe that blasted air at the rock face. In some areas the roof was about four feet high and water poured through like a warm shower. It felt more like the Amazon basin than Cornwall. To work in such areas took not just great skill and strength but stamina. It felt subtropical - no wonder most miners worked at the drills with their shirts off. And those that did leave them on, sawed the arms off. Red and blue check was the order of the day, with some subtle variations. All from the same tailor and issued by South Crofty. You came back out of the mine exhausted, having lost a lot of sweat. For safety reasons miners always worked in pairs to keep an eye on each other, and some worked together for many years. Quite often fathers and sons worked together in the same mine. With cap lamps supplying the only light you could often only just see your partner's face when working close together on jobs like wiring up the fuse wires for detonation. Faces became incredibly important and I was reminded of the Old Masters and those wonderful pictures of Industrial England by Joseph Wright of Derby (1734-97). Sometimes when a man was mining a raise, the water and rock debris and dust covered him totally and you could not see a thing. You just heard the deafening noise of the pneumatic drill.

Mining a raise was very difficult because everything had to be carried up the hole you were working on by clambering up on a chain, or a chain ladder. Bits would fall off - one slip and you too would go right down. Sixty feet was quite a drop and even more alarmingly many of the holes often had no safeguards - there might only be a narrow plank to walk across the winze. Many past miners have slipped or tumbled down. It must have been even worse in the days of candles which could easily go out (and then there was the problem of keeping matches dry...)

Our cover photograph was taken at a 410 sub level which I visited with George Wright in October 1997. The two men working there were Mervyn Randlesome and Micky Roberts, the oldest 'married couple' in the mine. They had worked together for some fifteen years. Mervyn had come from Wheal Jane, but Micky had been in South Crofty since he was a lad following his father into the mine. Mervyn was a fearsome rugby player and once took a bite out of someone's arm. Micky had also worked on the fishing boats. The day we photographed them Mervyn was putting in some safety bars and Micky was mining a raise in a cloud of dust, oil and water otherwise known as funk. His drill was powered by compressed air and had a telescopic leg which could be manoeuvred almost anywhere to get purchase. Working the drills was a hard job. In the old days they were known as 'widow makers', partly because the men's muscles were shot to pieces, but also because the early drills had no water in them, which meant the dust was a lot worse and the men died of pneumoconiosis and silicosis.

'These Britaines being meerly barbarous, as most of the Western parts of the known world then were, lived privately to themselves with scarce any commerce, or entercourse with any other nation: neither indeed were much known to forraine people, for a long time. For the first notice of them extant, was by Polybius the Greek writer, that accompanied Scipio in his warres about the year... two hundred and nine, before the birth of our Saviour Christ. Which Author nameth their Iland to be plenteously stored with Tynne: but of other things therein is silent...' John Speed, 1611

Geography: Did Cornwall trade directly with the Phoenicians? For many years it was believed as gospel even though there was no supporting evidence, except well-established Phoenician trading posts in the south of Spain. I think it's likely a link was made through middle men in France and Spain (Jews?). No one knows for sure

the true history of Cornish mining, but it certainly goes back at least 3,000 years and probably another 1,000 on top of that. Smelted tin was exported to France and Spain in the Bronze Age. The importance of tin in the Bronze Age cannot be overstated, for bronze itself is a mixture of tin and copper. The casting and manufacture of bronze powered the culture. Many beautiful artefacts, such as ceremonial axe heads, items of jewellery, swords and mirrors, have been discovered, and they bear witness to a major civilisation. Cornwall and West Devon were prime European sources of the necessary metals. Ingots have been found in boats trapped in the mud in the Carrick Roads, ingots in H-shape for carrying on horseback.

Smelting tin and copper was a difficult process. Charcoal from wood and peat provided heat. In those days streams of tin washed down from the mother lode could be collected as surface deposits. Geologically, copper and tin occur together. Many Cornish tin mines have also extracted copper, South Crofty included. The changing pattern of supply and demand is one reason historically why mines have closed and then reopened.

Pumping water has always been a major expense. On a turnover of £8 million the annual electricity bill at South Crofty was about £1.2 million. The main problem was that water had to be pumped from many old workings that still drained into the mine. The total was about 1.5 million gallons a day.

'Mad' water is water that falls back through the system and has to be pumped again. Once it's safely up to adit level, water can be led off into a surface stream like the Red River which flows out to the sea near Gwithian.

The Sharp End: This is where the real work was done. Ore was extracted by drilling then blasting. Everyday blasting was at 3.30pm when most men were clear from the mine. Think what a phenomenal amount of rock must have been taken out of South Crofty over the years! Left underground is a warren of tunnels, and where the lode used to be, gaps ranging from a few to a hundred feet wide. There were over thirty lodes at South Crofty, all followed ruthlessly until they were exhausted or became uneconomic.

The sharp end of my title also refers to the drills, which have to be razor sharp. They're driven by compressed air, which is very safe. The first air-powered drills were brought into the mines in the 1860s and were inevitably more cumbersome than drills today, but they were an incredible advance on the old system of hammer and borer. This consisted of a long iron bar with a cutting edge at one end which was used to drive a hole through the granite, back-breaking work. The borer or boryer often had to be worked at odd angles, one man held the bar, another wielded the hammer. The cutting edge of the borer, incidentally, is remarkably similar in cross-section to a Bronze Age axe.

In modern times men were paid by metres drilled, though allowances were made for particularly hard stretches of rock. Working a drill felt a bit like holding an old-style machine gun, and it made a racket like a road drill. Steels had to be changed every two metres and drill heads sharpened every few days by the mine's blacksmith. The drill bits were carried around in leather satchels a bit like large quivers.

The two main types of work carried out in pursuit of the ore were overhand shrinkage stoping for lodes up to 1.8 metres wide, and above that width sub level longhole open stoping was used. Each technique had its advantages, in the final analysis it came down to economics. Longhole stoping meant that miners had to drill holes up to twenty metres long in a star formation which sheared the lode off so it fell down to the bottom of the stope from where it could be extracted each day. The miners retreated gradually down a sub level. Shrinkage stoping meant that the men drilling were always scrambling above a mountain of broken ore,

REDRUTH TIN SMELTING Cº

and slowly working their way up to the next level. Once holes had been drilled they had to be primed at the toe with dynamite or powergel and then filled with ANFO, ammonium nitrate mixed with fuel oil. This was blown in with compressed air. The mixture was highly effective for giving a slow heave rather than a shatter. I have used it myself in a quarry in Cyprus, and underwater in sealed bags. It was a favourite with the IRA as fuel oil and fertiliser are to be found on almost every Irish farm that has a tractor. ANFO is responsible for the larger culvert bombs detonated from a distance behind a hedge, preferably across the border. You have to be careful mixing it up to avoid metal-to-metal contact or sparks. We used to employ a wooden trough and wooden shovel. For urban use, I believe Semtex is better. One miner in Geevor, who was Irish, never returned from a trip home. It had been rumoured that explosive was going missing and somehow finding its way north. I believe he ended up in a ditch. This must have been in the 1980s.

Anyway, back to those holes. Once holes had been primed and filled with explosive they had to be tamped and the det cords gathered. The appropriate detonators were then used to give millisecond delays between blasts. Sorting out the wires was like grandmother's knitting, a skilled process. No electrical detonators were used as they were liable to go off prematurely with static. Tamping the explosive was important as it helped to contain the explosion. In the old days many accidents occurred when gun powder would ignite with a spark and the iron tamping bar would shoot back and injure the man working.

Drilling: It's worth stressing what an art it was manhandling heavy and cumbersome equipment around the narrow confines of a mine. Even more demanding than the standard hand-held SIG drills - one can be seen on the cover of this book - were the Tamrock L500 long-hole drilling rigs. These needed special strength and power to drill holes of up to twenty metres, at very precise angles. The machines used to sit on the floor and, once they were set, the miner - like a chimney sweep - would feed in metre lengths as required, then retract them when the hole was drilled. Angles were always important as the final aim of the exercise was to blast off great sections of the lode.

The Reckoning: This was it at the end of the day. Tonnages of ore extracted, metres of holes drilled, cubic metres of ore shifted. Graphs were drawn of output per employee and in 1992 it was about 800 tons per man per year of ore, which meant about ten tons of tin per man per year. The ore at South Crofty, once raised, was trucked over to Wheal Jane about twelve miles away, a major operation on small Cornish lanes. Ken Tucker, driver of a massive loader, told me that he got approximately seven tons in each scoop, so it only took three scoops to fill a lorry. At Wheal Jane the ore was processed, first in a crushing plant with bars inside a large rotating drum a bit like a revolving boiler but stronger. The ore was then crushed again with steel balls about the same size as those used for a game of boules. Then through screens and hydro-sizers, before being sent along a series of Wilfley shaking tables, a gravity-separation scheme invented in the 19th century and little improved upon since. The sight of so much machinery vibrating was impressive to say the least, and the noise was deafening - as down the mine, you needed ear plugs. (Oddly enough, when earplugs were first introduced there was great resistance to them, but it was for the good - tinnitus could be an irritating problem in old age). Froth flotation and further chemical treatments would finally concentrate the ore into a heavy powder like fine sand, about twenty tons a day.

Geological Survey: No geologists, no mining - no survey, no maps. On the surface it's a matter of defining who owns what and where the boundaries lie. In the past lawyers did well out of boundary disputes. Underground, it is even more complicated, and techniques such as diamond-tip drilling are used for exploration. These produce miles of cores for analysis. Laser beams and computers have made life easier, but line of sight is still vital for theodolites. The geologists' job is to predict grades of ore and suggest promising directions for future mining enterprises, which could attract investment. Their maps can be very complicated as they have to present a 3-D view, usually in vertical section at various key points, normally where the shafts are. Levels, sub levels, and lodes are clearly marked.

When you see them down a mine, the thin veins of cassiterite (tin oxide $Sn O2$), stand out very clearly; at times they have a dull glisten, very different to the grey-flecked and quartzy granite. South Crofty still has plenty of good reserves, but there's always economic realities and the world price of tin to consider. Much of the surveyors' day-to-day work consisted of assessing volumes blasted and the progress made in driving tunnels. This then determined a miner's weekly pay by metre.

Language: Because of the noise, men working in pairs had to communicate through gestures instead of words. Those who had been together for a long time developed an intuitive understanding and worked by instinct. I am sure that being underground in the dark developed the senses. It was very much a family affair underground, with an atmosphere like a tribal gathering. It made me think of Tibetan monks, who in some disciplines undergo dark retreats in caves specifically to stimulate their awareness of more intuitive parts of the mind, likewise the Kogi in the Amazon Basin. Indeed the Kogi keep children chosen at birth to be priests in near darkness till they are fourteen. Maybe the Cornish Fogous, short tunnels into the ground, had more ritual significance than we realise. The role of the miner in the Cornish male psyche is just as important symbolically as it was economically. Add rugby, wrecking, shark-fishing, smuggling, wrestling, military service and sailing close to the wind, and there's a very powerful combination. I've heard it said that Cornish men on a parade ground took up more space than any other regiment because of their wide shoulders. Their regiment of course being the Duke of Cornwall's Light Infantry.

Croust, Morsel And Crib: For miners the only time of rest underground was at Croust, as it was called in the Camborne area, Morzel in the St Just region, Crib at Wheal Jane. Here men would traditionally eat their pasties, though in recent times most took down sandwiches, crisps, and cake.

A vast amount could be said about pasties. Over the years, contents have varied according to availability, but there was usually a bit of beef, such as brisket, chuck, skirt or shin. Other fillers included pork, bacon, rabbit, lamb, even mackerel. Anything to hand in other words. Sometimes they added leeks, onions, potatoes, turnips and pepper grass. The pastry could be black barley, with the pasty either cooked under the ashes in the oven or steamed in a cabbage leaf. I prefer pasties which include swede. It is said that miners would have their initial on one end, so that when they put their pasties down in a crack for later they could recognise their own. Some liked a sweet corner filled with jam to follow on from the savoury part. In some mines it is also said that the outer rib of pastry was discarded to stop arsenic getting from hand to mouth. But with rations being so important below ground, I think this would have happened only when there was a real risk. I can't resist mentioning squab pie. This had layers of apple, bacon, onions and mutton, and at the bottom a young cormorant or squab, alias shag... To quote Charles Kingsley, there was 'diffused through the pie and through the ambient air, a delicate odour of mingled guano and polecat'. Best eaten above ground I think!

But back to the mine. All groups of miners had their favourite hideaways or refuges where they could sit in safety and enjoy a degree of comfort. A wooden bench was considered luxurious... the main thing was to get out of the wet and have a chat. Superstition used to loom large in miners' lives and certain animals were never spoken about directly. An owl was called a 'braced farcer', the fox a 'long tayle', the hare a 'long ear', the cat a 'roker', and the rat a 'peeper'. Many older miners, even in modern times, believed in the so-called 'knockers', small men, mine spirits there to warn of disaster or hold out candles in times of need. Some mines were thought to be haunted by familiars, black dogs and white hares. The knockers (also known sometimes as noogies) could be troublesome and men who did not heed their voices often had bad luck, but, at other times, they could lead the way to rich lodes. They were said to be little withered dried-up creatures, the size of children about two years old, with big ugly heads, faces like old men and ungainly limbs. Sounds familiar... Witches and old ladies were treated with great respect and in one case, at North Basset Mine near Redruth in 1850, the appearance of Jack O'Lanterns led to the discovery of a good deposit of copper. The miners were led there by an old woman called Gracey. The mine yielded £90,000, and the amazing Gracey was given 5/- a year and a new dress in recognition of her advice. Geology on the cheap I call it... In Catholic times saints must have played a bigger part, as they do in Italy, Spain and France today.

In 1997 I saw Christmas trees brought down the mine for the last Christmas, which added to the poignancy of the situation. Just to see greenery underground was refreshing, albeit alongside girlie pin-ups in the fitters' bay at 420 level. At the same time there was a Christmas tree lit up on the mine's headgear, as everyone waited for the DTI to make up its mind...

The Gospel: It diminished in recent years, but religion used to play an important part in miners' lives. Chapel and Non-Conformist attitudes, steeped in rugged independence, were the hallmark and mainstay of the Cornish miner. Faith in a God was necessary when safety was questionable. Men used to sing hymns as their cage descended down the mine shaft, I imagine it was rather like sailors singing 'For those in peril on the sea'. The echo and the sound of the voices carrying underground must have been awe-inspiring and a real focus for the heart and mind. Miners trapped in accidents used to call out 'Praising the Lord' to guide their rescuers. Prayer either silent or vocal provided a measure of mental stability.

Danger is a great fuel for religion and miners' wives must have worried almost every day for the safety of their husbands, never knowing if they would see them again in one piece. Often in mining communities the thoughts and feelings of women are rarely expressed openly, but they should not be ignored.

The changing pattern of religious observance in Cornwall reminds me of what happened with Scottish crofters who, in the 1850s, managed to disassociate themselves from the churches of their land-owners, and led by the early 'Wee Free' ministers started the slow process of reclaiming their land. Their language - Gaelic - never died out (unlike Cornish) and in Stornaway today matters are decided in a bilingual parliament, called the Comhairle nan Eilean, Council of the Isles. In a similar way I think the Cornish moved away from established churches towards Chapel and Non-Conformism, and are now rediscovering their Celtic roots. Scotland and Wales have parliaments. I wonder how long it will be before Cornwall also has a fully bilingual institution with the black and white flag of St Piran fluttering overhead? Passports and exchange rates, five Pirans to the pound?

St Piran is of course the patron saint of Cornwall, who had a chapel at Perranporth among the Towans or sand dunes. St Piran came across from Ireland on a millstone and invented smelting, so it is said, though I should think smelting had already been around for quite a while. St Piran's flag is used today as a symbol of Cornwall's

independence. Some say the black and the white of the flag represent black and white tin. I once spoke to the Mayor of Redruth who was reading meters for SWEB. We met by chance in the main street beneath the clock tower and he said he risked life and limb for St Piran every time he put the flag up or took it down because the roof of the tower was so slippery.

In days of old the Cornish God led miners to rich lodes, looked after their safety, and sent wrecks and pilchards in time of need. Saviours of tin mines are harder to find in this computer-dominated age.

The Power of The Past: More than any other county in the south of England, industrial remains litter the surface of Cornwall. In some areas land is still contaminated by arsenic and other chemicals and heavy metals - tell-tale signs include a lack of vegetation and technicoloured water. In the 19th century farmers complained of animals dying after particularly heavy clouds of arsenic oxide dust blew across their land. Bees also suffered badly. However, some people - such as horse breeders in the Red River valley - claim their animals thrive on the land and pine away if grazed elsewhere. Maybe they have built up a local immunity.

Arsenic was a valuable by-product of smelting and kept many Cornish mines afloat between 1900 and 1950. There were smelting works at Angarrack, St Erth, Bissoe, Trereife, Penzance, Truro, Redruth, Lostwithiel and many more. There was far more money in smelting than mining and many smelters were also bankers. For example, the Bolitho family, who had a smelting works at Chyandour. The Bolithos were also tallow merchants and owned rights to auction fish at Newlyn. Tin was last smelted in Cornwall on a large scale in the 1930s at Sellegan, Carnkie, ore also went to Harvey's of Bootle. In recent years South Crofty's output was smelted in Thailand, yielding about 2,000 tons of pure tin a year, about the same as the total produced in Cornwall and Devon circa 1715. In the Middle Ages tin was smelted in blowing houses, the bellows powered by waterwheels. Many ruined blowing houses remain on the western edge of Dartmoor. They must have consumed vast quantities of charcoal. Later Welsh coal was brought across in sailing vessels. That sufficed for smelting tin, but not copper. So much coal was needed to smelt copper it was generally more economic to send copper ore to Wales (or, between 1689 and 1730, to Bristol, for Somerset had coal fields which only stopped production in the 1970s. Even today coal still outcrops in parts of the Mendips on what they call 'gruffy' ground).

The other reminder of the past, apart from the architecture and spoil heaps, is miners' gravestones. Recently an ex-miner at Geevor told me of old men he remembered in his youth who kept their cottage windows open an inch or two in even the foulest of weather simply to get more air into their already corrupted lungs. Arthritis and broken bones were common. White finger is when the nerve ends of the fingers have been shot away with vibration. Painful, it means that fingers get cold and numb in winter.

Naming The Mine: No county is as studded with enigmas as Cornwall. The name of a mine is but a riddling clue to a whole seam of history. A mine could become famous overnight with a rich strike, then disappear over the horizon like a comet. Every lode also had a name, sometimes linked to its discoverer, but that too could be extinguished as the minerals gave out or the cost of pumping water became too much or the price of tin dropped. Mines are black holes into which men and capital are sucked. Miners' culture was inward-looking and distinct, so mines had reputations for being warm or wet or cold, or famous characteristics, particularly in Penwith, where they protruded under the sea or were perched on cliff tops or, like Botallack, at the bottom of the cliffs. Often the large land-owning families, the Mineral Lords, had their names recorded for posterity in mine names like Grylls, Basset and Grenville. Each mine was

like a legend, a treasure trove of folk tales and daring, sudden death and great wealth, fertile ground for heritage and myth, interpreting the past.

The Roll Call: Many mines have extraordinary and enchanting names often belying conditions below ground. They have the same quality as ships' names, and indeed each mine went on its own voyage of discovery. Like ships they could be wrecked, filling with water at a moment's notice. In Victorian times they both needed miles of rope and chain, tons of coal for boilers, timber, large crews, good-looking engines and investors. The art of naming also came to the fore when allocating tin bounds, and very inventive they were on wastrel or unenclosed land. I have chosen the names in the poem from two sources. Mine names from *A Compendium Of British Mining* by Joseph Yelloly Watson (1843) and *A Guide to the Mines of West Cornwall* by DB Barton (1963). Names of tin bounds from AK Hamilton Jenkin's *The Cornish Miner* (1927).

Old Engine Houses: Vast as cathedrals or castles, they dot the landscape like giant chess pieces or old battle ships at anchor. Many have been stabilised, which is just as well, as the chunks of granite are enormous. Just building them was an achievement, and to see beam engines operating inside them must have been awe-inspiring. Some worked right up until the 1950s, the Robinson's 80" engine lasting until May 1955. The trick was to get a vast piston going up and down at the urging of the steam, and then to get a beam (or bob as it's known in Cornwall) to activate a pump. Thomas Newcomen succeeded in doing this as early as 1716, although others like Edward Somerset, the Second Marquis of Worcester, Denys Papin and Thomas Savery, had experimented with less successful engines from 1650 onwards. In Dartmouth where I lived as a boy I remember the Newcomen engine coming to town. It is still there in Dartmouth by the pleasure gardens. Further developments were made by James

Watt in 1763, he used condensers and double action and took the critical step of turning the power of the beam engine into circular motion. Cornish engineers then made many improvements and the engines went all over the world. They fulfilled the Victorian dream of industry, art, elegance and efficiency. Mines were kept dry and working conditions for the miners improved. Even the water they pumped was used in the various stamps, mills, and washing processes. Pollution was not really considered to be a big problem until the latter half of the 20th century (though some very early warnings were sounded. In the 1695 edition of Camden's *Britannia*, the publisher Edmund Gibson added a note about tinners healing cuts and wounds with Mundick, a mixture of iron pyrites, sulphur and arsenic. But what was good for miners - allegedly - was otherwise 'so venomous... that it kills the fish of any river it falls into').

'The real tinner or miner was, and is, differently created, being like poets, 'born not made.' AK Hamilton Jenkin, 1927

Ancestors: Important in Cornish mining because so many miners come from mining families. You have to be born to it and learn the ropes as seafaring families do. Every ancestor is logged and plotted, the names of the mines they worked in are handed down like memories of ancient battles.

In Cornwall a mine shaft too has many lives and when its work is at an end, when - to use the local term - it's knacked, all kinds of rubbish mysteriously appears, hovering near the edge. Cars, cookers... Local people no doubt exercising the ancient Cornish right to tip stuff anywhere. What's really interesting about ancient rights is the emergence of an early form of democracy in the Middle Ages with the Tinners' Parliaments, which stemmed from ancient privileges confirmed in the famous Charter of the Stannaries of 1201. Tinners could vote on their own affairs inside the Duchy, at least as far as mining was concerned. Devon also had a Parliament which met in the middle of Dartmoor at Crockerntor near Two Bridges, with a total of twenty-four members drawn from the towns of Tavistock, Chagford, Ashburton and Plympton. They had their own laws about mining which evolved from their decisions and were administered from the towns. There were Stannary courts dealing with everyday matters, and Stannary prisons. The one at Lydford, a Norman keep, still stands and was infamous. Then as Cornish tin became more important, the Cornish miners petitioned for a Parliament of their own. A further twenty-four representatives were chosen from the towns of Lostwithiel, Helston, Truro and Launceston. Bodmin and Liskeard came later. The Stannary Parliaments met and discussed larger issues every two years. The resulting sense of independence filtered down to the miners' Dutch auctions, held on the Count House steps once a month to divide up pitches.

I'm also intrigued by the opening up of some of the old mine shafts which had been capped. They have been known to swallow sheep, cows, even tractors. In the Mendips they are aptly named swallets. Some people make a hobby of exploring old mine workings, even abseiling down them, others - more lunatic still - go diving. More and more shafts are opening up as if the past is returning to haunt the present - like the acceptance of the Cornish language which is growing apace. No doubt it will be compulsory in schools before the year 2020.

Tho:Daniell: *TRURO.*

Old Faces: A great wealth of old mining photographs still exists in museums, records offices, books and private collections. Many were taken underground with the aid of carbide lamps or phosphorus flash. They are evocative and accurate. Few if any of the men are smiling, indeed they seem caught off-guard or in groups almost sullen as if the weight and seriousness of their occupation ran through every inch of their bodies. Some photographs were obviously posed but even that is interesting. We are all indebted to those early photographers who lugged their equipment down the mines, at great risk to themselves. Even today photography is not at all easy. Because of the great heat and humidity, lenses steam up and take at least an hour to equalise. (Surveyors try to get round this problem by keeping their instruments in a warm box before taking them down). Also, taking pictures in the dark is never easy, so lights are needed along with powerful batteries, leads and synchronised flashes. But then sometimes photographs containing too much light can lose out on the atmosphere. Photographing in a narrow space is yet another problem, though it has to be said that some places underground are cavernous, vast, endless, almost 'measureless to man' - but not to Cornish Man. It is thought that Coleridge's Kubla Khan experience derived from a trip to the caves at Cheddar or Wookey hole as well as a bit of opium... South Crofty must be one of the best photographed mines. After he went down there, George Wright was sent to Japan to photograph geishas. An interesting contrast.

'those mines do require a great deale of timber to support them and to make all these engines and mills, which makes fewell very scarce here; they burn mostly turffs which is an unpleasant smell, it makes one smell as if smoaked like bacon...' Celia Fiennes, 1698

Old Workings: These are legion and charting them is essential. Holding old water, they can break in at any moment. Water levels in a mine and its surrounding areas are constantly debated. When South Crofty closed, it was thought it might take four years for the water to reach adit level, and nobody still knows for sure where it might come out - it might even emerge where houses have been built. Old workings on the surface can also be

unstable, with horrifying consequences (remember the killer mudslide at Aberfan). Then there's the problem of arsenic. Some ground is poisoned for a long, long time. It can be 100 years before salt-tolerant species are able to survive... Thrift is a good example. Bryophytes too. Occasionally even plants new to science (like the willowherb at Wheal Maid).

As a boy I often explored Morwellham in the Tamar Valley long before it became a tourist attraction. Through the brambles were old docks, mine entrances, water wheel pits. It is no different in Cornwall where seemingly humble remains are so treasured by industrial archaeologists that, in a few years time, parts of the county may win World Heritage Site status from UNESCO, so shaped has the landscape been by historically significant advances. Devon and Cornwall led the way technologically; it's no coincidence that both Newcomen and Trevithick worked in mines. Even Boulton and Watt came down to see what was going on. And once the tin was at the surface and smelted, transport was vital - not just for the ore, but for iron, timber, coal, and other necessities. Good access to the coast and shipping was essential. Not surprisingly, consistent attempts were made to speed things up. Where I lived in Tavistock, a whole canal was built. Only four and a half miles long but nearly two miles of it went through solid rock. It came out above Morwellham and ended in an incline railway, which must have been one of the wonders of its day. Started in 1803, the canal took fourteen years to complete. I lived above the canal for several years and walked along it almost every day. It passes through some wonderful country, Drake's birthplace at Crowndale and the local tip... Nowadays the flow of water through the canal is used for a hydro-electric scheme.

A mile or two upstream from Morwellham lay the wealthy copper mine of Devon Great Consols. This played a key part in the life of William Morris, the famous 19th century designer, writer and Communist. Morris's father died in 1847, but as

Morris put it, 'as he had engaged in a fortunate mining speculation before his death, we were left very well off, rich in fact'. Morris went to public school at Marlborough, then Oxford University. At the age of 21 he was receiving an annual income of £900, more than £20,000 in today's terms. Three of the shafts in Devon Great Consols were named after the Morris family. William was obsessed by the idea it was all 'fortunate', all luck. By extension he believed the wealth of all bourgeois families had no attractive moral basis. Economics was just a question of windfalls. This primitive notion made Morris a confused writer and thinker - he did not fundamentally understand the social processes of the 19th century - but it also inspired him to try to improve the lives of the poor through the designs of fabrics, wallpapers, etc, which are still so popular today. Morris resigned his Great Consols directorship in 1875 - and symbolically sat down on his top hat.

Dick Trevithick: Born in 1771 near Carn Brea in the parish of Illogan on South Crofty land. Grew up to be so strong he could chuck a sledgehammer over an engine house, while at Cook's Kitchen he would stand on two stools and lift a 10cwt smith's anvil off the ground.

Trevithick was a great intuitive engineer and gambler with wild schemes. He pioneered railway locomotion and the use of high pressure steam boilers. Latecomers like the Stephensons claimed they invented the railway engine. Not so. The ancient Greeks came up with the theory of steam power, but Britain's first model locomotive (toy-sized and powered by a candle) was made in 1784 (and this is contentious, for it pitches Redruth against Camborne) by William Murdoch, who married the daughter of a local mine captain. Murdoch lived in Redruth, the house still stands, and he worked for Boulton and Watt as an engine erector, a job that Trevithick himself was after. Very much an unsung hero, Murdoch invented gas lighting and gasometers, he also pioneered the use of compressed air, and invented the oscillating cylinder engine.

Anyway, in 1797, Trevithick and his cousin Vivian made their own working steam engine models. Whether Trevithick ever saw Murdoch's model is debatable, but it didn't take long for him to design his own full-sized monster, basically a boiler on wheels with the circular motion transmitted by an eccentric. The beast was given its test run up Camborne Hill on Christmas Eve, 1801. It went very well, but alas, the machine came to grief a few days later when it hit a gully and capsized. Left alone - while its owners tucked into seasonal roast goose at a local hostelry - and filled themselves up with ale I suspect - the engine ran dry and the boiler burst. But still, Trevithick had succeeded, and uphill at that.

In 1802 he tried again. A small locomotive ran on rails in Coalbrookdale and then in 1804 for a £500 bet, a full-scale engine designed by Trevithick moved seventy men and ten tons of coal along a tramway nine miles long in South Wales, at Penydaren. This was a good twenty-one years before George Stephenson - Trevithick was way ahead of him - in 1810 Trevithick had an engine going round and round in London at twelve miles an hour. He charged people to come and look at it and try to catch it. Stephenson designed his own engine, and won a competition at the Rainhill Trials of 1829 with his famous Rocket, but he did not invent the railway locomotive, even if he did develop the idea and have the vision of connecting cities. Take a five pound note out of your back pocket, look at it carefully with a magnifying glass and you will see the error of the Bank of England's ways. When Cornwall gains full independence I trust the mistake will be corrected and Trevithick's image might appear on say a £20 note, if we aren't into Euros by then. Of course like any good hero Trevithick had his setbacks. Experimenting with high pressure steam, he built a pumping engine at Greenwich, which blew up in October 1803 because the boy who was supposed to be supervising it went fishing for eels instead. A passing labourer, who thought the engine might be running too fast, stopped it, but did not release the safety valve. Four men died in the resulting explosion (the boy survived). Bad publicity arising from this sensational incident set back the development of high pressure steam by twenty years.

Trevithick's wife, Jane, whose father ran the famous Harvey's foundry at Hayle, was very long-suffering. After Dick went abroad in 1816, he rarely wrote to his wife, let alone sent her any money. In Peru he was employed to work a number of his engines in rich silver mines at Cerro de Pasco, 14,000 ft above sea level. Local conditions made life difficult, disputes broke out and Trevithick moved on to work in a copper and silver mine in the province of Caxatambo. Here his bad luck continued; he was pressed into the army of Simon Bolivar, for whom he invented a brass carbine for which he was not paid. Eventually released, he returned to Caxatambo, but this time the Spanish army arrived to steal his money, tools and £24,000 worth of ore. So then it was back up to Cerro de Pasco, but just when things seemed to be going well, yet more soldiers damaged the mine during a battle in 1820. Trevithick headed for Chile. Here he pioneered a kind of diving bell which in 1821 enabled him to raise brass cannon, tin and copper from an old frigate that had sunk in Chorillos Bay. This earned him £2,500, not bad for a bit of underwater wrecking, but alas he then lost it all in a pearl fishing scheme in Panama. When Trevithick finally decided to return to England he was so keen to avoid travelling all the way round Cape Horn he became one of the first white men to walk across the isthmus of Costa Rica, and was very nearly eaten alive by a crocodile, being saved only by a timely shot in the eye, the crocodile's eye that is. After being dragged from the water by marksman Bruce Napier-Hall, Trevithick went to Cartagena in Colombia where he met Robert Stephenson, George's son, who after ignoring him for a while, eventually gave him £50 because he'd fallen on hard

times again. He arrived back in Falmouth in 1827, having been away eleven years. His wife had survived by running an inn in Hayle. What she said upon his return is not recorded...

Nothing daunted, the penniless Dick soon had more ideas. In Holland in 1828 he suggested pioneering ways of using steam-power to help drain the Dutch fens, techniques later used to great effect in the East Anglian fens and the Somerset Levels. After a move to the Kent town of Dartford in 1832, he worked for the engineer John Hall in experiments on turbines and high pressure steam-boilers.

Trevithick died of pneumonia in April 1833 at the Bull Inn, and was buried in a pauper's grave at Dartford. In the company history of J & E Hall, he is described as 'probably the greatest mechanical genius of the nineteenth century', and yet there is no Trevithick College or award that I know of, though there is the venerable Trevithick Society, not to be confused with the Trevithick Trust, that also does much good work saving engines and sites of interest to Cornwall's industrial heritage.

Arsenic And Strong Women: There were often as many workers above ground as below. The job of breaking-up ore by hand or stamps, then washing it and sorting the different grades into piles for auction, was a time-consuming business frequently done by women and boys. In the 19th century, when they were old enough, commonly at ten or twelve, boys went underground, but the women stayed above and were called bal maidens. Unlike in the coal mines, women never worked below. They wore head-dresses (known locally as 'gooks') to keep the wind and sun from their faces. Some of them had cardboard underneath for stiffening, but generally they were quite plain - not as elaborate as those found in Brittany, for example. The women tended to work out in the open spalling, that is breaking up the ore into walnut-sized lumps, while the boys went barefoot through the water tending the various buddles and launders where the fine ore was separated. Bal maidens were noted for their hard work and good looks and also for their singing in gangs as they walked to work through the fields and lanes at six in the morning. It was hard labour but the pay was better than agriculture and the hours shorter...

So to arsenic. In the 1870s half the world's arsenic came from just four mines. Enough was stockpiled in the south west of England to poison the world. Sulphur dioxide and arsenic oxide were removed from ore by roasting it (a process called calcining). The arsenic oxide condensed in special flues scraped out by young boys... Men wore primitive masks. They would cover exposed skin with Vaseline or fuller's earth and put cotton wool in their ears before work.

Agriculturally, calcium arsenate served as a killer of boll weevils in the cotton plantations of the southern states of America, and as a guard against potato-munching Colorado beetles. King's Yellow, arsenic sulphide, appeared as a medicinal tonic, particularly in the 19th century against syphilis. More commonly, it was used in sheep-dips as a protector against fly strike, keds and scab. The presence of arsenic in sheep dips was effective but controversial. In the 1930s the once-famous barrister Lord Birkett (he later served at the Nuremberg Trials) managed to save several women who had poisoned their husbands. One celebrated case concerned the death of a quarryman in the Forest of Dean, who had battered his wife over a long period of time. She took her revenge with sheep dip powder, but because he had kept a few sheep and often had cuts to his hands, Lord Birkett was able to plant an element of doubt in the jurors' minds. Surely there was a chance that arsenic got into the man's body during sheep-dipping? In another case in Cornwall a body was exhumed after two years and high levels of arsenic were found. Could it not have got there simply because there were also high levels of arsenic in the burial ground? Lord Birkett succeeded again - even though the woman had been lacing sandwiches.

Arsenic, incidentally, was also blamed for the alleged poisoning of Napoleon on St Helena. Traces were found in his hair, and some thought his doctor had laced his wine. With pure arsenic one sixth of a teaspoon would do the trick.

Industrially, arsenic was used in various paints and dyes. Copper arsenate was a good mordant for fixing pigments, though this is no longer practised. White Arsenic, arsenic trioxide, was used to produce that marvellous white decoration in the twisted stems of hand blown champagne glass. It was also later used extensively for de-colouring glass. Red Arsenic was the disulphite and Yellow Arsenic the trisulphite. The notorious Paris Green favoured by Victorians for wallpaper was made with copper sulphate, sodium arsenate and acetic acid. This unfortunately reacted with urban smoke to give off the deadly gas arsine. No wonder Sherlock Holmes was so busy...

Arsenic was a valuable part of the mustard gas used in the First World War. In 1914 the price of arsenic was £9 a ton, by 1918 it was £100 a ton... The formula for mustard gas was diphenylamine chlorasine, a bright yellow solid rather like Colman's mustard, hence its name. Hitler was affected by mustard gas in 1918 and more than anything else this very personal experience - blistered skin, corrupted lungs and temporary blindness - prevented him, I suspect, from gassing enemy troops in the Second World War, though of course he gassed civilians in concentration camps... Mussolini used mustard gas in Abyssinia in 1936. Vile as this was thought to be, the British took no chances. In 1939, mines around the Tamar valley were surveyed to see what resources were left, just in case they were needed. More recently, Saddam Hussein has used mustard gas against the Kurds and during the Iran-Iraq war.

A Rough Apprenticeship: Horses and ponies were used at the surface but very rarely below. Some pictures do exist of ponies underground at Levant. Whims were all horse-driven before engines came along, and the ore was raised in egg-shaped iron buckets called 'kibbles'. These were about three foot high with several chains, which made them very manoeuvrable. Their tops also tapered so they didn't get stuck on ledges while being hauled up. A clever design by our old friend Trevithick. Men too would ride up in them in the days before man engines and cages. Timber was a necessity both above and below ground particularly in unstable conditions or in areas of faults such as the Great Concourse beneath the Red River. Timber was also used for scaffolding, ore chutes and the building of stulls, artificial walls between footwalls and hanging walls designed to keep back hundreds of tons of waste rock.

Accidents occurred above ground as well as below. Boilers would sometimes explode, scalding everyone around them with super-heated steam. The main cause was metal fatigue and loose nuts not being able to take the strain. But incidents like this were nothing compared to what could happen at gunpowder factories and fuse works. Women and girls often worked in the powder factories and if the powder was ignited, the results were gory. One of the geologists who took us round the mine, Chris Rogers, said that his relations had run a lemonade factory at Perranporth near to the gunpowder factory there... When the factory went up, so did they, and he lost a fair chunk of his family. Nowadays Perranporth sprouts caravans amongst the dunes as well as the odd lurking chapel. With so many tourists the need for lemonade is more pressing than ever, if only to mix with rough cider, sometimes referred to as Rat's Piss or Cripple Cock, the latter name being dreamt up by a man called Dixey. For a detailed look at Cornish mine disasters see the book of that name by Cyril Noall (Dyllansow Truran, 1989). It makes interesting bedtime reading.

Two of mining's main safety inventions came from Cornishmen. The Davy lamp from Sir Humphry Davy (1778-1829) of Penzance had little application in Cornish mines but saved many lives in coal mines. It is still taken on routine examinations of old workings just in case. In the Newcastle area, incidentally, miners preferred a safety lamp invented by George Stephenson, hence the term Geordies... The other invention was the safety fuse developed by William Bickford of Tuckingmill, just below South Crofty in 1831. Prior to that they used goose quills filled with gunpowder, or a rush inserted into the powder by way of a long needle. Reliable fuses and detonators became a necessity when handling the more powerful but less stable nitro-glycerine explosives invented by Alfred Nobel in 1860. His profits later helped to endow the famous prizes for Peace, Science and Literature.

'A tinner is never broke till his neck's broke.' Old Cornish proverb

Uncertainty - The Final Act: On 13 June 1997 it was announced that development mining at 470 fathom level was to be temporarily stopped. In August 1997 it was further declared that South Crofty would close unless a rescue package came from the Government through the DTI. Either that or a new buyer. No buyer emerged, though several bright ideas were put forward. The crisis came as a surprise to many people, particularly after a share issue in 1994 was enthusiastically supported by many well-wishers in Cornwall and overseas. All seemed to be going well but the persistently low price of tin on the international market and an increased exchange rate against the dollar decreased profitability. All through the autumn of 1997 the mine expected to hear any day from the Government - but the world price of tin was still adverse. The Conservatives had supported South Crofty in the past, now the miners waited to see if a Labour Government would do the same... No offer was forthcoming, just a fax, not even a phone call or a letter.

The mine started to shut down even though three weeks of new development had been sponsored by the sale of tin tokens. Equipment was earmarked for sale, men were laid off and plans made for evacuating the mine. The last explosion took place at 3.30pm and the mine finally shut on March 6, to the singing of hymns, various television reports and the odd hosing-down. Union leader Mark Kaczmarek had led a determined campaign from the locker room, and at one stage he even climbed the headgear, but to no avail. Next day there were miners' marches from Camborne and Redruth which homed in to a beer tent in the field opposite the mine entrance and the lane leading to Robinson's shaft. There was a sea of faces, miners' helmets, Cornish flags and banners. There were pasties, a whole tent awash with beer, but no bitterness that I could detect, though some felt that the company (Crew Natural Resources Ltd from Canada) could at least have provided a barrel or two as a sign of goodwill. It was a celebration of Cornish mining and many felt the 3,000 years had slipped by in a twinkling.

The fight had apparently been lost - a mystery buyer from Wales was on the phone in the last few days but nothing materialised. The job of stripping out machinery began in earnest, the scrapmen went round with their bits of chalk. Men picked up their redundancies and signed on. Some went abroad. One night, even the boardroom grandfather clock disappeared, as if time had really run out. The water was creeping up the shaft like nobody's business and there was nothing anyone could do about it. It was a sad day for Cornwall, coming as it did swift on the heels of St Piran's day.

The Uses Of Tin

IF YOU paid for this book in cash, then tin will almost certainly have been involved in the transaction. The humble penny handed back to you after you proffered (say) your ten-pound note contains tin - though much less than it used to. The amount of tin in British coins dropped from 4 percent in 1860 to 0.5 percent in 1942 when supplies decreased as the Japanese took over Malaya and Indonesia. Zinc was used to make up the balance. After the war the level went back up to 3 percent but in 1959 it fell again to 0.5 percent and has stayed there ever since.

History with a capital H has always affected the uses of tin. The gathering Cornish tin mining crisis of the 1990s prompted moves towards diversification at South Crofty, including the jewellery which now makes up South Crofty's very own Tin Collection. This has an unusual lustre. Tin has always been worth less than gold and silver, but I think it's subtler than those two precious metals, which are so conventionally decorative. The tin for South Crofty's jewellery is smelted at Wheal Jane and cast in Penryn to designs made by local artists. The collection has mining, maritime and Celtic themes and is now widely distributed. See www.crofty.demon.co.uk/jeweller.htm

Or take another recent example, the experimental use of tin shot to replace the lead shot condemned as part of the great trend in the western world towards thinking more about the environment. Market research on ducks has been carried out, without, I fear, the ducks' consent. I heard one Exmoor farmer was worried that after a day's heavy shooting his twelve-bore might end up as a tin-plated sixteen-bore...

Tin was once so popular on the continent that merchants in Amsterdam had their own Duchy stamps to make ingots of smuggled tin look authentic. It is a versatile and under-rated metal: non-toxic, attractive, resistant to corrosion, with a low melting point - and it will take a shine. Among the middling range of metals tin is often priced higher than copper, aluminium, lead, zinc and iron. It's notoriously difficult to use tin in a pure molten state but it combines well with other metals. Brass and bronze are both mixtures of copper, zinc and tin, but bronze has more tin. Bronze of course was once so important it gave its name to a whole Age.

A history of the western world written by someone obsessed with tin would also perhaps feature a Pewter Age. The demand for pewter - a combination of tin and lead - helped power mines for centuries. It was widely used throughout Europe for plates, dishes, tankards and goblets. The dull shine and everyday elegance of pewter saw it adorn many a farm dresser. It was also relatively indestructible, unlike the posh china and porcelain which became the 'in' thing in the 18th century. When it did, tin miners fearing for their jobs rampaged through west Cornwall wrecking all the dainty stuff they could find... Pewter's only problem (in my eyes) is that when you combine it with cider, the cider reacts with the lead, particularly when boiled up for mulling.

Our imaginary tin history should pause for a musical interlude - it is the tin in church bells that gives them their good ring and, in a nearly pure form, tin is still used for organ pipes.

One of tin's vital properties is its ability to form a thin layer or skin over other metals, usually through hot dipping. The metal was used to coat the insides of cooking vessels in ancient times, but it was the invention of food canning that made it indispensable. Both Napoleon and Nelson recognised how essential food preservation was for keeping troops and sailors happy. Many mutinies - notably those at Spithead and the Nore in 1799 - arose from bad food and conditions as well as poor pay. Napoleon offered a prize of 12,000 francs to anyone who could find a way of keeping food fresh. The winner was Nicholas Appert of Paris who discovered that if food was boiled in glass and then immediately sealed it would last for several months. In 1810 he published a book on the art of conservation - this was fifty years before Louis Pasteur showed how heat should be used to destroy the bacteria which made food decay. An Englishman called John Gamble finally took up the challenge. He bought the English rights for £1,000 and headed back to Bermondsey to work with the engineering firm J & E Hall. Together they realised that tin-plated cans would be as effective as glass, and less fragile, so they started the first food canning factory. Their tins were very strong, almost requiring an armourer to open them. The first customers were the Royal Navy and Arctic explorers, who sometimes may have got more than they bargained for. On one expedition led by John Franklin the men became disorientated. One theory is that too much lead was used in the solder, it got into the food and they suffered lead poisoning...

Nowadays we live in the Solder Age. At its peak, canning took up half the world's tin. Today the same proportion goes into electrical solder, another mixture of lead and tin, vital for microcircuits and circuit boards. The circuits are moved over a molten bath of solder so that the electrical connections just touch. Tragically, the tin that was used in cans is not recoverable, the layers were so thin. These days, plastics are employed instead.

Who knows what uses of tin remain to be discovered. Maybe it could be Cornwall's Viagra. Take one part tin, two parts pilchards, three parts cider and four parts nationalism. Mix on the beach, stir, stand back and then take to your surfboard...

The Workforce

South Crofty employees in August 1997 when the mine's closure was first announced. Names have been taken from the payroll and put into alphabetical order.

Mining

Ronald Terrance Abel; David John Abraham; Terence Michael Allaway; Alan Michael Allison; Edward Charles Ball; Wayne Ball; Peter David Barnes; Ian Bawden; Robin Owen Bawden; Nicholas Julian Beere; Joseph Bende; Jonathan Paul Bowden; Stephen Sinclair Bowers; Paul Allan Brown; James Daniel Buckley; Stephen Arthur Burrows; David Busby; David Buzza; Nigel Paul Chapman; Richard John Cocking; Shaun Conway-Baker; David Robert Cunnick; Paul James Thomas Curtis; Stephen John Dadd; David Anthony Easter; Raymond Ellis; Bromley Steven Evans; Antonio John Fernandez; Nicholas Fox; Peter Alan Futcher; Paul Gallie; Kenneth John German; Ronald Gulliford; Evelyn James Paul Gunn; Malcolm Harris; Ian Nigel Harvey; Richard Phillip Harvey; Eldred William Hawke; Brian Head; Sidney Kenneth Hearn; Maurice Raymond Hennah; Gerald Henry Hinton; Roland Timothy Hocking; Neil William Hodges; Kenneth Roy Hooper; David Michael Ivey; Michael John James; Brian Jenkin; Phillip Jenkin; Wayne Jenkin; David Garfield Jewell; Derrick William Johns; Mark Anthony Kaczmarek; James Henry Keen; Bruce James Knights; David James Laity; Patrick Andrew Lloyd; Clarence James Matthews; Kenny John Matthews; William David Medlen; Christopher David Merton; Stephen Paul Merton; Brian Raymond Mitchell; Geoffrey Coad Mitchell; Nigel Mitchell; Adrian Mugford; Frederick Kenneth Mugford; Roger Charles Mugford; Vivian Andrew Mugford; Kevin Mutton; Richard O'Brian; Christopher Phillip O'Keife; Lewis Pascoe; Nigel Pascoe; Jim Henry Pellow; Danny Penhaligon; Kevin Penrose; Mervyn Reginald Randlesome; Carmelo Rizzo; Michael Ronald Roberts; Steven Frederick Roberts; Stephen William Roscoe; Thomas Leslie Rowe; Frederick Brian Rule; Alexander Eric Saundry; Neil Eric Saundry; Nicholas Shaw; Jaroslav Smejkal; Jason John Sobey; David Peter Southby; Mark Hellyar Spear; Brian Thomas Sweeney; Graeme Hugh Thomas; Roland Ronald Thomas; William Thomas; Adrian Tonkin; Godfrey John Tonkin; Sidney Michael Tregonning; Adrian Paul Tremayne; Graham Michael Tremayne; Ian Malcolm Tremayne; Kenneth Charles Tucker; Derek Clifford Uren; Irving Guthridge Uren; Michael Viles; Oliver Scott Warren; David Watkins; Eric Richard Watkins; Jason Austin Weeks; John Henry West; Clevedon Williams; Lee Bryn Williams; Brian Whitaker; John Peter Wyatt

Engineering

William Maynard Anthoney; David William John Bishop; Robert Peter Board; Benjamin Brook; Simon Davey; Albert Henry Evemy; Jonathan Peter Futcher; Charles Malcolm Gilbert; George Anthony Gilbert; William Rodney Harris; Richard Edward Harvey; Anthony Hewitt; Paul John Hoskin; Robert Peter Kellett; Anthony George Lanyon; Peter Kingsley Lanyon; Richard Love; Darren Mark Maudling; Peter Michael May; Rodney McAleenan; Paul Carter McCabe; Frederick Paul McDonald; Philip Gilbert Morcom; John O'Keife; Paul Grenville Oldfield; William Edward Palmer; Keith Pankhurst; Cedric Cecil Paterson; Geoffrey Cyril Riggs; Mark Stephen Rivron; Mark Anthony Rule; David Craig Smith; Steven Smith; Andrew James Solomon; Brian Charles Spargo; Alan Trerise; Paul Andrew Tyack; Philip John Vokins; Desmond Wagstaff; Kevin Waters; Ian William Webster; Eric Edward Williams; Kenneth Alan Williams; Michael Williams

Staff

Peter Aston; Kenneth Joseph Barnes; Sheila Margery Beattie; Rachel Beyer; Patricia Ann Brady; John Allen Buckley; Nigel Alex Clark; Michael George Clothier; Julian Paul Collison; Thomas Anthony Cullen; Kelly Jay Dawkins; Garry David Dunn; Eric Eckersall; Kathryn Helen Entwistle; Anthony David Giles; Geoffrey Harvey; Howard Heap; Stephen John Herbert; Jennifer Susan Hinton; Ernest Paul Johns; Gary Henry Kaczmarek; Nicholas Gerald Leboutillier; Brian Charles Leigh; Leonard Henry Matthews; Karen McCaig; Frank Mitchell; Derek Morgan; Michael Anthony Pereir; Adrian Lawrence Perry; James Alistair Pettett; Anthony Philp; John Robert Phillips; Dianne Roberta Price; Allan Reynolds; Robert George Risbridger; Chris Jason Dean Rogers; Andrew Paul Seager; Raymond Edward Sicolo; Tina Armstrong Simpson; William Beresford Storey; Rachel Louise Symons; Richard Colin Taylor; John Nkere James Usoro; Nicholas James Westley; Thomas Simon Williams; Martin Wolstenholme; David Michael Wood; John Pendarves Young

Mill At Wheal Jane

Clayton Wayne Abraham; Neil Mark Anthoney; Stephen Robert John Bartle; Nicholas Alfred Bauer; Kenneth John Bird; Keith Edwin Blunden; John Franklin Mark Bowden; Adam John Michael Brady; Martin Carlyon; Stephen Carlyon; Alan David Carswell; Malcolm Chivell; Johnathan Keith Collins; Keith Frances John Collins; Len Collum; Ivor Congdon; Peter Alan Cooper; John Benjamin Curnow; Malcolm George Fred Davies; Nathan Gay; Peter John Girdlestone; Grenville John Glasby; Kit Kelley Griffiths; David John Groves; Nigel Hambly; Rodney Howard Harvey; Maurice Hunt; Tyrone Richard Johns; Mark Anthony Kessell; Simon Kevern; Charles Henry Keyworth; Graham John Lloyd; William James McKinnon;

Raymond Moyle; Philip Anthony Mugford; David John O'Brian; Stephen Parnell; Anthony Martin Percival; Edwin James Perkins; Micky Rafferty; Derek Bertram Rice; John Edward Roberts; David Percival Rowse; Arlo Ian Smith; Keith William Smith; Francis Gerald Symons; John Francis Symons; Graham Thomas

Carnon Contracting

Malcom Roy Batchelor; Michael John Bryant; Sean Nicholas Bryant; Paul Coppinger; Anthony Patrick Crocker; Andrew William Daddow; Stephen Mark Dash; Kelvin Mark Gay; Hugh Henderson; Robert Lee; Jonathan Allan Nicholls; Joseph Robert Osborne; Nigel Gordon Reynolds; Karla Teresia Riekstins; Stephen Paul Rule; Christopher Tenbeth; Michael Tenbeth; Eric John Wedlake; Emma Jane White

Senior Staff

Bernard John Ballard; Alan Beattie; Robin Edmund Boon; John Brady; Kingsley Paul Bray; Roger White Davey; Stephen Gatley; David Maxwell Giddings; Michael Peter Hallewell; Peter Ivan Hughes; Clive Robert Jones; Howard Guy Midwinter; Mark Lyndhust Owen; Anthony John Pope; Reginald Thomas Reid; Clifford Rice; Keith William Smith; Robert James Smith; Barrie Tippett; Robert Frederick Wedlake

Further Reading

A History of South Crofty Mine, JA Buckley (Dyllansow Truran, 1997)

South Crofty Underground, PR Deakin, JA Buckley, KT Riekstins (Penhellick Publications, 1995)

Cornish Mining at Surface, JA Buckley (Tor Mark Press, 1990)

A History of Tin Mining and Smelting in Cornwall, DB Barton (Bradford Barton, 1967)

The Cornish Miner, AK Hamilton Jenkin (Allen and Unwin, 1927: repr. David & Charles, 1972)

Mines And Miners of Cornwall, Vol. X Camborne and Illogan, AK Hamilton Jenkin (Truro Bookshop, 1965)

Cornish Mine Disasters, Cyril Noall, ed. with an Introduction by Philip Payton (Dyllansow Truran, 1989)

The Meads of Love: The Life & Poetry of John Harris, Paul Newman (Dyllansow Truran, 1994)

Exploring Cornish Mines, Vols 1 & 2, Kenneth Brown & Bob Acton (Landfall Publications, 1994 & 1995)

Cornwall in the Age of Steam, A Guthrie (Tabb House, 1994)

Tin in Antiquity, RD Penhallurick (The Institute of Metals, 1986)

The Stannaries, GR Lewis (Harvard, 1908; repr. Bradford Barton, 1965)

Tin and Tin Mining, RL Atkinson (Shire Books, 1985)

Mining in Cornwall, Vols 1 & 2, J Trounson (Moorland Publishing, 1980)

Cornish Mining, Bryan Earl (Bradford Barton, 1968)

Cornish Mining, essays ed. Roger Burt (David & Charles, 1969)

Richard Trevithick, James Hodge (Shire Books, 1995)

Camborne, Redruth, Truro and Plymouth libraries all have good collections. For detailed information on tin, see the International Tin Research Institute's website at www.itri.co.uk

About Agre

AGRE BOOKS publishes non-fiction books of literary merit about South West subjects. Based in Dorset, it covers the South West peninsula. Agre takes its name from the legend of Actaeon and Diana as told in Ovid's *Metamorphoses*. Ovid names Actaeon's hounds and lists their attributes. 'The thicket-searcher Agre' was the hound with the keenest nose. Agre Books intends to search the thickets of its distinctly rural region to find interesting truths and intriguing stories.
Titles published or forthcoming include:

Islomania by Sara Hudston (£6.50). Illustrated, with Victorian photographs from the Gibson Archive. Islomania - an obsession with islands. Why are people so attracted to islands? Using the Isles of Scilly as its working example, this book explores the special place islands occupy in our imagination.

The Cornish Pasty by Stephen Hall. Illustrated, entertaining account of the original fast food. Includes authentic recipes never before published alongside details of pasty-making past and present, the pasty overseas and pasty myths and legends.

To find out more about Agre you can write to Agre Books, Groom's Cottage, Nettlecombe, Bridport, Dorset, DT6 3SS, or visit our website at www.agrebooks.co.uk.

About The Printing

THE WHEAL OF HOPE was typeset and printed by R. Booth Ltd of Mabe, near Penryn, Cornwall, in Monotype Imprint, plus Adobe Myriad on 130 gsm art paper. R. Booth is a family firm which prints books for several small publishers. Robert and Mary Booth started as a bookbinder's in 1971. In 1977 their son Steven joined the business and the firm expanded into printing. Steven Booth is now works manager in charge of production.

James Pascoe Crowden was born in 1954 and grew up on the western edge of Dartmoor. His middle name derives from his Cornish ancestors. He joined the army, read civil engineering at Bristol University, and in 1976 hightailed it to the Himalayas. He then studied anthropology at Oxford, and lived for a year in the Outer Hebrides, before returning to Bristol and working in the docks as a boatman. Now living in Somerset, he has also worked as an agricultural labourer, doing sheep shearing, night lambing, forestry and cidermaking. He recently retired from the land to concentrate on writing full-time. His other books are *Blood, Earth and Medicine* (1991), a collection of poems, *In Time of Flood* (1996), a collection of poems and notes with photographs by George Wright, ('Enjoyed it. Full of interesting effects. Unexpected things' - Ted Hughes), and *Cider - The Forgotten Miracle* (1999), an account of cidermaking and its history ('Well researched' - *Financial Times*). His most recent book was *Bridgwater - The Parrett's Mouth* ('Unusual' - *Western Daily Press*).

George Wright was born in London in 1950. From 1970 to 1973 he studied graphic design at Wimbledon School of Art and in 1975 he became a freelance photographer. He has worked internationally for many newspapers, magazines and book publishers. His pictures have appeared in *The Independent Magazine, The Observer, The Independent on Sunday Review, Departures* (USA) and *Istituto Geografico De Agostini* (Milan). He is also a stills photographer for Channel 4. His work has been exhibited at the Metropolitan Museum in New York and the Chicago Botanic Gardens, and he has a number of photographs in the National Portrait Gallery. His books include *English Topiary Gardens* (1988), *Ceramic Style* (1994), *Print Style* (1995), and *In Time of Flood* (1996), a collection of photographs of the Somerset Levels accompanied by poems by James Crowden. He has lived in West Dorset since 1983.